THE STORY
OF OLD NEW YORK

Old York, England, from which our city derives its name.

THE STORY of OLD NEW YORK

By

HENRY COLLINS BROWN, 1862—

ILLUSTRATED BY FRANK RENNIE

NEW YORK

E. P. DUTTON & CO., INC.

FIRST PRINTING......SEPTEMBER, 1934
SECOND PRINTING......SEPTEMBER, 1934
THIRD PRINTING......SEPTEMBER, 1934

TO THE

Big Six, The Adorable Five

and the

Tumultuous Nine

THIS BOOK IS LOVINGLY

DEDICATED

Preface

I HAVE always felt that the man who undertakes to write the Story of Old New York, should first offer the public some assurance that he is reasonably well equipped for his extraordinary and pretentious assumption, and is not merely a rabid rhetorician, exulting in the exuberance of his own verbosity.

For my own part I would offer as my foremost qualification, the inestimable value of a continuous residence of three-score years and ten in this whimsical, exasperating, lovable old town; my many acquaintances with old New Yorkers, whose interest in the city equaled mine, and who told me many things not found in history books.

I have seen this City grow from a half-mining camp to be the Mayfair of the Western World. I was here when the wooden cigar store Indian roamed the town and I have sat in the gutter chairs of Tillie Haynes' Broadway Central where Fiske was shot, and at Sim Ford's Grand Union, where the noonday meal of the cab horses, opposite, brought droves of pigeons to feast on the oats that dribbled from the feed bags. I have known Fifth Avenue when few persons were seen on it in the daytime, and practically none at night. I have wandered among the shacks of shanty town beginning at Fifty-ninth Street, and I have known South Street when it was a forest of masts. I remember the time when many of our best people went shopping in Washington Market and brought home their purchases in their own baskets.

There was no end of garden truck farms between Ninth

Avenue and Central Park to be seen from the car windows when the Elevated was first extended to Harlem; and when you came out of the tunnel at Ninety-sixth Street, on the New York Central train, there were no houses at all in sight—nothing but vacant lots except the Ruppert house on Fifth Avenue. Yorkville was still almost a separate village. Harlem was looked upon as a distant town and the quickest way to get there was by the speedy little East River boats—*Sylvan Grove, Sylvan Dell, Sylvan Stream*—all painted white and as pretty as their names. And what a glorious ride it was on a fresh sunshiny morning in Spring!

I was at the American Institute Fair—a marvelous organization in those days—and paid ten cents to talk over a wire connected with the other side of the hall. It was Bell's Telephone. I still have a program saying that you could talk over this contrivance for the modest sum of ten cents—one dime.

I remember when the stenographer first made her appearance. She wore a stiff sailor hat of some glazed material, a rather mannish suit of plaid checks, long trailing skirts, and was noted for her lack of pulchritude, which at that time was not considered an asset. Abigail Jones, who looked the part, was much more in demand than Hazel Kirke, who also looked the part. Wives are much more liberal today.

A by-gone race of giants walked our streets. Fine old Peter Cooper; vivacious Commodore Vanderbilt; Henry Ward Beecher. There may have been finer orators than Beecher, but I never heard them—nor anyone else. The poet Bryant; Morse the telegraph man; Evarts, the interminable; genial Bishop Potter; good Dr. Chapin; Lilliputian Stewart, the big dry goods man; Oil King Rockefeller, newly come to town; glorious Grover Cleveland; First Citizen Gen'l U. S. Grant; the fiery Sherman; and Morgan the Magnificent.

Looking backward, it seems as if it were another world. There were no movies, no motor cars, no telephones, no electric lights, and no radios. Yet this delectable era of Annie Pixley Cigars, red flannel underwear, statues of Venus de Melos with eight-day clocks in their tummies, and the introduction of toilet paper, was nevertheless a glorious decade in the unfolding of New York. Soon after that we permitted males and females to bathe in the same ocean together, and also allowed books of lady and gentleman authors to be placed alongside each other on the library shelves. When the Sombre '70's passed into history, it left us on the threshold of a renaissance, destined to eclipse in dazzling splendor, the mightiest achievements of all time, since the fall of the Roman Empire.

I revived that sterling old City publication, *Valentine's Manual*. I issued it regularly for twelve years and lost money every year. But out of it grew the Museum of the City of New York, the Liberty Pole in City Hall Park, the printing of the Minutes of the Common Council from 1789 to 1831 hitherto in manuscript form, and unavailable for public reference, and the removal of that eyesore in City Hall Park, the old Post Office, now in process of demolition. In only one of its measures did it fail—to remove the present buildings from Welfare (?) Island and turn it into a beautiful public Park. However, I was not shot at sunrise for thinking of this grand idea, which was something.

I remember writing Frederick Gallatin, then Commissioner of Parks, on a letterhead which bore the title, "The Museum of the City of New York." That was all there was at the time to the Museum. My note was on an altogether different topic, but Mr. Gallatin asked me to call upon him, which I did.

"Where is your Museum?" he asked. Being an old New Yorker, he was naturally interested.

"Well," I said, "it is not for publication yet, but it is the Vanderbilt Mansion on Fifth Avenue at Fifty-seventh Street."

"Oh!" he replied, "I congratulate you. I was going to offer you the Gracie Mansion in Carl Schurz Park."

"Mr. Gallatin," I answered, after I had recovered from the shock, "you are talking to the biggest liar since Baron Munchausen. In the words of Margery Daw, there isn't any old Colonial house, there isn't any Vanderbilt Mansion and there isn't any Museum!" But it was a great idea just the same.

I was taking no chances at that particular moment and the upshot of it was that I secured the Gracie Mansion for the first home of the new Museum. And now it has a magnificent building of its own on Fifth Avenue.

Although the *Manual* erected the Liberty Pole, a former President of the Sons of the Revolution paid the bill, as he has paid all the bills, with one exception, of the Governors and staffs of the various States who have brought a stone from a Revolutionary battlefield to build the base.

Many attempts to remove the Post Office had been made, but the present plans now being carried out are exactly those arranged with Will Hays, while Postmaster General, who really galvanized the project into life, even though it took ten years to get definite action. His prompt adoption of the idea should not be forgotten. New York owes him a debt of gratitude.

And in rescuing the old Minutes of the Common Council from obscurity, which were at last put in book form, a Mr. Williamson, then librarian of the Municipal Reference Library, played a prominent part. Although he had never heard about the Minutes, he quickly grasped the significance of my request and the importance of the project. He had been a classmate of Mayor Mitchel in college, and through this acquaintance, was able to put the matter through, where Dr. Hegeman Hall and I had repeatedly failed.

In preparation for this book, I spent a year in the countries of our origin—England, France, Holland and Belgium.

It was a wonderful experience. I think such a background is absolutely necessary to any man who attempts to write a History of New York. Some traces of this sojourn I hope are discernible in this book. Through the kindness of Mr. Ralph D. Blumenfeld, of the *London Express,* I was cordially received by many of the old families whose ancestors fought in the Revolution and gained an acquaintance with our English cousins, the charm of whom it is hard to describe.

The Duke of York collected an amazing amount of material pertaining to our City. It makes about fifty volumes in the British Museum. The library of the House of Lords; the Custodian of Documents in the Record Office; the Middle Temple; Somerset House, and the private correspondence in the libraries of the Earl and Countess of Howe, Lord and Lady Cornwallis, and others, provided interesting material. The Clinton and Gage correspondence was bought by a wealthy lumberman out West who promptly removed it to the forests primeval of Michigan. These papers cover the period of the British occupancy of New York, 1776–1783, and no doubt contain some interesting material of a military and official character. They are not available at present to the public, and I doubt very much whether the letters are what I want for a book of this particular kind. New York was made by its people— not by foreign fighters, and it is of their hopes, their fears, their achievements, that I write.

Exactly why any lumberman, steel man, glue man or any other kind of a man, living away from New York, should purchase a lot of valuable documents pertaining solely to this City and of no special value to any other place, and then cart them off to the arid wastes of his own home town, I do not know. But that is precisely what this lumber person did. They should have been presented to the New York Public Library and exhibited in a special room. Students, writers and others would then have gladly subscribed for a marble bust of the generous gentleman to stand in the very middle of the main corridor, or between the paws of the lions outside, if necessary.

At old Cambridge University, I was not so much interested in New York for the moment, as I was to look over those pothooks and cabalistic figures of our dear delightful friend—Samuel Pepys. I reveled in the pictures of London in the Sixteenth Century which this lovable old rascal has so magnificently portrayed. And I prayed that I might write a book on New York that would reflect, as he did, the manners, the customs, the life of the people of New York that *I* knew, as he has done of the London that *he* knew. But we haven't all the genius of Pepys, so we can only hope that our efforts may not be wholly writ in water. And I was also reminded that it was in old Cambridge, that Charles Kingsley, sometime professor of history in this venerable seat of learning, resigned his office, saying that "no honest man could teach history any more."

Anyhow, it was delightful to ramble through England. I happened to be in York when the guide was explaining to a group of tourists that the tablet he was now showing them was presented by the City of New York in America, its namesake.

"That's my home town," I called out. "I am glad the folks had the decency to do such a nice thing." My old friend's name, John F. Hylan, was at the head of the tablet!

There is probably no more interesting city in all England than old York. There is a legend that it was founded by a near relative of that greatest of all psalmists, David, the sweet singer of Israel. I think it was made by the angels. York was at one time another Rome; Roman Emperors were born and died in York, and the first Christian Emperor here took up the reins of government. And to-day there are relics of Rome the Great, in York, that are none the less interesting than are found in the Rome of Italy. And reminders of its Danish and Norman occupation are still plainly in evidence.

The great glory of York is of course its magnificent Minster, the gorgeous Church of St. Peter, built by the medieval Archbishops, through the munificence of the great York families. It is particularly rich in stained glass and the shrine of Archbishop de Gray is one of the most beautiful in the world of ecclesiastic art. No less than fifty churches stood in old York before the Reformation: some thirty of these still remain. In her ancient Guildhall hangs the brass tablet, just mentioned, presented upon the occasion of the three hundredth anniversary of the birth of NEW York, its namesake in America.

The quaint overhanging buildings in the Tudor style remain, many looking just as they did when the great Elizabeth passed through here.

I have sought to tell my tale simply. Such errors of detail as may possibly creep in will not lead to a false interpretation of the period; the nature of the subject does not lend itself to an unbroken narrative, but the unity of the volume lies in its effort to portray the rise and progress of New York during its three centuries. In the present volume I have conformed to the accepted theory that New York was founded by the Dutch. The claim of the Belgians as set forth recently by its amiable Ambassador at Washington is noted, and his facts duly recorded.

With the close of the eighteenth century, our city unconsciously became the whole United States, and has reluctantly and blushingly been compelled to play that rôle ever since; so the Story of Old New York is also a short History of the American People.

The present book ends where steam enters our civilization, and our whole social fabric changes. The next hundred years are dazzling. I hope to complete the entire work. Life's evening shadows sometimes slip disconcertingly into the big black night without warning. Some other pen will then be found to carry on. "The indispensable man," as the Honorable Joe Pulitzer remarked upon a memorable occasion, "is not very numerous."

The work of many other writers has helped me; also institutions and individuals, both here and abroad, not forgetting the little Public Library in my home town, White Plains, if I may single it out for special mention without incurring the hostility of the British Museum, the Bibliothèque Nationale, the New York Public Library or the New York Historical Society. A great deal can be learned from those who have gone before and left some records of their pilgrimage.

And now—

"I pray you,
let us satisfy our eyes,
with the memorials and things of fame,
that do renown our city."

THE AUTHOR

Contents

xiii

Contents

Contents

Illustrations

xvii

PAGE

THE STORY
OF OLD NEW YORK

t' Fort nieuw Amsterdam op de Manhatans

First view of New York ever shown to the world—about 1626–8.
Published by Joost Hartgers, Holland, in a book on Nieuw
Amsterdam written by a Yonkers man, Adrian Van der·Donck.

CHAPTER I

Who First Founded New York?

NOT far from the little fishing village of Palos de Mogues in Andalusia, there stood and stands at the present day the ancient Convent of Franciscan Friars dedicated to Santa Maria de la Rabida. One day a stranger on foot stopped at the gate of the convent and asked of the porter a little bread and water. While partaking of this humble fare, the Prior of the convent, happening to pass by, was struck by the distinguished appearance of the stranger, who bore himself with an air of dignity unusual in pilgrims, entered into conversation with him, and soon learned the particulars of his story. Disheartened with the many delays at the Spanish Court, Columbus determined to abandon his efforts with Ferdinand of Castile and Isabella of Aragon.

The Prior was a learned man. His attention in some manner had been turned to the science of geography and he was deeply impressed not only with the grandeur of the views of Columbus, but with his profound knowledge of navigation. It was rather an unusual experience for the little convent to entertain a stranger of such extraordinary character and to be made a partner thus unexpectedly in so vast an undertaking. For the worthy Prior at once realized that a golden opportunity was here presented, whereby Spain would become the ruler of the seas and possibly of a new and greater empire. He could not bear the thought that his dear country should miss so wonderful a prize. At one time, he had been Father Confessor to Her

Majesty. He knew that by the nature of his holy office, he could obtain access to her where more powerful men would fail. So he pressed Columbus to remain an honored guest, and meantime set on foot his own plans for reopening the project with the Government. He sent for his friend and confidant, Garcia Fernandez, a doctor living in Palos, who repaired immediately to the convent and was presented to Columbus.

His impression was in accord with the favorable one already formed by the Prior. The two friends laid their heads together, and finally, in the quiet cloisters of La Rabida, was evolved the plan which gave to Spain the undying glory of discovering the Western World.

The amazing result of the voyage of Columbus broke upon Europe with all the suddenness of a thunderclap.

When Columbus ceased to speak before the courtiers of Barcelona and told them of his discoveries—

> . . . The King and Queen
> Sank from their throne and melted into tears
> And knelt and lifted hand and heart and voice
> In praise of God, who led him through the wastes
> And the great "Laudamus" rose to heaven.

The whole world seethed with suppressed excitement. Daring navigators set out at once for the El Dorado beyond the seas. Power and glory, gold and dominion, beckoned them on.

England, France, Portugal, Holland, followed hard upon the tracks of the dauntless Italian. Cabot was the first to reach the mainland. Henry Hudson in *The Half Moon* entered the harbor of New York. He sailed up the river which now bears his name. The Dutch, a few years later, settled upon the little island at its mouth. The history of New York began.

It is hard to believe that only a little more than three

hundred years ago the great City of New York was a far-
flung outpost on the shore of an unknown rocky region
beyond the rim of the world. Wild beasts roamed where
now are concrete roads, and wilder red men lurked in
every shadow. Wooded shores were all around the island
even at its widest part. It was a mass of rocks, covered here
and there with straggling patches of scrawny earth crowned
with tufts of mangy grass. To coax a crop from such reluctant and belligerent soil was not husbandry—it was a
triumph of black magic and burglary. The shores on both
sides made a gradual ascent to almost a hundred and fifty
feet, and a path that ran along the high ridge thus formed,
commanded a sweeping view in every direction. This
strategic outlook was naturally the favorite trail of the
Indian. That trail is now old Broadway.

On the right was the lordly Hudson, called the *North*
River, though it isn't north of the city at all. It lies directly
west. At the top of the island was an estuary of this stream,
separating it from the mainland—the Harlem—and now
mistakenly called a river; on the left, a thin arm of the
blue waters of Long Island Sound, which we call the East
River—another error; and on the south, the most glamorous harbor in all the world. Only in our magnificently spacious bay can warships anchor almost at your front door,
where you can hear their "six bells," "eight bells" sound-
ing the knell of parting day. The noble Drive that skirts
the river is known the world over as the Street of the Lass
who loves a Sailor.

Overhead, a sunny sky bluer than Italy's; in the woods,
stately elms, oaks, birches, pines, and sycamores; wild
grapes, raspberries, strawberries, currant bushes, apple
trees and peach trees. There may not have been any peach
trees on the Island. The fact that they do not succeed very
well except in certain parts of the country, suggests that
possibly they were not indigenous. However, there was at

one time a song that was extremely popular,—"In old New York, in old New York, the peach crop's always fine." A fresh-water lake, deep enough to float an ocean liner, lay in the middle of the island like a diamond sparkling in the sun. This lake lay between Worth & Duane Sts. and from the Bowery to Broadway and is now covered by the County Court Buildings and new Civic Center. Rippling streams and gurgling springs flowed everywhere. It was, indeed, a realm of enchantment and a pleasant land to live in.

The island was peopled by a tribe of red men, who called it "Manhadoes"—Island of the Hills. It contained twenty-two thousand acres. A few portable wigwams, half-a-dozen canoes lightly tethered to the banks, were all that foreshadowed our present massive skyscrapers and our great transatlantic steamships. Any small moving picture house today would seat more than the entire population of the little newly discovered island. It was purchased from the Indians by the Dutch who gave in exchange a handful of tawdry trinkets valued at about twenty-four dollars!

With the coming of the Dutch, New York lost the name by which it had been known for almost a hundred years— Virginia. That was the name bestowed upon the whole region then known in North America, by the redoubtable navigator and explorer, Captain John Smith, whose work was one of the notable achievements of the reign of Elizabeth. He named the entire known continent "Virginia" in honor of the Virgin Queen who made him first Captain, and later Admiral, of Virginia. This included all the territory we now call New England, which Smith had discovered and explored. The little settlement of Jamestown, founded under James I, was fifteen years old before Plymouth was born, alluding to which, Shakespeare wrote,

Shall make new nations.
His honor and the greatness of his name,

But even before Jamestown, Sir Walter Raleigh planted a colony on Roanoke Island, which has a romantic tie with New York. To this day, in this region, are still preserved many of the old customs and of the English of Elizabeth's time. They still speak of a "couthy" woman, meaning a capable one, and say "heerd," "disremember," "wine" for vine; and they drop the "g" in words like aimin', singin', goin', etc.

Five days after the arrival of the second expedition in 1587, a little girl was born to one of the passengers, and the place where this child, Virginia Dare, the first English native of America, saw the light of day is marked by an attractive monument on the site of old Fort Raleigh. Little Virginia lived with her companions on the island for three years and then all trace of the colony is lost. Nothing was ever heard of it again, and but for this curious lingering of Elizabethan speech, it would be as if it had never existed.

The tie with New York, of which we would speak, centers around a portrait of Theodosia Burr, daughter of Aaron Burr, which was found in the hut of an old woman on Nag's Head just across the channel from Roanoke Island.

In 1812 Theodosia was on her way to rejoin her father in New York. The boat on which she sailed was said to have been captured by pirates and all hands made to walk the plank to a watery grave. Even to this day, echoes of this tragedy reappear in items in the papers from time to time purporting to be the confession of some mysterious person who claims to have been one of the pirate gang.

Be that as it may, the boat itself, the *Patriot* on which she sailed, was cast up by the sea on Nag's Head. As was their custom, the pirates scuttled the abandoned vessel, and one of them, the narrator's sweetheart, had kept, as his part of the loot, a portrait in oil painted on mahogany.

For nearly sixty years it had been hidden away by this woman, before she decided to hang it up.

Dr. W. G. Pool of Elizabeth, North Carolina, was called to minister to this woman, and noticed this picture on the wall. His patient told him the story and offered to give it to him in lieu of a fee. The doctor recognizing a possible likeness to Theodosia, submitted it to members of the Burr family, who declared it bore a striking resemblance to that young woman. The portrait eventually found its way to a reputable art firm in New York, by whom it was sold to Mr. Herbert L. Pratt of our city and whose collection of early American portraits is considered the finest in the country.

So there is quite a tie between Raleigh's first settlement and Old New York, by reason of this portrait; which is our excuse for printing this interesting little romance.

England's great admiral, Sir Francis Drake, also appears in this picture for a moment; he was Sir Walter's Commander-in-Chief in the great battle of the Spanish Armada, and his personal friend. He rescued the members of the second colony sent out by Raleigh, who were obliged to return to England.

Company after company was subsequently formed in London for development of different sections. These sections took the names selected by their proprietors and the old general name gradually disappeared, till it applied to only one of the Thirteen Original States.

On Star Island, one of the Isles of Shoals off the Maine coast, there is a monument to Captain Smith—a triangular shaft of marble rising eight or ten feet above a craggy rock. Its situation is on one of the highest eminences of the island and the monument is crowned with heads—the three Moslems slain by Smith, of which we shall speak later. There is no other instance of decapitated heads being set up in New England since King Philip's was struck off and stuck on a pike in Plymouth in 1676. Two of the heads have since fallen down and the third seems doomed to follow. Captain Smith was all over this coast and made many maps of it.

This monument stands in a silent place forever removed from the noise and the clamor which marked the militant career of this fierce warrior. It is in singular contrast to the peaceful lives of three half-forgotten graves of the little children of a missionary, which lie at the foot of Captain Smith's monument. They are wholly covered by dwarf willows and wild rosebushes. On the stone that marks the grave of the eldest—Mittie, seven years old—are these touching and tearful words, "I don't want to die, but I'll do what Jesus wants me to."

Captain Smith's grave is in the old Church of St. Sepulchre in London over against Newgate, where Kidd was tried and condemned. In an otherwise admirable pamphlet given to visitors by the church people, it tells us about his romance with Pocahontas. She thought he had been killed, and married John Rolfe. When Smith afterwards turned up alive, the shock was too much for the poor little Indian maid and she died of a broken heart. This is touching and very romantic, but, alas, has nothing to do with the real facts. Smith disappeared all right enough; that was the life of an explorer—here today and gone tomorrow. So Pocahontas was wooed and won by John Rolfe, one of Smith's companions. They lived for many happy years together in Heacham, Norfolk, where Rolfe took her when he returned to England. To this day the Royal Family of England retain a decided personal interest in Virginia. In the Spring of 1933, Her Majesty Queen Mary paid her annual visit to Heacham where Pocahontas first came to live with her husband. She called on Mrs. Torney, a direct descendant of John Rolfe. This charming old lady —she is past eighty—still lives near the spot to which Pocahontas came as a bride. A monument to the memory of Pocahontas was erected in 1933.

The Queen does not take that trouble except for reasons of more than ordinary importance. Three hundred years ago, Pocahontas was fêted and received at the Court of a Stuart King and the memory of that incident is kept green in England by Royalty to this very day. She is still spoken of in that town as "The Princess," and a stained-glass window has been erected to her memory in the little Church of St. George at Gravesend, near the mouth of the Thames, where she lies buried. She was on the eve of sailing to revisit her native land when that dreaded disease, smallpox, seized her and she died. The descendants of Pocahontas and John Rolfe, however, gave us two Presidents, General William H. Harrison, an old Indian fighter himself, by the way, and his grandson, Benjamin Harrison.

But what that robust and romantic warrior, Captain Smith, did for us in the way of genealogy is something little short of marvelous. It is so awe-inspiring that mere words utterly fail to portray the inestimable benefits to mankind which he conferred upon them in this direction. He was undoubtedly the creator of that now well-known primrose path of dalliance. Wherever he wandered, young Smiths sprang up immediately, as daffodils grow in the Scilly Islands or tulips in Holland. Our telephone books are testimony to his activity and fertility.

But there is another side to this picturesque and valiant soldier of the Queen. In the ancient church of which we have just spoken, there is a beautiful memorial window depicting his adventures and an illuminated brass tablet recounting his exploits as a knight errant in the service of Good Queen Bess. It was here that he received Holy Communion before setting out on his great adventures, and in a house on Snow Hill, just opposite the old church and within the shadow of its tower, he breathed his last.

On the tablet erected in loving memory, we read an account of his life and

> In honor of his God and Christendom
> That he did divide from Pagans three
> Their heads and lives, proof of his chivalry.

The great Sigismundus of Hungarion, ruler of that great Eastern Empire under which he fought, was so pleased with this delicate accomplishment, that he bestowed upon young Smith the privilege of decorating his coat of arms with the three severed heads. You see them in the stained-glass window.

He was a member of the ancient and worshipful Company of Cordwainers, in London, and in their files is preserved a letter from Smith setting forth how his men's shoes gave out and how they "Had to tie the bark of trees around their feet to keep them from being cut by the shelles among which we must go or starve."

A right colorful figure was John Smith, sometime Governor of Virginia and Admiral of New England and a worthy representative of that gallant company of sea dogs assembled by the Virgin Queen. He was among the bystanders who heard this great Queen harangue her troops at Tilbury, when England stood at bay to repel the insolent Spaniard and his Invincible Armada.

The popular name of the remnant of Virginia, that former huge section, which originally embraced all the Colonies—"The Old Dominion"—has quite a romantic origin. It appears that during the exile of the Second Charles in Holland, the Colony of Virginia fitted out a small boat which they sailed to Breda, and there presented to Charles a formal invitation to become King of Virginia. The sudden change in English political opinion, by which Charles was called to the throne of his father, prevented an acceptance. But Charles always recalled that offer with affectionate gratitude and when he was crowned, he styled himself "King of England, Ireland, Scotland and the *Dominion of Virginia*," and caused the arms of the Colony to be quartered on the Royal Standard.

This ancient name of Virginia for New York, therefore, should be carefully borne in mind, as it was afterwards made the basis on which England expelled the Dutch, and later the French, from the Western World. When this great section was finally subdivided into the thirteen original Colonies, some curious results, now wholly forgotten, were achieved. Had the boundaries of these thirteen States remained as laid out at that time, Chicago and Cleveland would have been in Connecticut; Detroit in Massachusetts, and St. Louis in Virginia.

The directory of London is over six hundred years old; the directory of New York a hundred and forty-three. Rome this year, 1934, celebrated her 2686th birthday, and Paris was a little fishing village on the Banks of the Seine long before the Christian Era began.

There are no buildings in New York of which we can say, "In that church is buried the Captain of the *Mayflower*," or, "On that parapet Jacob Leisler passed the last agonizing moments of his life." No streets of hers have echoed to the martial tread of Cæsar's Roman Legions; the tramp, tramp of Cromwell's stern warriors, or the gentler footsteps of Chaucer's Canterbury Pilgrims. Compared with the other great cities of the world, it is a mere infant still in swaddling clothes. Yet its claim to be the leading city of the Western World and second in size in all the world, is undisputed. What it will be a thousand years hence, the mind of man cannot foretell.

The claim of England to all of North America was primarily based on the discoveries of John and Sebastian Cabot, who set sail from Bristol in 1498. This was long before Smith appeared on the scene. The spot from which the Cabots embarked from the quayside in the ancient English city, and the splendid Cabot Tower which has been erected to commemorate their work, are interesting sites in their old home town. There is good reason to believe that Bartholomew Columbus, a brother of the great explorer, may have had much to do with suggesting this voyage. He had come to interest the English King in his brother's behalf, and stayed at Bristol with the Cabots several years.

It is now widely believed that the Cabots gave the name "America" to the new world. There was a collector of customs in Bristol at that time, called Richard Ameryk who was largely instrumental in raising funds for the expeditions of the Cabots. Several payments at various times to John Cabot are recorded in his books. As the origin of the name rests largely upon conjecture at best, these seem excellent ground for the belief that America was suggested by the Cabots in honor of their paymaster. It was no harm then, as now, to pay whatever compliments you could, to the gentleman who disburses the cash.

Amerigo Vespucci at that time was unknown. He was an obscure clerk in the office of the Medici at Florence and later a dealer in secondhand ship-chandlery. Many years before he appeared as a navigator, the name America had already been printed on various contemporary maps. So the supposition that America was derived from Richard Ameryk rests on very tangible ground.

Researches in history constantly bring new facts to light, and one of the strangest is that a considerable French settlement existed on Manhattan Island a hundred years before the Dutch. The name of the settlement was Norumbega. You will find it spread all over many of our early maps, extending over a vast region from New England almost to the Great Lakes. It is not the name of an Indian tribe, as has been supposed. It is Norman French. It is clearly indicated on a map drawn by the celebrated cartographer, Mercator, published in 1569. Mercator is one of the few map-makers upon whom we can rely, and this map showing Norumbega appeared in the first map ever published showing geographical projections, and marks an epoch in map-making. A copy is in the British Museum.

There is not much known about this little settlement, yet it seems to have been quite an important trading post. It was located on the shores of Collect Pond where now stands our new County Court House. Its location had some economic advantages. It was between Albany from whence came the peltries, and the Long Island shores where wampum was made, the money of the Indians. Wampum was the gold standard of these days, and it was a convenience to the traders to have a supply of this money within easy reach. So there was a practical reason for the selection of Manhattan Island as headquarters.

This settlement by the French is interesting, but apparently of no great importance. It left no lasting impression on Manhattan Island; and long before the Dutch arrived, all traces of its existence had been swallowed up. The devastating wars which followed the cruel and needless Massacre of St. Bartholomew provoked reprisals which, for the next hundred years, engaged all the resources of the Gallic Empire and distracted her attention from the magnificent possibilities in the New World, foreshadowed by the enchanting discoveries of Frontenac, La Salle, Cartier, Champlain, and Pere Marquette. When she finally awoke to the real situation, the British lion had his forepaws on the Atlantic, and his tail wagged on the Ohio.

We have, however, in Norumbega, quite unconsciously, the first recognition of the natural advantages of Manhattan Island as a center of commerce. Although its marvelous harbor, its miles of landlocked wharves, its lordly river, tapping the wealth of the West, were not recognized till more than two centuries later, it never ceased, after its start, to press forward to its manifest destiny. That Salem, Newport, and Boston were, for nearly two centuries, the leading maritime ports on the Atlantic Coast—with Salem far in the lead—is admitted. But New York slowly but surely outstripped them all both in commerce and population, and today even the fame of so great and so ancient a maritime port as Salem is all but forgotten. And it is with a recital of how this progress began and continued that our story deals.

The New York with which we are concerned came into view by reason of its discovery by Henry Hudson and its settlement by the Dutch. In the little Church of St. Ethelberger in London, adjoining the imposing office building of the Hudson Bay Company, is a stained-glass window to commemorate the attendance here of Hudson and his crew for the blessing of the Church before starting on their dangerous adventure. It is a gift from the venerable corporation which he created and which recalls the memory of their intrepid founder.

Hudson was an Englishman. His father was an Alderman in London and a member of the famous Muscovy Company, of which Sebastian Cabot was the first Governor and of which both Hudson's father and grandfather were factors, and under whom Hudson had made two unsuccessful voyages seeking a supposed northwest passage to the Far East. As a result of his failure in this direction, he was not in high favor and was naturally held in low esteem by the Muscovy Company. He had at this time a very warm friend in the learned historian van Meteren, the Ambassador from Holland to the Court of St. James's. It is rightly conjectured that Hudson was prevailed upon by this friend to accept service under the Dutch. No encouragement being offered by his old employers, Hudson felt free to en-

gage with anyone in need of his services. So he signed up
with the Dutch West India Company in command of *The
Half Moon*. For his perilous journey in the frailest of frail
crafts, Hudson was to receive the stupendous sum of three
hundred and twenty dollars. In case he never returned, the
Company magnanimously agreed to pay his bereaved
widow a further sum of eighty dollars in cash.

Men who went down to the sea in ships, those days, did
not rate high in the economic scale. In the Record Office
in London, you can see a letter from Elizabeth to Martin
Frobisher about to start on one of his voyages: "I have sixteen men to whom you are welcome," writes the great
Queen. "They are already condemned to die; so if anything happens, it won't matter." And so Hudson sailed—to
gain not only a few paltry dollars but to achieve undying
fame as one of the world's greatest discoverers, and to link
irrevocably his name with one of the mightiest and greatest achievements in all history.

He was born, no one knows exactly when or where. He
died—no one knows when or how. Even his portraits are
imaginary, and we do not know his age. He comes into our
knowledge on the quarterdeck of a sixty-foot shallop. He
goes out of it in a leaky rowboat manned by eight scurvy-
crazed sailors, turned adrift from his ship, the victim of a
cruel mutiny, and left to perish miserably in the frozen
wastes of the Arctic Seas.

On this, his last voyage, he took with him a young man
named Henry Green, of worshipful parents but of forward
and unseemly life, whom he sought to reform and to have
for his secretary. It was this viper who devised the mutiny.
Our chronicler tells us with satisfaction that before reaching the ocean, the faithless Green and his abettors were
slain by the Indians. On arriving in England, the crew
were thrown into jail and an expedition was sent out in

search of the great navigator; but in spite of diligent seeking, no more was ever seen or heard of Henry Hudson.

The man who came to such an untimely end was a notable victim of the irony of human destiny. In all that he attempted, he failed, and yet achieved great results that were not contemplated in his original plans. He started two immense industries, the Spitzbergen whale fisheries and the Hudson Bay fur trade; and he brought the Dutch to Manhattan Island. But no realization of his dreams, however wild, could have approached the astonishing reality which the incoming voyager now beholds in sailing up the Bay of New York. What perhaps might have surprised him most of all would have been to know that his name was to become part of the folklore of the beautiful river to which it is attached; that he was, in spite of himself, to figure as a Dutchman, in legend and story; that when it was thunder weather on the Catskills, the children would say: "It is Hendrik Hudson playing at skittles with his goblin crew!"

Perhaps it is not an unkindly fate. Even as Milton wished for his dead friend, Lycidas, that he might become the genius of the shore, so the memory of the great Arctic navigator will remain a familiar presence among the hillsides and the gurgling streams which the gentle fancy of the whimsical Irving has clothed with undying romance.

The scene when Hudson and his crew of the *Hopewell* appeared at the ancient Church of St. Ethelberger the Virgin Within, Bishopgate in London, to receive Holy Communion before starting out on one of his first voyages, is well worth recalling. The little church was founded in the Eleventh Century and was miraculously spared in the great fire of London in 1666 and still stands directly opposite the imposing offices of the Hudson Bay Company which was founded as a result of his discovery. It is a diminutive building only 30 x 60 feet, but has a steeple and two quaint little shops in the porch facing the street in which books were sold as was customary in Tudor days. It has three beautiful stained-glass windows in memory of Hudson, one built by subscriptions from our own country. They represent Hudson before starting on his first voyage; Hudson meeting the red Indians; Hudson cast adrift with eight men to perish miserably in the frozen waters of the Arctic Ocean. Underneath the last is a scroll reading:

> He sleepeth beneath the radiant vault of peace,
> among the brave who lie forever still,

and below the first:

> They laughed at dangers and scorned the delights
> of easeful lives.

The record of the Communion Service is delightful reading.

Anno 1607 April the nineteenth, at Saint Ethelberger in Bishop Gate street did communicate with the rest of the Parishoners these persons Seamen, purposing to goe to sea foure dayes after, for to discover a passage by the North Pole to Japan and China, First Henry Hudson Master, Secondly William Colines his Mate, Thirdly James Young, Fourthly John Coleman, Fifthly John Cooke, Sixthly James Benbery, Seventhly James Skrutton, Eighthly John Pleyce, Ninethly Thomas Baxter, Tenthly Richard Day, Eleventhly James Knight, twentiethly, John Hudson, a boy.

A word might be said about these early discoverers before we proceed with our story. There is something peculiarly moving in the trials, disappointments and the final triumphs of those intrepid old navigators, a feeling not unmixed with a pang of deep regret that they never knew the great work they had accomplished.

Stained glass memorial window to Henry
Hudson erected by Hudson Bay Co. in
Church of St. Ethelberger the Virgin,
London. *1930.*

Not only did these intrepid sailors suffer incredible hardships sailing uncharted seas, but they were also continually harassed by the superstitious fears of the crew who constantly imagined frightful and ghoulish forms arising out of the vasty deep seeking their destruction. It was common belief among seafaring men, that beyond the horizon was inferno, that it was peopled by a horde of demons. But that they were not all abhorrent creatures, is apparent from an entry by Hudson himself in his journal describing the voyage to New York in *The Half Moon*. He says:

This morning, one of our companie looking overboard saw a Mermaid and calling up some of the companie to see her, one man came up and by that time she was come close to the ships side looking earnestly on the man; a little later a sea came and overturned her; from the navel upward her back and breasts were like a woman's (as they say that saw her) her body as big as one of us; her skin very white and long haire hanging down behind of colour blacke; in her going down they saw her tayle which was like the tayle of a porpoise and speckled like a macrell. The names that saw her were Thomas Hilles and Robert Raynor. Written by myself, Henry Hudson.

Hudson, apparently realizing that there were many doubting Thomases in this poor world of ours, takes the precautionary measure of affixing the names of the eyewitnesses to the exciting circumstance which he records.

These incidents, however, were rarely as diverting as this. Usually the apparition breathed fire and brimstone and was consumed with a deadly fury against those who had invaded his heretofore inviolate domain. It caused much trouble among the crews and was a prime cause of the mutinous spirit that frequently broke out.

There is a portrait of Hudson in our City Hall which is said to have been painted from life and to have hung in the original Dutch Stadt House in Coenties Slip. This is all bosh. There is no authentic likeness of Hudson known to exist.

Of Verrazani, whose statue adorns the Battery and who is known to have viewed Manhattan Island from a distance but passed it up, we have but little to record. His career was brief. He was soon after captured by the Spaniards and hung as a pirate.

Bartholomew Gosnold, Sir Francis Drake, Martin Pring, George Weymouth, Christopher Newport, Sir Walter Raleigh, Ferdinand de Soto, Champlain, de la Salle, Marquette, Vincent de Gama, and many others, all died without the slightest knowledge of the great continent they had seen. They are all entitled to a monument as much as Verrazani.

When we speak of "the Dutch coming to New York," we unconsciously repeat what all historians have taught us concerning the founders of our great city. But it is ever the task of the seeker after truth to delve farther and still farther into the dusty documents of the past in the elusive hope that he may discover some new facts or correct old statements proven to be no longer accurate. The loss of all the correspondence, public and private, contained in the papers of the West India Company and which were unforgivenly sold to the junkman in 1821, has left an irreparable blank in the early history of New York and leaves many things to conjecture.

As Montaigne remarks, "Nothing is so firmly believed as what we least know." And so in this chapter we shall discuss casually, and without bias, the claims of the Huguenots or Belgians to be the first settlers of New York. This claim of late years has grown more and more insistent. Only recently, the accomplished Ambassador from Belgium, His Excellency, Mr. Paul May, spoke over the radio on this subject; Mrs. Robert de Forrest who has had access to unusual source material, and Professor Henry G. Bayer of the University of New York, have each contributed an important monograph. Yet we do not think any New Yorker proud of his distinguished Dutch ancestry need be alarmed; even if he has to share his glory with the Walloons, there is still enough left to go round.

We have already alluded to a settlement by the French on Manhattan Island in 1525, a hundred years before the coming of the Dutch. A map drawn by Gerard Mercator, shows this settlement on the Island plainly marked "Norumbega." This name is also attached to the hinterland, covering all New England and west to the Great Lakes. This name was copied by other map-makers at a later period, and in time came to be considered as of Indian origin. The Curator of Maps in the British Museum, however, says it is Norman French. It is also applied to the Hudson River. In cases like this where other knowledge is lacking, a map by a cartographer of established reputation is a formidable document and is regarded as convincing evidence. It is outside the realm of conjecture or speculation.

Harrisse, the authoritative writer on early American Voyages, has but little to say in detail about Norumbega. He mentions the fact that such a voyage was made, but says it had no official connection and was just a casual trip by some adventurous sailors. Beyond this mere statement of fact he does not go into any further details. Stokes in his *Iconography* records this map, but is also reticent regarding particulars. John Fiske, however, in his *Dutch and English Colonies in America*, goes much deeper into the subject.

This first appearance of the French on Manhattan soil is regarded, by the adherents of the Walloons, to be of vast importance. In matters historical a century is but a day; and they point to this fact with increasing insistence and offer it as

Exhibit Number One. Perhaps tradition may have handed down some legends among the Walloons concerning the New World and thus planted the germ of future migration.

But when the Walloons read that "The fact remains undisputed that to Henry Hudson belongs the honor of being the first to attract public attention to the Island of Manhattan as an advantageous point for a trading post in the New World," they are convulsed with laughter; and point out with glee the fact that Hudson had been dead over seventeen years before the first settlement of New York was attempted. Henry was no doubt a good navigator, but as a publicity agent for the Island, they question whether he would even qualify as a guest speaker at Grover Whalen's famous noonday forums at the Advertiser Club.

They also make much of the absolute indifference with which Hudson's discovery was actually treated by the Dutch. It was placed by them on a par with his subsequent voyage to the Artic Seas, and rated as another complete and colossal failure. They defy you to connect Hudson's voyages with any plan whatever to settle New York.

Furthermore, they point significantly to the fact that his name was not even mentioned in connection with the River till 1809. Upon the occasion of a dinner given by the New York Historical Society in that year, to commemorate the two hundredth anniversary of the discovery of the River, the suggestion was made that his name be given to it hereafter on all Maps, Drawings and Documents. This idea was taken up with enthusiasm. In due time the old name was dropped except on the portion flowing past the city. From Spuyten Duyvil to the Battery, it still retains the old appellation—North River; but beyond that it is the Hudson. So Hudson's work is conceded to have been confined to an effort to find a shorter passage to the East Indies, and had no colonization idea in it whatever.

The Walloons or Belgians base their claim to be the first
settlers of New York on the voyage of the *New Netherland,*
a ship which sailed into the harbor from New Amsterdam
in 1623 and landed thirty Walloon families. The formal
purchase of Manhattan Island by Peter Minuit (also a
Walloon) acting for the West India Company, did not
occur until three years later. All of these thirty families did
not remain in New York. Some went to Albany and elsewhere, so that they had part in settling not only the City,
but several other adjacent towns as well. This voyage is a
matter of record and is not disputed.

In addition to this voyage, however, the Walloons point
to other and perhaps more pertinent and convincing evidence—the existence of two contemporary maps showing
the region under discussion. One of them portrayed "New
Amsterdam" for the first time on any map. This is the now
famous Visscher map, as it is known to students. The striking feature about this map from a Walloon point of view
is that the formal title is not "New Netherland" as one
would naturally suppose, representing as it does a new possession of the Dutch Republic, but *"Nova Belgii"*—New
Belgium. In the interior, the land is again called *"Nova
Belgii,"* but as a sub-title the words "New Netherland"
also appear. As if to reënforce this Belgian claim, the first
seal of the City, 1623; the second, 1654, and Governor
Stuyvesant's private seal, 1659, all carry that same *"Nova
Belgii."* These exhibits are at least interesting, even if they
have no vital bearing on the topic we have brought up.
Doubtless, the reason for their existence would be found
in some of these old records, now so hopelessly lost. They
also claim that Stuyvesant is not a Dutch name, and we
can agree with them that Judith Bayard, his wife, was certainly not Dutch, neither is Nicholas Fish.

Who first settled New York, will probably never be
known. A certain Father Jogues, a well-known Jesuit Mis-

Courtesy of New York Historical Society.

Seals of the City.

sionary in those days, paid a visit to New Amsterdam about two years after the town was started. He reports the astounding fact that no less than eighteen tongues were spoken there. From a drawing made at this time (1628), the "Hartgers View"—the first ever made of the city—we find that there were thirty houses in the settlement, besides the Fort and the Church—perhaps a total population of a hundred and sixty people. When you come to divide this population into eighteen different languages, you get about nine persons to a tongue. As the Dutch were not included with the Walloons, it makes about four and a half of each, against a foreign population of nearly eight times their numerical strength. These foreigners seem also to have been among the "first settlers."

No doubt, some gallant champion will arise to put the bird on the hired assassins who would rob the Dutch of their glory, and in this event we hope he will at the same time clear up the Ugly Duckling atmosphere that has always enshrouded this darling of the gods. Even after thirty years of occupation in 1653, when it was organized as a city and local officers appointed Sheriff, Schouts, Burgomasters, etc., it had a population of only 750, most of whom were English, French, Portuguese, German and Spanish. Some say that barely ten per cent were Dutch—not exactly, one is tempted to say, a shining example of fostering care by the Motherland.

In this book we shall conform to the accepted tradition. To deny the Dutch the credit of founding New York, is a matter requiring infinite research and irrefutable documentary evidence—a task which we must leave to scholars more profound. Meanwhile, we will let the matter rest as it is.

The flour barrel on the city's coat of arms, is a reminder of the time when New York enjoyed a monopoly of bolting flour. No flour or bread could be exported except from the Port of New York. It was first granted by Gov. Andros, in 1680. The bolting monopoly was renewed by Gov. Dongan in 1684, and under it the city prospered mightily. In 1694 however Gov. Fletcher declined to renew the privilege, and in 1697 it was ended by an act of the General Assembly. The City made several ineffectual attempts to have it restored, but did not succeed.

The beaver likewise is significant of the very earliest trading done in New York—when it was headquarters for skins and peltries of fur-bearing animals, chief of which was the humble beaver.

The eagle and hemisphere are taken from the Arms of the State adopted in 1778. A crown originally had the place where the eagle now is.

The figure of the Indian is said to be an authentic copy of the Coastal Algonquins, to which the Manhattan Indians belonged. The sailor represents sea borne commerce but there is nothing apparently to represent the Dutch West India Company.

CHAPTER II

When the History of New York Begins

THE announcement of Hudson's great discovery created
profound excitement in Europe where all the nations now
vied with each other in the quest for new worlds. England
showed her appreciation of the great navigator by locking
him up on his arrival on her shores and keeping him a
prisoner several weeks. He eventually arrived in Amsterdam and made his report.

Several other expeditions at once set out from Holland,
notably one under the command of Captain Adriaen
Block. Block crossed the ocean successfully in a small sloop
called *The Tiger,* but while his boat was lying at anchor
off what is now the Battery it suddenly burst into flames
and was utterly destroyed. His men escaped by swimming
ashore, but they lost everything except what they had on
their backs. To make matters worse, winter was approaching and they had no shelter.

But Captain Block proved himself the man of the hour.
He carefully studied the structure of the Indian wigwams
and quietly ordered his men to build something like them
for themselves. With the kindly assistance of the Indians,
this was successfully accomplished, and Block and his men
made comfortable from the cold weather.

A very important fact which Block and his men did not
know at the time is now common knowledge. Unwittingly
though it was, they were the first white men actually to begin the settlement of what was one day to become the great

City of New York—ten years before its formal occupancy
by the Dutch West India Company. There had been, of
course, from time to time, a few trading vessels which
stopped here a few hours; but until Block's men arrived,
none had built houses or made preparations to remain
permanently. A bronze tablet on the building at 39 Broadway, the spot where they landed, now records the event we
have just related.

Lower Broadway is, therefore, not only the scene of the
first permanent occupation by white men of Manhattan
Island, but also of the first shipyard—an industry that was
later to assume enormous proportions along the East River
and to produce many of the celebrated Yankee Clipper
ships and that most famous of all yachts, *America,* winner
of the Blue Ribbon of the Seas. As early as 1631, a vessel
of eight hundred tons equipped for thirty guns, one of the
largest of the world, was launched. More than two centuries were to elapse ere the shipbuilders of our day were
to emulate this pioneer craft.

But what was still more remarkable, Captain Block,
with only the aid of such tools as he could fashion for himself, contrived to build another vessel to take the place of
the lost *Tiger.* How he managed it, no one knows; but
necessity being ever the mother of invention, Captain
Block succeeded in some miraculous manner in complet-
ing his self-imposed task and presently launched the *On-
rest* or *Restless,* which was the name he chose for his new
caravel. In this home-made affair, he explored all the
neighboring harbors and Sound. He located a trading
place where Hartford now stands.

Notwithstanding Block's really wonderful and valuable
contributions to the knowledge of a little-known land, no
particular honor has ever been accorded his discoveries;
and but for naming an obscure island at the end of the
Sound, his very existence would probably have long ago

been forgotten. The little island in question had a beautiful Indian name, "Manisseas." To the everlasting regret of the antiquarian and the lover of tradition, Block substituted his own unromantic and plebeian cognomen in its stead. That was a shame. He published an account of his explorations which attracted much attention at the time, and described many little coves, inlets, islands that are now very familiar in the society columns of our newspapers—Watch Hill, Narragansett, Newport, etc. He explored the Connecticut shore as well as Long Island, and it is nice to read a description of it in those far-off Indian days by one who had actually seen them. He was, undoubtedly, a resourceful person. In order to return at once to Holland, he traded the *Restless* for a more seaworthy vessel which had just arrived under the command of Captain Cornelius May, who was subsequently to explore the coast where now stand Cape May, Atlantic City, Long Branch, Ocean Grove, Asbury Park and other delectable New Jersey resorts.

Desultory trading had sprung up between Manhattan Island and Holland, but nothing definite in the way of permanent colonization began till 1623. In that year as we have noted, a group of Walloons came over under the patronage of some wealthy directors of the then newly formed West India Company, to whom large grants of land were made conditioned upon their being colonized by fifty persons or more. They were not Holland Dutch, but came originally from Belgium. They did not settle on the Island, but on the Jersey Shore opposite New York— Pavonia, and along the shores of the Hudson, principally in the neighborhood of Albany and beyond. Kiliaen Van Rensselaer, who was one of the company, gave his name to the territory given to him which was located in what is now Rensselaer County. These Walloon settlements afterwards gave some trouble to the authorities in New Amster-

dam, as they insisted that they were independent settlers
and not subject to the jurisdiction of the officers holding
forth at New Amsterdam. At all events, they were the first
settlers to occupy what was officially called for the first
time Nieuw Amsterdam.

In 1626, however, the formal purchase and settlement
of New York was effected by Peter Minuit representing the
West India Company, as we have already noted, and from
that year its history begins.

Two private letters at this time contain items of absorb-
ing interest concerning the young settlement. One is from
Peter Schagen, dated 1626, and is the first letter of any
kind written from the coming city of New York. He says:
"Our people are in good heart and live in peace here." He
also records, in the same letter, the birth of the first girl in
New Netherland—Sarah Rapaelje, born June 9, 1625, to
Jan Joris Rapaelje and his wife, Catelina Trico, at Fort
Orange, Albany. The first boy was Jean Vigne. The second
letter is from the Rev. Dr. Jonas Michaelius, the first min-
ister of the Dutch Reformed Church in the United States.

While visiting Holland, some fifty years ago, the late
Hon. Henry C. Murphy, an eminent Brooklyn lawyer and
a distinguished member of the Long Island Historical Society, had the good fortune to come across this fascinating
document, hitherto unknown. It is particularly valuable as
it gives the first actual glimpse of real life in the new settlement.

The good Dominie had just arrived and his letter is addressed to Dom. Adrianus Smoutius, minister of the Dutch
Reformed Church at Amsterdam. It begins in that quaint
but appealing manner of the time, with a Latin salutation:
"*De Vrede Christi.* Honorable Sir, Well beloved Brother
in Christ, Kind Friend." It was found among the papers
of the late Jacobus Konig, clerk of the fourth judicial district of Amsterdam. Further than this, its history is un-

known; but it is undoubtedly owing to the importance of its contents that we are indebted for its preservation. We read with interest the picture which the writer draws of the privations of the first settlers, of their struggle to coax a harvest out of a reluctant soil, of the natural wealth of the country and of the manners and language of the Indians. We must content ourselves, however, with the portion bearing directly on the people and the city itself.

The good Dominie meets with a deep sorrow immediately upon arrival. His "amiable" wife dies, leaving him with three little children, far from home and friends. The voyage was long—almost three months; storms and tempests were many; the food abominable, and rendered still more unpalatable by the conduct of "a wicked cook and a drunken captain who annoyed them in every way." No wonder the poor woman died. But, says the brave minister, "The Lord himself has done this and knowing all things must work together for good to those who love God, I hope to bear my cross patiently nor lose my courage."

He is soon in the midst of his duties and he gives a very excellent photograph of his surroundings. His description of the red man is not at all flattering, and is somewhat prophetic of the troublous future from this source.

"As to the natives of this country. I find them entirely savage and wild, strangers to all decency, yea uncivil and stupid as pests, proficient in all wickedness and Godlessness; devilish men who serve no one but the Devil. They are thievish and in cruelty more inhuman than the people of Barbary. How," he adds plaintively, "these people can best be led to the true knowledge of God, and of the Mediator Christ, is hard to say." The letter continues:

"The country yields many good things for the support of life, but they are all to be gathered in an uncultivated and wild state. . . . We want ten or twelve farmers with

horses, cows and laborors in proportion, to furnish us with
bread and fresh butter milk and cheese. . . ."

Already are noted beginnings of Indian troubles. "The
business of furs is dull on account of a new war of the
Mohawks against the Mohicans at the upper end of this
river. There have occurred cruel murders on both sides."
The letter concludes:

They fell much wood to carry home to the Fatherland, but
the vessels are too few to take much of it. They are making a
windmill to saw the wood and we also have a gristmill. They
bake brick here but it is very poor. There is good material for
burning lime, namely, oyster shells in large quantities. The
burning of potash has not succeeded; the master and his
laborors are all greatly disappointed. We are busy now in
building a fort of good quarry stone which is to be found not
far from here in abundance. There is a good means for making salt; the water is salt enough and there is no want of heat
in summer. Besides as to the waters, both of the sea and rivers,
they yield all kinds of fish:—and as to land it abounds in all
kinds of game wild and in the groves, with vegetables, fruits
roots herbs and plants both for eating and medicinal purposes working wonderful cures. . . . The country is good and
pleasant; the climate is healthy, notwithstanding the sudden
changes of heat and cold. The sun is very warm; the winter
strong and severe and continues full as long as in our country. The best remedy is not to spare the wood and to cover one-
self well with rough skins which also can be easily obtained.

On the whole this is a good letter and gives us an excellent view of the little clearing in the wilderness which one
day was to be the Eighth Wonder of the World.

Notwithstanding the marvelous opportunity thus afforded the Dutch, they allowed this valuable possession to
trickle through their fingers until it was finally lost. During their occupation, the population between 1626 and
1664 increased but little—from about two hundred to fif-

teen hundred, while the English around Boston had increased from their original few hundred in 1628 to over fifty thousand in the same period. The Dutch figures, moreover, include not an inconsiderable number of French, German, Swedish, Portuguese, English, and Negroes, thus materially reducing the already small population of Dutch.

Their occupation was important, however, not so much for what it actually accomplished as for what was to follow as the result of these pioneer efforts. With the exception of Stuyvesant, the Dutch were most unfortunate in the selection of the Governors appointed by the States General. In addition to this, their scheme of settlement was fatally defective. It permitted no ultimate ownership of the land by the settlers except under conditions that were far from attractive. The Colony was regarded merely as a lemon to be squeezed by whomever was in power. A dream of empire never entered their minds. Minuit, Van Twiller, and Kieft were men of surpassingly low executive caliber. Stuyvesant was of a higher type in every respect, intellectually and every other way. Yet his administration was disgraced by almost childish ignorance of the growing desire for popular government which he ruthlessly repressed, and by shocking cruelty to the helpless Quakers and Indians, which must ever remain a blot on an otherwise fairly glamorous record. Much may be forgiven a man of acknowledged probity whose chief failing came from mistaken zeal for the welfare of the Company and the State whom he served.

Minuit seems to have been a rather capable, enterprising sort of a man. He brought over with him a competent engineer, Kryn Fredericks, who built the fort on the site of our present Custom House, which has been called successively Fort Amsterdam, Fort James, Fort Orange, Fort Nassau, Fort George, according to the changes in its

checkered career. Although merely a block house of red
cedar palisades and walls of sod, around it clustered all the
thirty-odd houses that formed the settlement. In time it
was greatly strengthened and it speedily became the headquarters of the activities of the island. It was a five-pointed
building in design and had a commanding position. It
had a naturally strong defensive situation, hemmed in as it
was by huge ledges of rock. Years later, a battery of thirteen guns was mounted outside the fort, and from this circumstance we get our present name of Battery Park.

During Minuit's administration, two comforters of the
sick were sent over; and a year or two later, Jonas Michaelius, a very learned prelate and schoolmaster, was employed to preside over religious meetings and instruct the
children.

Minuit was recalled in 1632. He was arrested by the
English on his arrival at Plymouth whither his vessel was
driven in a storm. He was eventually released and on
reaching Holland was dismissed from the country's service. He died a few years later.

He was succeeded by Wouter Van Twiller, a henchman
of the powerful Van Renssalaer, and easily the stupidest
selection that could have been made. A specimen of his
opéra-bouffe administration is delightfully recorded in his
treatment of an English vessel that announced its intention of sailing up the river to Fort Orange for the purpose
of trading with the Indians, in express violation of the
orders of the States General.

Van Twiller regarded the audacious movement with in-
credulous wonder. Instead of halting the impertinent
stranger on pain of sinking him, this perfectly preposterous
Governor ordered a barrel of wine opened and, after drinking, waved his hat and shouted, "All those who love the
Prince of Orange, follow me in this and assist me in re-
pelling the violence of that Englishman!"

Van Twiller's soldiers, accepting the invitation, proceeded to punish the wine instead of the intruders and only wished "that they had six barrels of wine instead of one," so that they could show the English what valiant warriors they were upon occasion.

But the Englishman laughed derisively at this war-like (?) gesture and proceeded up the river.

Of course, a report of such fantastic and bizarre conduct on the part of the Dutch Governor spread rapidly, not only through New Netherland but the English Colonies as well. It did not enhance the reputation of the Dutch for either courage or wisdom.

But with all his faults, Van Twiller was undoubtedly a gentleman of culture and exceeding good taste. He cast an envious glance on that pearl of New York Harbor, Nutten (now Governors) Island. With the aid of some shiny trinkets, he acquired this delectable spot from the Indians and converted it to his own personal use. He was subsequently forced to disgorge this appetizing morsel, but not before its advantages were disclosed to those who followed him. Under the English, Lord Bellomont converted it into what became popularly known as "The Smiling Gardens of the Governor"; and Lord Cornbury, a cousin of Queen Anne, built a pleasure house for himself on it.

In a way it became what the White House is now as a social center. Such visiting officials from neighboring Colonies as came to see the Governor were formally received in the Fort. But when that ceremony was concluded, a barge would carry them across to the Island, there to sit under the Governor's vine and fig tree in seclusion and content. It would be hard to select a more delightful place in which to entertain and impress the visiting statesman. There is a suggestion of these far-off days in the afternoon teas and receptions that are a part of the private life of Governors Island even now. All through the summer, gay

parties of distinguished strangers are entertained by the
Commandant; and the guests at these impromptu gatherings are distinguished for their prominence in the social as
well as the official and commercial life of the country. .

The little island in its long history has passed through
many curious changes. In Mr. Huntington's great library
at San Gabriel, Cal. there is a little book written by the
first passengers on the *Sea Mieuw* who landed on the Island
before proceeding to the mainland. This little book records a meeting at which a tentative plan of procedure was
adopted regarding their life on shore. So-and-so was to be
invested with certain powers. Minuit was, of course, to be
supreme. But a sort of plan looking to an orderly conduct
of affairs was agreed upon. It somewhat resembled the
famous *Mayflower* Compact, but was not so formal or so
tremendously important.

The Island, as a landing place, occupied this position for
a long time. During the great Palatinate exodus of more
than ten thousand persons, the arrivals were taken there
first before being sent up the country in 1710. There are
more than two hundred and fifty graves on the Island of
these Palatinates. The plague broke out on several of their
ships and many of them succumbed as soon as they landed.

A most interesting description of the Island is given by
an observant writer in the *New York Advertiser* of July 11,
1791:

Nature seems to have placed this spot at the entrance of
our harbor, on purpose for a pleasurable occasional retreat
during the spring, summer and fall seasons. The soil, naturally
good, and consisting of about seventy five acres, when improved into walks, groves and gardens, cannot otherwise than
present a delightful scene of recreation. . . . The island
abounds with excellent fresh water, and a clean gravelly shore,
washed by waves that are poured in upon us, twice every
twenty four hours, directly from the bosom of the Atlantic, at-

tended by a fresh sea breeze, offers every inducement to those
who are fond of bathing and swimming, or wading in the
water. The prospect from the plains and rising grounds is delightful; on one side a spacious and beautiful bay, covered
with vessels of every description, either leaving or coming into
port, from all parts of the continent, and every quarter of the
globe. . . . The city of New York, (the Naples of America)
exhibits from the place, an elegant appearance, which will
daily become more so, as the improvements are completed in
the neighborhood of the old battery, and new buildings
erected in the room of stables, barracks, and other petty edi-
fices, which ought always to be in the background or less
noticed parts of a large city.

Later on it became a favorite race course of the young
city and many spirited contests were held there. It rivaled
the famous Union Course in Long Island established by
Nicolls, and its proximity to the city made it popular.

COLUMBIA RACES
On Governor's Island, near the City of New York.

Commencing on Wednesday, the 30th day of November on
which day a Saddle, Bridle and Whip, will be Run for, the
best of three one mile heats, free for any Horse, Mare or Geld-
ing, carrying Catches; to shew and enter at 3 o'clock, the day
before Running. No crossing or jostling or any kind of foul
play will be countenanced, which if detected, the Riders will
be pronounced distanced. To start precisely at the hour of
11 o'clock of the aforesaid day. If it should be bad weather,
the next fair day.   1790.

This day at 11 o'clock, there will be a Horse Race, on Governor's Island, which, if the weather is fine, will give satisfaction to the Public.   Wednesday Nov. 30, 1790.

It was frequently let out to one man for general farming
and for caring for livestock. The *New York Journal* of
May 17, 1790, prints this:

Pasture for horses and cows very fine may be had on Governor's Island both fresh and salt. For terms apply to the subscriber on the island or leave a line at Mr. William Hillyards near the Albany pier. Any of the passage boats at the Whitehall will bring or take off horses or cattle at a small expense.

N. B. No disordered horses will be received.

There is something alluringly naïve in that neighborly message—"Leave a line at Mr. Hillyards near the Albany pier." It doesn't seem possible that it could ever have been written in the great City of New York.

Here is a rather scandalous item:

To be sold not for any fault but because she is with foal— (supposed to be by a black stallion lately Capt. Chadwick's as they got loose together once last year on Governor's Island) a chestnut mare belonging to Dr. Moore of the 16th Regiment.

But perhaps the strangest experience of the Island was to find itself in the possession of Columbia University and that the rentals and other emoluments accruing to the College from its ownership were to be applied to the "better advancement of science and literature in the said College." Such, however, was duly set forth in the following act of 1790:

By an act for the encouragement of Literature passed March 31, 1790, the Regents of the University of the State received a grant among other lands to be used for the benefit of Columbia College—of a certain island lying within the county of New York commonly called Governor's Island with power to lease, grant and demise from time to time for one or more lives or for years and on such rents and considerations as they shall judge most beneficial . . . and to apply said sums from rents from time to time for the better advancement of science and literature in the said College.

The threatened war with France brought the Island once more into prominence. It was suddenly realized that its capture by the enemy would mean that New York could be destroyed at their leisure from such a vantage point. So

By an Act passed March 26, 1794. George Clinton, Matthew Clarkson, James Watson, Richard Varick, Nicholas Fish, Ebenezer Stevens and Abijah Hammond were appointed commissioners for the purpose of repairing or erecting fortifications for the defence of New York.

Feverish haste was now made to erect fortifications thereon and citizens everywhere were drafted to assist in the work as the following item shows:

1794 May 24, Saturday: As I was getting up in the morning, I heard drums beating and fifes playing. I ran to the window, and saw a large body of people on the other side of the Governor's House, with flags flying, and marching two and two towards the water side. It was a procession of young tradesmen going in boats to Governor's Island to give the state a day's work. Fortifications are these erecting to defend the harbor. It is a patriotic and general resolution of the inhabitants of this city, to work a day gratis, without any distinction of rank or condition, for the public advantage, on these fortifications. To-day, the whole trade of carpenters and joiners; yesterday, the body of masons; before this, the grocers, school masters, coopers, and barbers; next Monday, all the attorneys and men concerned in the law, handle the mattock and shovel, the whole day and carry provisions with them. How noble is this! How it cherishes unanimity and love for their country! How much does it tend to unite all ranks of people, and render the social compact firm and united.

One curious result of the work on the Island is thus noted in the papers:

No marriages in the city during the last week. The citizens probably too busy digging fortifications. Next week one marriage.

To facilitate passage to the Island

... a ferry was established at 3d. each person—but all fatigue parties to pass gratis. The fort was now erecting on the island.

There must have been some permanent residents on the Island soon after, as we find this notice in the Museum, probably the marriage referred to previously:

Married on Saturday evening last by the Rev. Mr. McCloy, Sergeant Major William P. Harris to Miss Barbara Monroe, both of Governor's Island. August 15, 1814.

Governors Island was also the scene of the first attack by a submarine on a warship. During the Revolution, the British ship *Eagle* lay close inshore. A mechanic named Bushnell hailing from Saybrook, Conn. had constructed a "Marine Turtle" able to go under water. Washington, upon examination, approved of the contrivance, which was built to hold one man.

A small magazine filled with powder, so arranged as to be secured to a ship's bottom, was part of the equipment. This machine was to be attached to the bottom of the enemy ship, with a clockwork attachment which exploded the charge after the operator had time enough to escape to a safe distance.

Unfortunately for the inventor, the *Eagle* had a copper-sheathed bottom, and the young operator, Ezra Lee, was unable to penetrate this protective covering. Washington and a few officers watched the attack from the Battery, but the calm waters of the Bay remained unruffled and the watchers thought the young man had perished.

At dawn however, a column of water shot up from the sides of the *Eagle;* the cables of the ship were instantly cut and the ship floated safely out of harm's way, but with evidences of much confusion on board.

Lee had been under the water two hours, trying in vain to penetrate the thick copper. He could hear the sentries on the deck say that a floating log had struck the ship when the shock of his "Turtle" was first felt; when the charge was finally exploded a short distance from the ship, they took alarm. Lee managed to submerge, coming to the surface beyond musket shot and landed safely. He received the congratulations of the Commander-in-Chief and the other officers. Young Lee was afterwards employed by Washington in secret service and was in the battles of Trenton, Brandywine, and Monmouth. It was certainly an audacious undertaking and shows a submarine to have been in use in warfare before the world conflict.

Curiously enough, Fulton took up the same idea some years later. His model propelled itself nearly four miles under water. He afterwards took it to Paris, hoping to interest Napoleon. Of that we shall speak elsewhere. Fulton afterwards built an ironclad warship—the first of its kind—and sailed it off Governors Island.

There is a letter in the Paine Memorial House at New Rochelle, from Paine to Joel Barlow. In it the writer asks, "Has Fulton hired any whales yet to pull his boat under the water?"

In 1800 the State of New York formally ceded the Island to the Federal Government and ever since then it has been United States property. It was soon after made headquarters of the War Department of the East, and has so remained ever since.

In spite of Van Twiller's spectacular life on Governors Island, he did not improve otherwise; so, tiring of the ridiculous antics of this burlesque official, influential men in the Colony finally preferred charges against him. He was finally recalled and made to disgorge all his property, his fine herds of cattle, and all the rest of his plunder.

His administration, however, should be remembered for one important thing. The first schoolhouse and Adam Roelantsen, the first schoolmaster, commenced operations

under his reign. The school was established jointly by the
West India Company and the Established Church of Holland at Amsterdam. It has continued to this day as the
Collegiate Reformed Dutch Church. In 1933 it celebrated
its 300th Anniversary. Many descendants of families prominent in the early history of New York are associated with
this school.

Besides teaching the young idea how to shoot, Mr.
Roelantsen also took in washing. It is on record that he
sued a man Gillis De Voocht for pay for washing his linen.
The defendant did not deny the soft impeachment, but
claimed that he was not to pay till the end of the year. So
the Court decided that poor Mr. Roelantsen must perform
his duties until that time before he could collect any
money.

The early Dutch schools were mostly low-ceilinged,
small rooms on the second floor of the house, looking on a
dirty little street or back yard. Sometimes they were damp
moldy basements in some old public building. In summer, school was frequently held under an awning outside
the house. Inside the "catheder" stood a chair, on the
right side of which hung the A B C board, and beside it an
iron comb with a wooden handle, the mere sight of which
is enough to make us shiver when we remember that it
was used also to curry unclean scalps. A single stroke was
enough to make the blood trickle down the face. On the
left, hung the dunce's or ass's board, which was hung over
the chest of the scholar who was too stupid or too lazy.

Doors and windows were left open for ventilation. When
it grew dark, tallow candles on wooden blocks or in iron
candlesticks were lighted. In these low, dark, and damp
rooms, and in an atmosphere reeking with the flicker of
the tallow candles, children were kept sometimes from
seven in the morning until seven at night. School was
opened in summer at six and in winter at seven in the

morning. The children kept their hats and caps on, removing them only at prayers and when they said their lessons.

Punishment consisted in striking the palm of the hand with the "plak" (a flat piece of wood on a handle), and flogging with the rod or switch. The "plak" was often an instrument of horrible torture, of different makes and sizes. Some "plaks" were finely made with a twisted handle; some coarse and unfinished—a round piece of board with a handle. There were round and oval "plaks," thick and thin of blade, some with a smooth surface and some carved in diamonds; "plaks" with twisted copper wire, and with sharp points or with pin points, which tore the flesh of the palm.

The punishment with the rod was even more severe. According to the gravity of the offense, this was administered on the naked body, or with the clothes on. In some schools, boys were strapped with leathern belts. In the yards of some others, principally the poor and orphan schools, there were whipping posts where boys and girls were whipped; and in the school of the poorhouse in Amsterdam, there was a bench whereon the small malefactor was put with his head through a board, fastened down, and smartly punished. In another school, a block was fastened to the leg of the culprit and had to be dragged home through the streets and to church on Sundays. Nobody blamed the master if he beat or kicked the boys, or if he made them stand on a table and hold two or three heavy school books above their heads during the lesson. We also read of leather cushions with tacks pointed upwards on which unruly girls were placed; and of girls being beaten, kicked and bruised. In some cases the schoolmasters were veritable tyrants; but fortunately, they were the exceptions.

Looking backward, it hardly seems possible that out of such unpromising material, we could have developed such a marvelous educational system as we now have in New

York, or that these little stuffy Dutch rooms would have been succeeded by such truly palatial structures as George Washington High School, De Witt Clinton High School, and a score of others.

In Van Twiller's reign occurred another outstanding event—a real estate transaction destined to loom large on the annals of that business for many years and to provide more litigation than was ever achieved by any parcel of ground in Manhattan. That was the granting of a tract of land sixty-two acres in extent, to Rudolph Jans, beginning south of Warren Street, extending along Broadway as far as Duane Street, thence northwesterly a mile and a half to Christopher Street, with its base upon the North River. This is the very valuable estate subsequently bestowed by Queen Anne on Trinity Church. A valuable legal industry sprang up in connection with an alleged flaw in the title, and for years unscrupulous lawyers reaped a rich harvest from gullible clients who were persuaded that they and not Trinity Church were the real owners of this gold mine. The nuisance finally became so persistent and with such great losses to the innocent victims, that the Legislature finally had to step in and pass a law whereby no one could ever bring suit against Trinity for its land on any pretext whatever.

Van Twiller was succeeded by William Kieft and the little province stepped from the frying pan into the fire.

The shocking cruelty and inhumanity of Kieft in his treatment of the Indians rouses our anger and indignation even to this day. He started all the trouble with them in the first place by levying tribute on all the corn, furs and seawant made by them on the grounds that he had "defended them against all enemies," which was nonsense.

As an instance of his brutality, we may cite one example out of many. A tribal war had forced a band of terror-stricken savages to seek refuge among the whites. Half-

naked and defenseless, they were an easy prey. Every sentiment of humanity and decency dictated that they should
be treated with kindness and protection extended. Instead
of that, Kieft determined to exterminate "whom God had
thus delivered into his hands."

The story of that night is a blot upon the pages of Old
Amsterdam history. It was the most shocking massacre that
ever disgraced a civilized settlement. Eighty in one camp
were butchered as they slept, forty in another. Not one was
spared and every cry for mercy went unheeded. Later on,
vengeance was exacted an hundredfold.

The misery and wretchedness resulting from the reprisal which followed is sickening to contemplate. To the
white woman taken captive, death was a welcome release.
In the case of one woman who was in a delicate condition,
the usual Indian custom was followed—she was sent into
the woods, there to make a fire in the snow and look after
herself as best she could. Only a short temporary halt was
made ere the march was resumed, the infant tied to a sway-
ing cradle formed of branches.

Men were burned slowly at the stake with every devilish
torture the savage mind could devise. Short splinters of
resin wood were stuck all over the body, then lighted, and
the poor captive set at liberty. As he ran frantically along
the road, the breeze fanned the splinters into roaring
flames. It is a sad page in our early city's life and one that
we would cheerfully omit.

The net result of Kieft's deviltry was that all the Dutch
had accomplished in twenty years had to be done over
again. As a result of this counter-attack, little or nothing
was left of what had been a promising settlement. The
little colony was all but destroyed, and New York almost
died a-bornin'.

The whole story of our treatment of the Indians in the
early days of our city is probably as black a page as any in

history. A little Indian girl caught helping herself to some peaches in an orchard on Broadway near Wall was cruelly shot to death. Revenge followed and many innocents suffered. In New York we have interred in old Trinity Churchyard, Colonel Michael Cresap, one of the shining lights of this period. His headstone is now in possession of the New York Historical Society. About the only thing that can be said of this gentleman is that he unconsciously, if also atrociously, inspired one of the finest contributions to our annals of Indian literature. It deserves high rank in American eloquence. No more touching, no more dramatic recital of what these Indians were sometimes called upon to endure, has been preserved to posterity. It is familiar to many persons from schooldays. It was printed in most of the old readers, and is known as "Logan's Lament."

Logan was a friend of the white man. His tribe had gone to war with them in one of numerous disputes over territory seizure, common in those days. Sir William Johnson, than whom there was no better authority, often called attention of the authorities to these frequent outright stealings of land from the Indians and repeatedly requested the Council in New York to examine into their complaints and condemn all spurious patents and rights. The incident in which Colonel Cresap figures occurred about this time. A canoe loaded with Indian women and children sailed down Yellow Creek. There was only one man in it and he was unarmed. Cresap and his party hid in the bushes till the canoe grounded on the shore. Picking out each his victim, the wretches fired, killing every one of the occupants of the canoe. It so happened that these poor people comprised the entire family of Logan, a Mingo chieftain, who was afterward invited to attend a conference looking toward peace. He declined to come but sent the following letter:

I appeal to any white man to say if ever he entered Logan's cabin hungry and he gave him not meat; if ever he came cold and naked, and he clothed him not. During the course of the last long and bloody war, Logan remained idle in his cabin, an advocate of peace. Such was my love for the whites that my country-men pointed as they passed and said "Logan is the friend of White Man." I had even thought to live with you but for the injury of one man—Colonel Cresap who last Spring in cold blood and unprovoked, murdered all the relations of Logan, not sparing even my women and children. There runs not a drop of my blood in the veins of any living creature. This called on me for revenge. I have sought it. I have killed many, I have fully glutted my vengeance. For my country I rejoice at the beams of peace. But do not harbor a thought that mine is the joy of fear. Logan never felt fear. He will not turn on his heel to save his life. Who is there to mourn for Logan? Not one.

Few can read this touching lament without emotion. It epitomizes in a few sentences, all the sufferings that came to the red man as a result of civilization.

But the slaughter went on unchecked. It was deemed necessary.

If Stuyvesant's management of the Indians was not all that could be desired, he deserves credit for recognizing the genius of John Underhill, the first white man who proclaimed the "divine" doctrine that the only good Indian was a dead one. He made an arrangement with Underhill whereby the Indians that were harassing New Amsterdam, were to be destroyed root and branch. Fourteen years of peace was the result of this bloody and perhaps necessary policy, and it saved New Amsterdam.

A puzzling feature of these Indian depredations was the curious result that captivity had upon some of the children. Eunice White, for instance, whose mother was cruelly murdered in the Deerfield massacre, her whole family scattered among various tribes as prisoners, was adopted herself by a tribe of the Abankis. Under the teachings of the Jesuits, she renounced the faith of her fathers, was baptized, and in time married one of the young chiefs, who thence forward took her family name and called himself Williams.

Many years after, she came with her husband to visit her relatives in Deerfield dressed as a squaw and wrapped in an Indian blanket. Nothing would induce her to stay, though she was persuaded upon one occasion to put on civilized clothes and go to church; after which she impatiently discarded her gown and resumed her blanket. She repeated her visit the next year, bringing her two half-breed children. No attempt was made to detain her. She was kindly treated and a tract of land was offered her husband if they would settle in New England, but she positively refused. She lived to a great age, a squaw to the last.

So numerous are similar instances, that it creates confusion in the mind of the reader regarding the cruelty of Indians as a whole toward their very young prisoners. Children had no economic value and the wonder in their case is all the deeper.

There are still many admirers of the red man left in our midst. Our neighboring village of Allentown, New Jersey, in 1883 elected a cigar store Indian a justice of the peace by a majority of seven votes over the then incumbent, the Hon. Samuel Davis. We regret to add that Mr. Davis resigned in a huff when the result of the contest was made known.

It must not be inferred, however, that the Indian was never at fault. He was a willing ally of the whites at all times, selling himself usually to the highest bidder. The shameful alliances of the French with the Indians in the war of that name, and of the British in the war of 1812, come to mind.

But to return to Kieft. He was, providentially for the city, recalled to Holland. In addition to his Indian blunders, he was also called upon to answer serious charges of maladministration. The evidence disclosed the fact that he was entitled to rank as the first of that long line of distinguished citizens known, in the language of the streets, as "grafters." The boat which carried him back had also as fellow-passengers, his accusers. Nearing Holland, the vessel was wrecked on a rock in the English Channel. It looked as if all must perish. Fearing his end was near, Kieft humbly confessed that he was guilty of all the charges against him and humbly begged the forgiveness of all whom he had wronged. He had no sooner ceased speaking, than a huge wave carried him off and he sank despairingly into the sea. His companions miraculously escaped. Help reached them a few moments later and they were safely landed in Holland. Their tragic tale created a great sensation. The Government took such steps as were possible to redress the grievances of the petitioners and thus ended another troublous chapter in the checkered career of the West India Company.

Kieft was succeeded by Petrus Stuyvesant, the last and the only really great Governor sent over by the Dutch.

CHAPTER III

A Glance at Stuyvesant

THE administration of Stuyvesant was much more states-
manlike, but could not be called, by any stretch of the
imagination, absolutely flawless, or forever be looked upon
as the last word in Colonial government. Far from it. The
detailed records seem to reveal him as a good deal of a
petty tyrant, and without the slightest inclination to admit
that the lower orders could know what was good for them
in the way of government. He was arbitrary and dictatorial
to an inordinate degree; but nevertheless he was zealous in
protecting the property confided to his care, and his personal character, so far as it applied to his official life, was
blameless.

It came about, despite his objections, that the first seeds
of popular government were sown during his tenure.
Burgomasters, Schepens and Sheriffs were appointed by
the home office and a measure of popular representation
enjoyed for the first time. This innovation did not arouse
the Governor's admiration to any extent and he did not
coöperate with the enthusiasm a more liberally minded
ruler would have shown. Some of his personal interpreta-
tions were provocative of deep resentment and, no doubt,
in a legal sense, clearly violated his limitations. Constant
quarrels and bickerings with other influential men in the
settlement were the result. Matters reached such a point
that charges were formally drawn up and Allard Anthony,
one of the disaffected group, was sent to lay them before

71

the States General. The latter decided to recall the Governor, but the Amsterdam Chamber interfered, and persuaded the States General to recall the papers; that in view of the war with England, they needed a man of his experience and military training to guard their American possessions. The burgher form of government, which they now decreed for the Colony, would, they thought, placate the discontented faction; and so Stuyvesant avoided this humiliation for the time being, at least. It was a narrow escape, as Adrian Van der Donck, the messenger with the recall papers, the man who later founded Yonkers, had already boarded a ship sailing on the morrow.

It would have been a miracle man who could have satisfied all hands at this juncture of affairs. Desperate and bloody Indian wars raged incessantly on every front. English encroachments, at one point coming down to the shores of Manhattan Island itself, were a constant source of irritation and anxiety, and revolts on Long Island added to a situation already well nigh insupportable. Added to that was the niggardly policy of the West India Company in the way of military equipment, and the same attitude on the part of the Holland Government in respect to soldiers, armaments and supplies. It was an exasperating period and possibly Stuyvesant was equipped neither by nature nor training to handle it with the suavity and diplomacy which circumstances demanded. Added to all this was the knowledge that the West India Company had already figured their losses in colonizing New Amsterdam at over ten tons in gold! A not very pleasing result and with additional deficits inevitable. A less courageous, less resolute man would have found himself hopelessly involved, and Stuyvesant deserves credit for keeping the little Colony alive under such circumstances.

Strange though it may seem, in spite of all the difficulties just mentioned, Stuyvesant added further fuel to the

flames by his outrageous treatment of the Quakers. A body
of them, expelled from Boston, landed at New Amsterdam
in August, 1657. Several were at once arrested; but one of
them, Robert Hodshone, kept on to Heemstede, on Long
Island, where he spoke to several persons about the new
Society of Friends and its benevolent aims. While walking
in an orchard he was seized and taken before the local
magistrate, Richard Gildersleeve, who locked him up and
went over to consult with Stuyvesant. Presently Gildersleeve returned with a squad of soldiers, who took away
Hodshone's Bible and papers, tied him to a cart's tail, and
dragged him over a rough road to the Brooklyn ferry. On
arriving in New Amsterdam, he was thrown into a filthy
cellar among vermin and kept there half starved for several
days. Then he was brought before Stuyvesant and the council, but was not allowed to speak in his own defense. He
was sentenced to two years' hard labor with a wheelbarrow,
or else to pay 600 guilders. As he had no money, the first
alternative was imposed upon him. So on a sultry August
morning, the poor Quaker was brought out from his dun-
geon, chained to a wheelbarrow, and ordered to load it.
He said he had done no evil and broken no law, and he
would not obey. Then he was stripped to the waist, and a
stalwart Negro with a piece of rope beat him until he fell
to the ground. This was repeated for several days, on one
of which Hodshone was brought before Stuyvesant, who
warned him that the whipping would go on until he
should submit to his sentence. This, he assured the Director, he would never do. Then he was kept for two nights
and a day without bread or water, and then hung up to
the ceiling by his hands while a heavy log of wood was tied
to his ankles. In this position he was cruelly beaten with
rods. As he remained obdurate, the same torture was repeated after two days. But public sympathy was now
aroused for Hodshone. An English woman came and

bathed his wounds, and her husband sought to bribe the Schout with a fat ox to let him go to his house until he should recover. It could not be done, said the Schout, unless the whole fine were paid. There were those who were ready to make up the sum, but the Quaker would not allow it; a principle was at stake, and he would rather die. At length Stuyvesant's sister, Mrs. Bayard, a woman of sense and spirit, came to her brother and implored and berated him until in sheer self-defense he was obliged to set the prisoner free.

In our day, the memory of these old-time heartless persecutions of the Quakers sometimes produces curious repercussions. In 1659, for instance, Lydia Wardell, a Puritan in Boston, became a Quakeress and was publicly whipped for her fall from grace. In 1663, Colonel Edmund Scarburgh rode through Maryland, at the head of the King's troops, marking with the broad arrow of the King the houses of the Quakers, and returned to punish them severely for their nonconformity. At a dinner in New York, the late Governor Wise of Virginia smilingly admitted that Lydia Wardell was his grandmother, and Colonel Scarburgh was his grandfather.

But events moved rapidly in the development of New York. A fleet of British warships suddenly sailed into the harbor and cleared decks for action. They were within a few hundred yards of the fort and their guns yawned for cannon fodder. Stuyvesant is talking. A group surround him.

"Stand back, I tell you—I'm going to fire!"

"Sire, 'tis madness! They outnumber us ten to one. For God's sake, stay your hand! Do you not see that there is no help for us, either to the north, or to the south, or to the east, or to the west? What will our twenty guns do, in the face of the sixty-two which are pointed toward us on yonder frigates? Pray, do not be the first to shed blood."

Just then a petition was brought to Stuyvesant signed by ninety-three of the principal citizens including the Burgomaster, Schepens, and his own son Balthazar. They pointed out, in all fairness, that should he fight, he would doom the city to pillage and ashes, and the inhabitants to the sword. The sacrifice would even be worse than useless —it would be an atrocious crime, as it could avail nothing in the end.

He read the missive with white lips and unspeakable agony in his every feature. "I had rather," he answered, "be carried to my grave."

Five minutes later, the white flag waved above the Fort, and the little Dutch settlement at the tip end of Manhattan Island passed into the hands of the English and became New York in honor of James, Duke of York, who himself was to perish a fugitive from his own land.

In the Admiralty offices in London can still be seen the magnificent gold mace carried before the Duke of York when he was Lord High Admiral of the British Navy. A more beautiful insignia of office does not elsewhere exist, I believe; it is richly embellished with handsome carving and is solid gold.

Our genial diarist, Samuel Pepys, was Clerk of the Acts in the Navy at this time, and undoubtedly issued the orders to the fleet to attack New York when it was decided to capture that city from the Dutch. The actual desk at which Pepys worked no longer exists, as the old Admiralty building was long ago torn down.

Pepys remained with the Admiralty until James was driven into exile. By this time Pepys had risen to be Secretary. On his way to France James, disguised as a common servant, in a small sailing boat, threw the Great Seal into the Thames, where it was afterwards found by a fisherman. So passed the first ruler of New York and the last of the Stuart Kings.

We now bid good-by to our Dutch founders, and to the little town which they planted. It presented a picture of alluring simplicity, preëminently bucolic. Like the pioneer's daughter who gave birth to Lincoln, the little Dutch mother who now bids it a fond farewell had no conception of the mighty giant she had brought into being, nor of the dynamic part it was to play in the tremendous affairs of a turbulent world. No shadow of its coming greatness crossed her mind as the white token of her submission streamed from the ramparts of old Fort Amsterdam.

CHAPTER IV

The English Rule New York

PROBABLY no more amicable transfer of a conquered city ever took place than that of New Amsterdam to New York. New York is the only city on our continent that has ever been captured by a foreign foe. It was captured by the English from the Dutch; by the Dutch from the English; by the Americans from the English.

It was a fortunate thing for both New York and New Amsterdam that the new English Governor was such a fascinating personality as Richard Nicolls. He united the qualities of a brave soldier with the charm of a polished diplomat. He possessed a knowledge of both the romantic and classical tongues. But above all he was considerate of the feelings of his conquered foes and sought to make the changes in rulership as little irksome as possible. He continued the Dutch form of local government with the Burgomasters, Schepens and Schouts for a limited time; and modeled his Mayor, Alderman, and Sheriff which succeeded them, very much on the same pattern. His high character, undoubtedly, served to redeem the reputation of a community that had become a jest among its neighbors. But his charming personality was, perhaps, his greatest asset. From all the accounts that have come down to us, he seems to have been abundantly blessed with the rarest of all virtues, common sense and courtesy. They were invaluable attributes at this particular time, and the results were speedily shown in the amiability which marked the relations of the two former foes from the first. The Dutch were confirmed in all their previous rights and were undisturbed in person and property and soon felt that their rights were better protected than ever before. It is a marvelous thing to win all hearts at sight, and that was the good fortune of Governor Nicolls. Even when the English Church followed hard upon the occupation of New York, there was no clash. Nicolls arranged matters so that the Dutch continued to worship after their own fashion and in the same old church. The only innovation was that the English services according to the Episcopalian ritual was established. These services were held in the same church, but *after* the Dutch services were concluded; and the Dutch were left with their usual session undisturbed—an admirable arrangement and greatly appreciated. And the Dutch language was also added in the Courts as an official tongue. These seem trivial matters; but had such a spirit prevailed generally throughout the world at that time, much bloodshed and undescribable misery would have been averted. New York was indeed fortunate in having Governor Nicolls as its first ruler when it at last was started on its marvelous career.

Fort Amsterdam was now changed to Fort James. The towns along the Hudson had a similar experience, Fort Orange became Albany, and a few street names were changed. On the whole, the transition was effected with the minimum of discomfort to the Dutch.

One curious result of Nicolls' splendid treatment of the Dutch was to impart to the original settlers of New York a distinction of their own so that in time it came about that, to have been one of the conquered race was to be a member of a respected and distinguished ancestry. That spirit has continued to this day. The descendants of these old families point with pride to their Dutch origin, and it is now considered a patent of nobility to have been a member of the old régime. And that splendid feeling is largely due to the kindness and courtly attitude of Governor Nicolls who refused to play the part of a tyrant and bully. He preserved the strain of Dutch blood and Dutch customs in New York and they lived to enrich the English blood which eventually absorbed them, not by fire and sword, but by the more romantic and possibly more peaceful means of matrimony.

The changes, as we have just noted, worked little or no hardship on the Dutch. In fact, they were distinctly to their advantage. The administration of justice was altered in favor of the trial by jury system instead of the Dutch method of referees—a great improvement; support of clergymen by the citizens instead of by the provincial government; the abolition of the great burgher rights, thus effecting a reform desired by the Dutch themselves and the quartering of soldiers among the people instead of herding them in the Fort. While the latter change provoked some hostility at first, this gave way when the real reason for the objection was found to be in the unsatisfactory sum allowed by the Government in payment for the soldiers' upkeep. When this was increased, all objections vanished. The soldiers had a pleasanter existence and enjoyed a social freedom which had hitherto been denied them.

Private affairs demanded Nicolls' presence in England and the Duke accepted his resignation. In New York there was deep and sincere regret at his departure; seldom was a public man so beloved. Had the Colony been so fortunate as to secure men of the same high standard as successors, it would have been a great thing for the little town. But, starting with James himself, a man of limited intelligence and abnormally bad manners, we could hardly expect such good fortune. In that respect, we were not disappointed.

An engaging picture of social life in Dutch Manhattan is fortunately revealed in the farewell dinner tendered by the leading citizens to the retiring Governor. It was held in the home of Mayor Cornelius Steewyck. We cannot present a list of the viands and wines consumed on this occasion; but a charming picture of the home itself has fortunately come down to us, and the majority of our readers will no doubt be surprised at its elegance and luxury.

Tapestries hung on the walls, with exquisitely covered French cabinets. The spacious velvet and Russian leather chairs, the muslin and flowered "tabby" curtains, the stately grandfather clocks, the delicate table china, the charming blue delft tiles, the choice collection of books and Old World paintings on the wall—all speak eloquently of a refinement wholly unsuspected in a hamlet on the shores of an untamed continent thousands of miles from civilization. The Dutch standard of living in Europe at that time we know was much higher than that of any other people. Apparently they carried the same high standards to the New World. Some of us think these old Dutchmen were continually wreathed in dense clouds of smoke and floundering hopelessly in a perpetual sea of schnapps. It might be a good idea to revise this conception.

Some years later, when the news reached New York that Nicolls had fallen in the first naval engagement in the new war between the English and the Dutch, the grief of the little Colony was deep and sincere. Special memorial services were held in the little church in the Fort, and his character and services lovingly recalled. No other ruler of New York was ever similarly honored.

Before entering upon the English period, let us for a moment, recall the everyday life in the old Dutch City.

Walking through the shiny, well-kept streets of that section of our city known as the Financial District, one would find it hard to believe that the habits of that familiar barnyard annex, the ordinary hog, would, at one time, have been an object of solicitude to the Dutch City fathers on whom rested the care and up-keep of public highways. But the early records of our city are filled with no end of regulations, laws and complaints concerning this valuable agricultural asset. We, of our day, are quite familiar with the road hog of the biped species, but the four-legged prototypes appear to have been equally objectionable. They were allowed to run at large, with the result that they rooted such huge holes in the streets and highways, that wagons and carts found it almost impossible to pass. The animals grazed alike on private and public property, and the damage was especially great in Spring when the first shoots of green grass appeared. Not satisfied with a luscious mouthful, the hog would dig and dig, thinking more grass would be found underneath. The Common Council first decreed that each inhabitant stick a ring through the nose of all they owned. This apparently did not solve the problem, for another resolution decreed that as "Goats and hogs are in the habit of daily committing great damage in the orchards and plantations hereabout Fort Amsterdam, it is ordered that all goats and hogs shall be kept in their own enclosures."

During and after the erection of the Wall or Palisade, the hogs were especially annoying and destructive. They would dig around the newly erected structure, uproot the posts and cause wide breaches in the wooden palings. They were a constant source of trouble and caused one or two rather amusing lawsuits. One plaintiff sued a neighbor for breaking the leg of a fine sow about to farrow. The defendant said he had already paid damages for depredations by the sow to his neighbor's garden and it was decreed by the courts that out of the damages he was to erect suitable barriers to prevent a repetition of the trouble. This he failed to do, and the sow, knowing nothing of the court's order, entered the garden as was her wont, and in consequence broke her leg escaping from the irate owner. Judgment for the plaintiff.

As a matter of fact, the city with true municipal economy relied largely upon hogs in those days for the discharge of the duties now performed by the Street Cleaning Department.

It was not till long after the Revolution that this nuisance was abated.

It was at the meeting of the Common Council held on Sept. 20, 1786, that the great question came up. Shall or shall not hogs be allowed to roam the streets at will?

The meeting seethed with excitement. The Committee who had been appointed to draft a law were ready with the report. First it was decided to postpone the matter: then it was decided to go ahead. Finally it came to a vote. The Board was evenly divided, so the Recorder cast the deciding vote in favor of the motion.

Thereupon, [says the minutes] the law passed accordingly which with the Title is as follows:

A Law to prohibit the going at large of hogs within this City. Whereas, the going at large of Hogs, Shoats and Pigs in the Streets or Highways of this City is attended with many inconveniences to the citizens at large and with great injury to individuals.

Be it ordained etc. that after Jan. 1st next no person or persons shall permit his, her or their Hogs, Shoats or Pigs to go at large in any of the streets or highways of this city under the penalty of forfeiting such Hogs, Shoats or Pigs to the use of the poor of said city.

And be it further ordained by the Authority of the same that from and after the first day Constables and Marshalls of the said City and any other person is hereby authorized to take up and secure all such Hogs, Shoats or Pigs as they or any of them shall find going at large contrary to this law and to deliver them to the keeper of the Alms House of the said City who is hereby authorized and required to receive them for the use of the poor as aforesaid and to pay such Constable, Marshall or other person for their trouble the sum of four shillings for each Hog, and the sum of two shillings for each Shoat or Pig.

Nevertheless and notwithstanding, hogs continued to thrive and were constantly in evidence. Even fifty years afterwards during the great parade to mark the introduction of Croton water, a pig managed to get mixed up in the great crowd and at the approach of the procession was left in the middle of the road. Nothing daunted, he proceeded blithely and nonchalantly to lead the marchers to the end of their jaunt. People were so used to seeing pigs at large that his presence at that particular place and at that particular moment, excited no comment whatever.

A great many of them today ride in their own motor cars.

The courts were especially interesting. They always opened the session with prayer for Almighty help in dispensing justice with mercy, after which they would condemn some poor woman found guilty of a trivial offense to be stripped to her waist, receive thirty lashes on her bare back, and to be driven out into the wilds, there to meet a still crueler fate by starvation or capture by the Indians.

In one instance, some stored wheat trickled from a sack on the floor above where rats had gnawed an opening. Sweeping up the handful or two of grain, thus providentially added to her larder, a poor woman suffered the penalty just described, on a charge of theft.

Libels, scandalous allegation, and cruel gossips occupied no small part of the Court's time.

Sheriff Van Tienhoven arrested Jacquest de la Motte and haled him before the magistrates that he might be compelled to answer certain questions regarding what he

had seen at Landaert Aerdens' house between Nicholas
Hoylsteyn and Geertie, the wife of Geurt Coerteus.

Mr. Aerdens lied like a gentleman and said he saw nothing. Several other witnesses testified in the same way. The
Court was puzzled, but finally decided that where there
was so much smoke there must be some fire. So they locked
Geertie up in the hoosegow and remanded Mr. Aerdens
in the custody of the Sheriff till his memory should improve.

There was a regular tariff for fighting. If you struck a
man "one simple blow with fist," the fine was 25 florins.

"For drawing blood with said blow," 100 florins.

No male and female shall be allowed to keep house like
man and wife before they have been legally married.

A rather unusual case was that of Hans Tommer vs.
Mme. Anna Van der Donck. The plaintiff demanded to
know why she had forbidden the publication of banns of
matrimony between himself and Maeyken Huyberton, in-
sisting that she be ordered to give her consent. Defendant
answered that Miss Huyberton might not marry without
the consent of those who hired her; also, that the young
man promised his father not to marry anyone in a foreign
country.

Their worshipful masters had a sorry time settling this
case, but their ultimate decision suggested another Daniel
come to judgment. Their report reads:

No lawful reasons exist why this marriage should not take
place. Delay under such circumstances might create a situation
between the aforesaid two young people which would bring
disgrace on both families. 'Tis true that our theologians say
we must not tolerate nor permit lesser sins in order thereby to
avoid greater ones. Therefore, we think that by a proper sol-
emnization of marriage, the lesser and greater sins are prevented. Therefore, the Burgomasters and Schepens of this city
are of the opinion that the banns of marriage between the

aforesaid young people should be published followed by marriage at earliest opportunity.

Thus was Maeyken restored to her lover's arms.

Roelef Johnson had been bitten by Philip Gerardy's dog and brought suit for damages. Defendant said plaintiff might kill the dog and that he had sent him by his wife four pounds of butter and was willing as a charity to send him four pounds more. The judges said "fair enough" and dismissed the suit.

Some of these cases were bizarre, to say the least. For example, a number of friends went off together on an outing. Upon their return, somewhat elated, they indulged in broad jokes and clumsy witticisms, wherein they alluded to the wife of one of the party in a manner that we would characterize today as rather familiar. So the gentleman whose wife was thus made the subject of their merry quips had the principal jester brought before the Court.

The testimony offered by the plaintiff was to the effect that the defendant took him severely to task because he (the husband) had failed to coöperate and further the desire of the defendant to possess himself of the affections of the plaintiff's wife. In fact, he had gone so far as to complain loudly and bitterly that the plaintiff had actually, with malice prepense, declined to provide him with a *lettre représaille*—permission to help himself.

From today's point of view, we must admit that such a request, strictly speaking, could hardly be called reasonable. We might go further and say it was decidedly bad form. In fact, the Court as much as intimated that such a conclusion might be permissible.

A great mass of testimony was offered pro and con to the utter confusion of the worthy justices. They finally decided to remand *all* the merrymakers to their homes to remain there till some decision could be reached. This took so

long a time, and interfered so seriously with the avocations
of the accused that it was finally decided to annul the
charges and call it a day. The case is Joost Goderis vs
Guilyam de Wyt, N A Records 1635.

John Adamzen, a prisoner, escaped from jail. After the
proclamation and ringing of bells, he did not return.
Thereupon, it was decreed that when found he was to have
a red hot bodkin stuck through his tongue and banished
from the province. In a suit concerning some beer alleged
to be bad, the defendant invited the court to come over to
his place and sample the brew for themselves. If they
found fault with it, he would pay damages. If not, he was
to go free. The offer was accepted, the beer found satisfactory and the case settled amicably all around.

On the whole, justice was rarely tempered with mercy
despite the opening prayers.

A few years later when the Dutch temporarily regained
the city, it was decreed necessary to remove certain houses
that were too close to the fort and were in the line of fire
should the Fort be attacked. Notice was accordingly issued
to the property owners and they were requested to state
what, if any, compensation was desired. Their answers are
deliciously naïve.

Peter de Riemer is willing to remove his house but requests
Muyen's lot or one at the Water side instead.

Lodewyck Pos requests the house next the City Hall; otherwise 't will be impossible for him to move.

Jacobus van de Water requests Pattison's house in Pearl
Street, or a lot as near his former residence as possible, with
satisfaction.

George Cobbett says he is unable to move unless assisted.

Jan Dircksen Meyer says he knows not whither to turn, but
finally requests a lot behind The Five Houses, in Bridge Street.

Andrew Meyer in like manner requests a lot there.

Gerritt Hendricks, butcher, says he has been ruined by the
English and is unable to move; requests help and assistance.

Peter Jansen Slott, by his father, requests a lot behind the City Hall.

Simon Blanck requests accommodation for the winter, as his house cannot be moved; asks a lot behind the Five Houses.

Peter Stoutenburgh, absent.

Martin Jansen Meyer says he is not able to move; is offered the lot next to Kip in the valley, or recommended to look up another.

Lysbeth Tyssen is told that her small houses will be examined, to see whether they cannot be spared.

Peter Harmensen's little house is in like manner to be examined.

Peter Jansen Mesier requests a place on the Water side; otherwise cannot remove.

Ephraim Herman requests satisfaction with others.

Dr. Taylor's wife says that her husband is willing to risk his house, and to abide the result.

So it was all very rural and very unpretentious. Soon, however, the little city began to forsake cowpaths and substitute regularly planned roads. When the first street was opened it was generally referred to as "the new street." It ran along the west front of the present Stock Exchange building, and singularly enough is still called New Street though it is now nearly three hundred years old.

In 1695, the Rev. John Miller resided in New York as Chaplain to His Majesty's forces, and for three years lived in the Fort at the foot of Broadway. He was apparently a close observer, and made many notes and also drew a very excellent map of the city as it then appeared. This map bears a striking resemblance to the Costello Plan, but adds a few new buildings and especially the new shipping docks —quite substantial affairs—constructed where the barge office now stands. This was an important addition to the city's public improvements and showed that its sea-borne commerce had grown materially.

On his way back to England the good doctor had the misfortune to fall into the hands of a French privateer

and was made prisoner. Fearing lest his drawings might
disclose to the enemy valuable information regarding the
defenses of New York, the plucky Reverend, before he was
searched, threw all his papers into the sea.

During his long confinement, he beguiled his time by
"endeavouring to retrieve some part of what I had lost and
put it such method as would promote . . . the service of
my sovereign and the benefit of my country." The result
was a small book dedicated to the "Right Reverend Father
in God, Henry, Lord Bishop of London."

The doctor praises the climate of our city and recom-
mends it to those suffering from rheumatism or almost any
kind of chronic illness, particularly consumption.

He rather laments the fact that it is possible to make a
comfortable living here without the heartbreaking toil
and unceasing labor inescapable in the old country. This
worries the man of God seriously. He cannot understand
why anyone should be willing to live except by the sweat
of his brow. He is also genuinely disturbed at certain other
social conditions which exist without anyone getting excited about it. He writes in his book:

There are many couples live together without ever being
married in any manner of way: many of whom after they have
lived some years or so, quarrel and thereupon separate and
take unto themselves new companions.

Another custom which he found much in vogue and
which caused the good man much perturbation of spirit
was that chaste and refined practice of "Bundling"—an im-
portation from pious New England. If he had stopped
to reflect a moment, he would have known that nothing
evil could have come out of that righteous God-fearing
community. But no, he could see no merit in the idea of
permitting young people to conduct their courtship in
bed. That was abomination to him. He never thought of

the long winter evenings, the deadening chill of the average fireless house nor the rigid necessity of conserving fuel. Every concession was made to convention; a thick wooden board was always supplied by the old folks to go between the couple; and although they were snugly ensconced beneath the blankets, they never removed their clothes. The custom had the sanction of our best families.

This is the chaste and delicate manner in which he alludes to his aversion:

Those who in earnest, do intend to be married together, are in so much haste, that, commonly, ante-nuptial fornication is enjoyed before marriage to which they seldom come till a great belly puts it so forward, that they must submit to that or to shame and disgrace, which they avoid by marriage.

He is further mortified to find that such accidents, when marriage follows, are not looked upon as sinful or scandalous. The holy bands of matrimony wipe the moral slate clean.

The city at the time of which he writes had about eight hundred and fifty families and six churches. Altogether, Dr. Miller's little book is an interesting item, and it is a matter of deep regret that the original manuscript found a watery grave. There was doubtless much more in it.

The chief business of the young metropolis at this period was not confined to the sale of firewater to the Indians in exchange for peltries, as is generally supposed, but in the more romantic and exciting realm of piracy. All this talk about Kidd's piratical career being a great shock to his virtuous friends, Bellomont and others, is sheer nonsense. They were all tarred with the same stick. Kidd committed the unpardonable crime of being caught. Therein lay his unforgivable crime. He sank in the Mediterranean some English ships belonging to the great East India Company and made their crews "walk the plank." To do this to the race of sea dogs that Elizabeth had raised, was fatal. They went after Kidd like a terrier after a rat.

No one had the sense to tell these virtuous upholders of the law that Kidd's capture would spatter mud on a king's throne. In his testimony, Kidd says, in part, "I hope I have not offended against the law, but if I have it was the fault of others who knew better and made me the tool of their ambition and avarice, and who now think it to their interest that I should now be removed out of the world." When one remembers that among Kidd's associates and shareholders in the enterprise was King William himself who was to receive half the profits; Lord Bellomont; Robert Livingston; the Earl of Oxford; Sir Edward Dressel, first Lord of the Admiralty; Sir John Somers, Lord Keeper of the Great Seal; the Duke of Shrewsbury, Secretary of State; and the Earl of Romney, Master General of the Ordnance, it is small wonder that no time was lost in stringing him to the yardarm. Dead men tell no tales. Master Will Shakespeare could have had Kidd in mind, as well as Wolsey, when he wrote, "Had I but served my God with half the zeal I served my King, He would not in mine age have left me naked to mine enemies."

When first arraigned, Kidd tried to avoid pleading, but he was tried first for the murder of William Moore, an insubordinate gunner. After an altercation, Kidd hit Moore on the head with a bucket and he died. It was probably manslaughter, but the jury sustained the indictment for murder. After being condemned for murder, Kidd was tried unfairly in several particulars and condemned for piracy. He was hanged at Wapping on the shores of the Thames, May 23, 1700—*infra fluxum et refluxum maris*—between high water and low water mark.

A doggerel that enjoyed great popularity at that time was widely sold as "Kidd's Farewell." It was sung everywhere. The first verse is:

My name is Capt. Kidd who has sailed (who has sail'd)
My name is Capt. Kidd who has sailed (who has sail'd)
   My name is Capt. Kidd
   What the laws did still forbid
Unluckily I did, while I sail'd, while I sail'd.

etc. etc. for about twenty more stanzas.

The great Frederick Phillipse, lord of Phillipse Manor, was also in this business up to his neck. No mention of this claim to a nation's gratitude, however, is recorded on the pious tablet erected to his sainted memory in that fine old cathedral in Chester, which is the first thing that strikes the eye of the American visitor to that old Roman town.

Henry Morgan who captured Porto Bello in 1668, Maracaibo in 1669, Panama in 1671, and whose wonderful exploits were carried out with great bravery, had a change of heart at the end of his life and became Governor of Jamaica, 1674–1688, and dwelt in an atmosphere of probity and righteousness till he died.

The late John Pierpont Morgan, "the senior Morgan," as he is known, once told me that Henry Morgan was an ancestor of his. The conversation occurred in his office in the back room of the building which preceded the present structure. I paid no attention to the remark at the time until I afterwards recalled that all the yachts that Morgan owned, and he had three of them, were named *Corsair*. The fourth of these yachts recently built by the famous son of this famous father also rejoices in the same romantic appellation. But Morgan the Buccaneer becomes a privateer and eventually is Sir Henry Morgan, thrice Governor of Jamaica, knighted by Charles II for his services against the Spaniards, and hero of the exploits against Porto Bello and Panama. When he died, the Duke of Albemarle ordered a State funeral with military panoply and a salute of twenty-two guns, one more than the regulation number for great public holidays. Thus was he given the obsequies of a dead Viceroy, and his tomb the atmosphere of a conqueror.

When we recall that John Fillmore, great-grandfather of Millard Fillmore, thirteenth President of the United States, was also tried for piracy on May 12, 1724, it gives us food for thought. He, however, was a pirate from necessity and not from choice. Sometimes the prisoners turned the tables on the pirates and drove them from the ship, they becoming masters. Such was the case of Fillmore. He was a prisoner on board the *John Rose Archer* when he made his successful coup against his captors. He started proceedings by killing a boatswain with a broad ax. The testimony clearly established the fact that he was no pirate but rather a hero, and he was acquitted before the Admiralty.

Some of these pirates were certainly remarkable figures. One of them, Bartholomew Richard, had a short but spectacular career. In the few short years between 1718 and 1724, he took more than four hundred sail before he himself was captured. A description of his costumes supports all the romantic tales that have come down concerning these spectacular figures. The man himself was a gallant-looking figure: wore a rich, crimson damask waistcoat and breeches. A gold chain wound ten times around his neck, a red feather in his hat, a sword in his hand, and two pairs of pistols hanging at the end of a silk sling, which was hung on the shoulders, according to the fashion of the pirates, completed his costume. His meteoric career lasted but four years. It was great fun while it lasted. He was killed by the captain of the H.M.S. *Shallow* in an encounter off the West Coast of Africa.

The great rendezvous of these gentry was in the Island of Madagascar off the East Coast of Africa. This Port of Missing Men was financed by Frederick Phillipse of Phillipse Manor. He shared in the profits of all the pirates who made this famous African seaport their headquarters. To this point all the pirates resorted with their stores of captured loot. Here they took the luckless women who had fallen into their hands. High jinks and carnival were the order of the day. Eat, drink and be merry, for tomorrow we die.

In dealing with the authorities of New York, the pirates anchored at a point near the east end of Long Island and sent men ashore to bargain with the Governor for permission to enter and for protection. Bellomont in his letter to the Lords of the Board of Trade, July 8, 1699, in the Public Office Record, detailing the arrest of Kidd, says that Kidd had sent a messenger to arrange a meeting at Oyster Bay and settle terms that would include a pardon. Bellomont further says that Robert Livingston, first lord of Livingston Manor (who had posted from Albany upon news of Captain Kidd's design of coming hither) hastily joined the party. And that Livingston was very peremptory in his manner, threatening that unless Kidd was immediately released, he would sail away with his great ship and its valuable cargo but would first satisfy Livingston out of that cargo. And much more of the same sort.

Kidd married a lady, who was the widow of John Oort, merchant of New York. He lived at 55 Wall Street. Frederic De Peyster in his reminiscences says she is said to have been a lovely and accomplished woman. Lovely, she undoubtedly was, as she captured four husbands, but she could not write her own name and always signed her documents with a cabalistic "SK" which correctly interpreted meant "Sarah Kidd—her mark."

Before we bid farewell to the Pirates of Old New York, let us recall to our readers the still more dreadful punishment which overtook the luckless buccaneer who happened to be captured in New England waters. In Boston, it was customary before execution, to march the con-

demned men under a strong guard to some church on the
Sabbath preceding the day on which they were to suffer.
There, marshaled in the broad aisle, they listened to a
discourse on the enormity of their crimes and the torments
that awaited them in the other world. The Rev. Dr. Cotton Mather usually officiated upon such occasions. Some
years later such "cruel and unusual punishment" was prohibited, and the poor wretches escaped with nothing worse
than a broken neck.

Whole books have been written about this piratical era,
and there seems no doubt that New York for a glamorous
half-century was but little better than a sublimated Madagascar. Sinister stories are told of dark and noisome re-
treats along the river front with concealed trapdoors
through which luckless victims were dropped when they
knew too much; the tide was swift and the water deep.
One more or less in the shifting, lawless population of
that time excited no remarks. A significant shrug of the
shoulders was all the explanation offered and that sufficed
—if you were wise.

The legitimacy of piracy was more or less recognized by
the various governments. Letters of Marque and Reprisal
were issued by all. Under them the right was conferred
upon the master of a sailing vessel to capture or destroy
any of the enemies' ships he could conquer. To give it a
semblance of respectability, this was called "privateering"
and was supposed to be in a measure an auxiliary force
to the naval strength of the country under whose flag the
privateer sailed. As most of the European nations were
constantly at war on some pretext or other, this made privateering to such a city as New York a highly profitable
field of exploitation. Even when brief lulls in hostilities
ceased, the privateers rarely heard of it. The result was
that the sea swarmed with these marauders. A peaceful

merchant ship was constantly in danger and they rarely sailed alone.

British warships when ordered home advertised in the papers that "all merchant ships ready to sail within ten days could enjoy the convoy of the warship to England."

When Franklin sailed from London to New York in 1765, his group comprised no less than nine sail and they were convoyed past the dangerous points by a warship. Only when the open sea was reached and they were safe from sudden attack from some near-by coast did their protector leave them.

A trip from Liverpool to New York in those days, despite its danger, was not without its compensations. The ships kept close together and, when becalmed, they indulged in that peculiar pastime known in nautical circles as "gamming." Coming to anchor, boats would be lowered and visits exchanged between the passengers of the different ships. The ladies would have tea, the men would exchange, no doubt, some jokes current among the Roman soldiery before the walls of Jericho (and which are still doing duty), and a good time was had by all. Franklin writes most entertainingly of such an incident on the trip we have mentioned.

The fleet stopped at Madeira. It was at the height of the grape season. The natives were delighted with the unexpected diversion and showered hospitality upon their welcome visitors. When the party reëmbarked, they carried with them immense clusters of grapes which they hung on the ceilings of their cabins. The fragrance and sweetness of the luscious fruit added greatly to the joy of their trip, and the unlooked-for visit to the little island formed a pleasant topic of conversation for many a day. With fair winds and no storms to blow them out of their course, the voyage could be made within eight or ten weeks. It must have been nice to have had such a genial companion as the engaging Pennsylvania philosopher, even then admitted to possess one of the great minds of the world. It is unfortunate that he had no Boswell along. Enough wit and wisdom, no doubt, fell from his lips to make *Poor Richard's Almanac* more famous than it is.

When the ship finally reached New York, the sail up the bay must have been a wonderful experience. There were no official reception committees in that day to welcome the distinguished. Not even a tugboat. The ship sailed up to her wharf, was berthed by the skipper's skillful manipulations of her sails and came to a stop without so much as a jar. The late Captain Nat Palmer of the *Houquah,* a famous tea ship of the Roaring '40's, brought his ship into its pier in the East River in this manner long after tugboats were available and it never failed to arouse a huge acclaim from the admiring crowd that quickly gathered.

After Kidd's arrest and execution, New York's chief industry suffered an eclipse. It looked for a time as if its inhabitants would be reduced to the dire necessity of having to work for a living. There seemed no escape from this cruel fate. The herculean exertions, by which this frightful catastrophe was finally averted, will be revealed in the further course of this story. In this rejuvenation we are happy to say that the old-time seafaring pirate or merchant was not neglected. And hereby hangs a tale.

At the beginning of the last century, Robert Richard Randall, son of Capt. John Randall, a retired sea captain, devised the benefaction now known as Sailors' Snug Harbor. He then owned a farm fronting the Bowery Road and extending west as far as the present east side of Fifth Avenue. It ran from about 8th to 11th Streets. The Wanamaker Buildings are on this farm and the aristocratic residences of the old Knickerbocker families on the north side of Washington Square above the Avenue. For obvious reasons the buildings that were to house the old sailors were located on Staten Island on a rather sightly tract of land of about four hundred acres. This afforded scope for effective landscaping, trees, shrubbery, walks, etc., all designed to make the old sailor feel perfectly at home.

The father of Mr. Randall, so it was rumored in polite circles, was in his younger days an ardent devotee of the gentle art of privateering, a marine diversion much esteemed by our best families in those times. It was a highly lucrative profession, perfectly legal and, generally speaking, not what you might call extra hazardous. Occasionally some old-fashioned, sour-tempered sea dog would be encountered who had, with malice aforethought, armed his ship with cannon, filled his chests with powder, pistols, poleaxes and bludgeons. He was also so far lost to all sense of human decency as to drill his crew in the use of these objects of art. His language in declining a perfectly civil and polite invitation to surrender, was, I regret to say, wholly unprintable. This particular species of mariner also inherited a perfectly fiendish dislike of both privateers and pirates, whom he rated as one. He even took a savage delight in concealing his heavily armed men till the boarding party arrived. Once on deck, he fairly reveled in dropping them back, one by one, into the sea. This was considered bad form in refined privateering circles, but nothing could be done about it. This type of unregenerate sailor man positively refused to mend his ways and as the more elegant privateers' man disliked roughhousing of any sort, every care possible was taken to avoid an encounter with such ill-bred and annoying persons, unquestionably members of the lower orders.

Be that as it may, Randall's son inherited a comfortable fortune, removed to New York, and proceeded to enjoy his affluence. As he grew old, he added to it both piety and benevolence. Having no near relation, he sought some suitable avenue for the distribution of his wealth and sought advice from his lawyer, Alexander Hamilton.

"You got your money from the sea, why not give it back to the sea—why not a refuge for old worn-out sailors?" suggested Hamilton.

"The very thing," said the delighted Randall, "a sort of snug harbor for them when the voyage is over—that's fine."

So was born the Sailors' Snug Harbor.

At the time the will was written (1801), the universal common carrier of the world was the sailing ship. The Seven Seas were dotted with square-rigged beauties from the ports of all nations. Helpless alike in calm and storm, the commerce of the world moved or stood still according to the whim of Father Neptune. Man's mastery of the sea was merely a poetic license.

That Randall's great benefaction would be of inestimable good to the world no one questioned. So long as men went down to the sea in ships there would be an unending stream of old and decrepit mariners to whom the vision of a snug harbor at the end of a storm-tossed life would be a constant source of comfort and an inspiration when even hope itself seemed lost. But in life, as in Wall Street, it is the unexpected that always happens. Right in his own city, within a stone's throw of his home, so to speak, a man was at work on an idea that was in time to sweep the ocean as clear of ships as foam disappears from the crest of a wave. When Robert Fulton on the deck of the *Claremont* poked her nose into the North River, the beginning of the end of sailing ships was at hand. It might be in one era, it might be many. But it was inevitable.

Meanwhile the great city was growing, growing. It grew up and past the old Randall Farm. The farm was graded and cut into streets. Lots were leased but never *sold* to the tenant. Values enhanced rapidly. Buildings that were erected on the land became the property of the Snug Harbor Corporation unless renewed at a handsome advance. The revenues increased tremendously and the surplus began to assume formidable proportions. But the supply of indigent sailors began to decline. The great romantic and spectacular era of the American Clipper Ship had come and gone. The gold rush to California by way of Cape Horn was merely a memory. Our great Civil War and the opening of the Suez Canal had transferred the carrying trade of the world from American bottoms, where it had been safely stowed away since the Napoleonic Wars, to the speedier steam-driven ships of England—which had steadily developed the marine engine and which had now made important progress. And the greater the development of steam power at sea, the greater the value of real estate on land—especially in the limited area of Manhattan.

We are all familiar with the situation of outgo exceeding income, but few of us know the horrors of income exceeding outgo with no possible means of adjusting the balance and so keeping within the law. The consternation and dismay of the kindly and benevolent gentlemen in charge of Mr. Randall's Snug Harbor who had solemnly made oath to spend his money on blowzy old sailors and hadn't enough sailors on whom to spend it—can better be imagined than described.

The provisions of the will as drawn by Hamilton are inexorably correct legally and there is no loophole of escape. The money is for the relief of Ex-Long John Silvers and for nothing else. The hunt for these sanctified derelicts is constant and unremitting. When information reaches headquarters that one has been sighted in the offing, word is at once telephoned to the Reception Committee to get ready and give the hero a royal welcome home. When he is safely delivered to the custody of the Snug Harbor, usually to his intense amazement, the French chef prepares a banquet fit for a King; the Governors and Trustees join him at the festive board and a good time is had by all.

One of the young internes earned speedy promotion and princely salary by a happy idea.

"You see," he explained to the Board, "sailors love the sea. Now, to get at the sea from our place he has to cross a road—a forty-foot road, and on that road automobiles frequently pass. And if one of these automobiles hits one of our honored guests, he will probably fall into a thousand pieces and we are shy another mouth to feed."

Here the speaker was interrupted by cries and groans from the Board, some of whom were observed in tears. "My idea therefore," he continued, "is to bring the sea into our own back yard. I have, as you see, the plans for a Roman swimming pool of Carrara marble. I have carefully omitted guard rails. That permits me to substitute twelve life savers in three shifts of eight hours each. That makes a wonderful increase in our pay roll."

"Splendid!"

Bowing gratefully at this spontaneous recognition of his genius, the young interne continued:

"You will also notice that the place I have selected for the pool is the depression at the foot of the hill where we have our own cemetery."

"But won't the Board of Health object?" ventured the Chairman timidly.

"Yes, I am sure they will."

"Are you *positive?*" said the Chairman. "I think I see where that might be very important. I would like to be sure on that point."

"Exactly. Well, *I* am the Board!"

At this modest statement the cheers of the Board were

deafening. The whole plan was at once understood. The Board of Health could condemn the pool as soon as completed and endless litigation would ensue. Enormous fees would be paid to high-priced lawyers. As the full significance of the unlimited expenditures possible under this plan suddenly burst upon them, the members of the Board were radiant with happiness.

Upon motion of the Chairman, the young man was unanimously appointed a fourth assistant to the third assistant Medical Director, at a salary of $50,000 a year, and a beautiful house, motor car and maintenance for life. So shines a good deed in a naughty world. The meeting then adjourned.

The pool was immediately built as planned, and immediately condemned as planned, everything proceeding exactly according to schedule. The hunt for superannuated seamen was resumed, but this time with the aid of a high-powered observatory.

And still the money pours in.

CHAPTER V

Pastimes in Early New York

THE little hamlet which was turned over to the English conquerors in 1664 was the least important, by far, of the seacoast cities in the New World. It stood at the bottom of the list and was rated as only a tenth-rate Dutch fishing village by its neighbors, if they thought of it at all, which was seldom.

Yet few ports could boast of the colorful life that made New York the fascinating little wench it then was. In front of the Fort, the streets were thronged with gay pageantry; with motley and weird groups. Striking beauties with the olive skins of the Orient in shawls of flaming scarlet, of passionate purple; skirts of soft clinging silks from the Indies; sparkling diamonds, glowing rubies and milk-white pearls glittered on their voluptuous bosoms. These strange exotic women were the consorts of still stranger swarthy, raven-haired men, with long tresses that fell in curling clusters on their broad, powerful shoulders. Shining gold earrings hung from their heavy lobes, and the hilts of jewel-studded sheath knives sparkled in the sun. These swaggering blades, in many-colored coats trimmed with gold lace, mother-of-pearl buttons, white silk knee breeches and embroidered hose with silver buckles on their shoes, gave the town the aspect of an El Dorado. A shower of gold followed their footsteps. No Treasure Island was ever more splendid. The modest clam shell, hitherto used to eke out the meager currency of the little

From Stokes' "Iconography."

The old Dutch Stadt House, Coenties Slip and Pearl Street 1640.

settlement, gave place to shining pieces of eight, the Louis d'Or of France, the dinars of Arabia, and the bysants of Greece. The tinkle of the guitar and the soft murmur of the lute hung on the air. Strange, seductive perfumes imparted a carnival atmosphere to the shore front. It was the Golden Age of Piracy, and New York was a second Madagascar. These strangers were a joyous, free, devil-may-care people; adventure was their handmaiden and danger was their God.

They formed a striking contrast to the stolid Dutch housekeeper and the few comely English women who were gradually becoming more numerous. But that's what New York likes—something unusual—bizarre—and in these revelers of the Sea, she enjoyed an element of relief from the endless psalm-singing of her pious neighbors. She got angry when she heard she was called *"l'enfant terrible."* But when she learned that this meant only "tough baby," she merely grinned. The Cavalier (?) States, Virginia, the Carolinas and Georgia, were so busy raising tobacco and First Families that they knew only in a vague way that such a wicked city as New York even existed. Her growth in population did not keep pace with the rapidly expanding census achieved by the Puritans with their lovely families of from sixteen to twenty-five little olive branches. Had they not passed a law prohibiting the kissing of wives on Sunday, there is no telling to what dizzy heights New England might have attained in the way of population.

But vast changes were now at hand. Piracy was to disappear and maritime commerce was to take its place. Already New York was looming in the distance as a formidable rival to her New England neighbors. Newport, however, was still conceded on all sides to be the natural gateway to the continent. Her natural advantages were unsurpassed. She was everywhere looked upon as the coming Venice of the New World. To a great extent she has realized this ambition, but her wealth comes from New York.

Although to the stranger things looked somewhat semi-barbarous, there was, nevertheless, a distinct atmosphere of approaching civilization everywhere. The red man who roamed its roads at will, had largely disappeared; the dock front, moreover, had been shored up and something approaching organized shipping had been attained. The Rattle Watch now patrolled the streets in greater numbers. Every hour you could hear them calling—"Four o'clock a cold and frosty morning. All's well." Fire protection in a limited way had been installed and fire buckets were, by law, part of the equipment of practically every dwelling. There were no engines yet. To quench a blaze water was pumped from the nearest well. Men formed in lines and buckets were passed along as fast as filled. Those at the end of the line threw the water on the flames. Sanitary arrangements were yet extremely crude. Out houses, however, had been removed by decree from direct sight in the public roads and were gradually being relegated to the rear. Sidewalks, slightly elevated, were hard-packed dirt roads, sometimes planked; but the streets were seas of mud, in every degree of consistency. After it rained puddles were frequent, and not at all bashful; they would crawl right up to your knee.

There were no theaters or other public resorts for entertainments. Social diversions, among the Dutch contingent particularly, consisted in little evening gatherings at each other's houses beginning at six o'clock and ending at nine. This select company was probably as bright and cheerful as a "Ladies' Aid" in the Gay '90's, but much more refined than some of the bridge parties of today. The evening was spent in decorous conversation and academic bromides. The younger set were much given to "bundling" parties. Our present necking party is just the good old Colonial bundling custom, with the alcoholic content greatly reduced. Card players were known as "Lost Souls." Cakes and wine were sometimes served, but not always. We would not today vote it a very smart evening.

In summer the long twilight was spent more pleasantly. The walks along the shore were vastly alluring and the view of the harbor by moonlight was never without its charm. Then there were kissing bridges at convenient intervals, and at a kissing bridge you were privileged to kiss your fair companion and it was considered perfectly proper. Two of these pleasant places are officially recorded on old plans and records of the city, but no mention is made of the twenty and two that the young people discovered for themselves and never put on any map.

Horse racing grew in favor. From the first race track established by Nicolls in the Union Course at Hempstead, the sport has been continued to this day; and at a later period, in the social history of New York, the Annual Horse Show at Madison Square Garden attained the position of a major social function. Until the coming of the motor car, the horse held high and undisputed position in affections and was, by far, the most popular sport among all classes than anything that has ever occurred in the annals of our city. A man and his horse are familiar companions in the history of our country from its beginning.

Means of transportation were necessarily limited. A solitary horse and rider could occasionally be seen on the landscape, but that was all. What little communication there was between the settlements was mainly by water. The sea was regarded as a highway and not as an obstacle. All of the English towns clung close to the seaboard where alone the necessities of life could be supplied. Only a few miles separated those hardy Colonists from the primeval forest where existence was possible only to the savage.

And curiously enough, each little port developed a type of boat best suited for its waters and the work it had to perform. The Hudson river craft were quite a different model from those used on the waters of the sound; the ferry crossing to the Jersey shore differed from the ferry crossing to Brooklyn; and in winter, ice choked both rivers and made sled crossing at times the only connection.

On land and around settlements, a type of wagon came into use for hauling produce and heavy material by horses. In winter the wagon gave way to the sleigh and it did duty for many months every year. Perhaps our climate has changed, though the Weather Bureau's records since they were established do not show much variation. But snow in those days lay long on the ground when it did fall. And a storm precipitating a few feet of snow early in the season would provide a hard-packed surface that lasted well into the Spring. This was especially true of the country just a few miles back of the coast line. The Dutch sled, judging by its substantial build, was meant for hard and continuous service and did it.

By dint of superhuman labor and courage, a post road had been opened to Boston. Huge gashes on the bark of trees were the only guideposts that pointed the way; only the eye of an Indian could detect the trail made by the horse.

Travelers enjoyed the right of demanding a night's lodging wherever night overtook them. Perhaps demanding is not the right word. It was a privilege freely extended. Something like our Western "Light and Hitch" was the universal greeting. Food for the horses and stabling were included in the welcome.

When the traveler happened also to be the mail carrier, he was doubly welcome. He brought news from the outside world and sometimes a letter and sometimes a "pacquet" as well. The post rider was required to conduct himself "seemly in all things; to comport himself truly and soberly." He was to treat all persons who desired to travel with him civilly and afford them all the help and assistance he could. He was warned not to make a longer stay anywhere than "necessarily belongs to refreshing himself and his horse" and otherwise conduct himself "as a good postmaster ought to doe." He is not to accept tips. He was a ray of sunshine in the lives of these lonely settlers.

As population grew and weekly stages between the larger cities became feasible, small taverns appeared along the routes at intervals. They were not over-comfortable. The stages had fixed posts at which they changed horses, took meals or stopped for the night. Smaller inns in less frequented roads answered the same purpose for the occasional traveler. Some idea of the differences between the

RULES
OF THIS TAVERN

Four pence a night for Bed
Six pence with Supper
No more than five to sleep
    in one bed
No Boots to be worn in bed
Organ Grinders to sleep in
    the Wash house
No dogs allowed upstairs
No Beer allowed in the
    Kitchen
No Razor Grinders or Tinkers
    taken in

hotel of today and the tavern of yesterday may be gleaned
from the rules and regulations promulgated by one of the
more pretentious establishments of that time.

Even in these early years of its existence, New York developed that capacity for attracting strangers that it pos-
sesses today. Beginning with Paul Koch's tavern outside
the Fort, it was not long before Martin Krueger opened
the second, to be followed at intervals with more and more
as the city grew. But the custom of stopping at boarding
houses continued for a long time. As a matter of fact, the
average tavern was merely a taproom and had little or no
accommodations for transients. The boarding house idea
flourished and New York was without what could be called
a hotel till long after the Revolution. John Simmons' tavern on Wall Street, on the site where the Bankers Trust
Company now stands and where the first Mayor of New
York was appointed, was a very small affair. Fraunces Tavern where Washington took farewell of his officers, is still
standing. It has been remodeled to its original proportions
and shows so small a building as to be incapable of caring
for more than a dozen guests at a time.

Just before the century closed, however, Burns Coffee
House, which had previously been the residence of Ettienne De Lancey, was torn down and New York's first
hotel—the City Hotel—rose in its place. The slate roof was
laid by Grant Thorburn, who was afterwards to become
famous as our leading seedsman. He was taken ill on the
street upon his arrival and staggered into the nearest house
which happened to be Robert Hoe's, the press builder, but
at that time unknown to fame. He took the lad in and
nursed him back to health. The City Hotel began a distinguished career and played a large part in the social life
of the city for many years. It marked a tremendous advance
over the old Tavern days and it soon attracted a huge following. Society flocked to it for all its public functions—

the Patriarch Ball was first given here; the dinner to Stephen Decatur on his return from his spectacular victories over the Barbary pirates; the dinner to Washington Irving on his return from Spain and to Charles Dickens on his visit to America. It marked the emergence of New York from a frontier town to a metropolitan city.

There are several very interesting contemporary views of the city about this period which are worth looking at. The one on page 111 shows the city as it looked about the middle period of Stuyvesant's administration. This is easily the most interesting and most beautiful view of New York that has come down to us from these early days. The artist is unknown, but it ranks among the dearest treasures of the Dutch Government and is preserved in the Royal Archives in The Hague where it is jealously guarded. It was found in a portfolio with other papers quaintly labeled

Collection of Sea Charts relating to the navigation of the East and West Indies, mostly drawn with pen in detail, together with some pictures of important islands, cities and fortresses situated as well in the Spanish and English as in the Dutch Indies; all painted in water colors very nearly from life and arranged in alphabetical order.

The view is taken from a point a little west of Governors Island and shows the East River shore extending as far as Coenties Slip. The most important buildings shown in the drawing are

1—The Windmill
2—The Fort
3—The Church
4—Governor's House

5—The Officers' Quarters and Storehouses
6—The Weighing Beam and Crane

The tall post at the water's edge is the so-called gibbet or gallows. No record, however, has ever been found of the erection or even the existence of a gallows at so early a

NIEUW AMSTERDAM ofte NUE NIEUW IORX op't TEYLANT MAN

Artist unknown.

Collection of the author.

New York in 1653. From a colored lithograph. Original in the National Archives, The Hague, Holland. The best view that has come down to us.

date, although there was evidently a gibbet or something answering this purpose as early as 1641 when a negro named Garret the Great was sentenced to be hanged. The rope broke under his enormous weight and the sentence was never actually carried out. It seems not unlikely that this structure was used for hoisting goods from the ships.

The first picture of our city ever shown to the world appears as an illustration in a book on New York written by Adrian Van der Donck who founded the city of Yonkers. It was drawn probably as early as 1628 and shows the port and the little cluster of thirty houses that then comprised the whole of the settlement. It is, of course, very crude but extremely interesting nevertheless.

But two still later views possess almost equal interest, partly because of their later date, but more especially because they show the city as it appeared when it was surrendered to the English; one of them is known as the Duke's Plan and the other was the Costello Plan, both showing a bird's-eye view of the city divided into streets, farms and residences. The Costello Plan is, by far, the more important.

The Duke's Plan was the drawing which Nicolls sent over to the Duke of York to show the extent and importance of the city which he had added to the Duke's province. The original is part of the extremely valuable collection of maps, plans, views, etc., made by the Duke of York. He left them to George III. The Fourth George presented them to the nation where they now repose in the British Museum.

It was at first supposed that Nicolls had the Duke's Plan drawn when he took possession of the city. Recent researches, however, point to it as of Dutch origin, probably drawn by Augustus Herrman from a survey made in 1661 by Jacques Cortelyou, well known for work of this kind and who is supposed to have laid out the plans for Har-

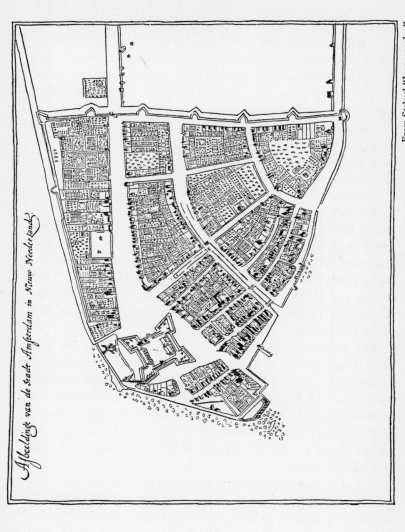

From Stokes' "Iconography."

The city as it looked enclosed by a wall. The famous Costello Plan. See page 112.

lem. He had an office in the Marketfield, which he rented from Peter Jacobsen Buys, where the original Costello Plan was also drawn. He lived in Brooklyn and was the first of the present vast army of commuters that come to New York every morning.

The English planned an invasion of New York in 1661 which was deferred. The Duke's Plan has several notations on it referring to 1661, and the supposition is that it was originally stolen from the Dutch and copied by English spies for the use of their army. Nicolls, however, sent it along to the Duke of York as if it had been newly prepared. The changes between 1661 and 1664 were probably slight, so the plan was a very fair representation of the city at the capitulation.

The Costello Plan is now regarded as the most valuable drawing of all the early views. It shows how the streets were laid out, where the principal private dwellings stood and, of course, the Fort, the Wall and the Broad Street Canal, and other public structures. It also foreshadows the substitution of streets for cow paths, and, a definite step toward the planning of a city. The number of houses shown is about three hundred. It was probably drawn in 1665–70 from the survey by Cortelyou in the summer of '61. The only changes between '61 and '65 would probably be in the number of houses, which had increased from one hundred twenty-four to three hundred. It is in the possession of the Costello family of Italy and now reposes in the Villa Costello near Florence, Italy. It is owned by the Italian Government.

As showing in all its details the city as it was when the Dutch relinquished control, the Costello Plan is invaluable. Our picture on page 113 is an exact reproduction of a re-draft from the original made by Mr. I. N. Phelps Stokes, who first discovered the plan some years ago. It is well worth intensive study.

Other very interesting views were those made by the celebrated Labadist travelers, Danckers and Sluyter, men of extraordinary intelligence and who have left an account of their visit to New York in 1670. While not accomplished draftsmen, they made a number of excellent sketches, one in particular showing the great improvement to the waterfront that was made by shoring up and by the construction of docks and a breakwater. It proved that New York was growing rapidly and gave definite indication that her destiny as a great maritime port was inevitable. Although these drawings are amateurish in workmanship, the fact that they were drawn by men who actually made them from personal observation imparts to them a value far in excess of their merits as an artistic achievement. They put down only what they saw with their own eyes.

In this connection, reference might be made to what is known as the "Restitutio View." This was an engraving made by the Dutch in the exuberance of their joy at having recovered the city from the English in 1674. They naturally exaggerated the appearance of the city they had taken, adorning it with docks of enormous strength and a waterfront so impressive as almost to dwarf even the ancient ports of Antwerp and Rotterdam. The little Fort has been transformed to a second Gibraltar. Cannon are belching forth death and destruction. The victorious Dutch troops are parading outside the breastworks. It is a vainglorious picture, quite pardonable under the circumstances, but of very questionable historic value.

A walk through the little city at this juncture, which was destined to become the "Sweetheart of the Western World," will no doubt prove of great interest.

Landing on the yellow sands of Pearl Street, we find that most of the houses cluster naturally around the Fort in which was also located the only sacred edifice on the island —the "Church of St. Nicholas in the Fort" now located on

Fifth Avenue and 29th Street. The next important structure was the Governor's House just inside the Fort, which was later changed by Governor Dongan to Whitehall, after its London prototype.

A really diverting spot in the town was, undoubtedly, the market place—a small open space in front of the Fort. This was where the annual Fair was held. It was also used as a bowling green, whence its name today; and it has the honor of being "Number One" in New York's prodigious and magnificent Public Park System.

The most noted structure of the city, undoubtedly, was the Wall or Palisades. This was a barrier of considerable strength across the city from river to river. It had several gates—one on the East River called the Water Gate; another (at Broadway and Wall Street) called the Land Gate, to which a bastion of heavy stone was added mounting several guns. It was called "Hollandia." Another similar defense was where William Street crosses Wall—Zeelandia. The wall was subsequently built along the steep bluffs facing the Hudson where Greenwich Street now is and later on was continued southward till it joined the Fort facing the sea at the foot of Broadway. This was as near an approach as New York ever made to being a walled city. While the Wall existed, the cattle of the settlers were each morning collected by a herder and taken through the Land Gate to pasture on the site of the present City Hall Park, then known as Common Lands. In the evening they were driven back to their owners. The herder made a picturesque sight as he went his daily rounds, and was something unique in the growth of American settlements.

It is hard to imagine these stolid Dutchman giving themselves up to an hour of leisure. But it is a fact, nevertheless; and the young men and maidens made merry with music and dancing in Bowling Green at the great annual Fair. It is pleasant to think of them without the inevitable

long-stemmed pipe and the ever-present bottle of schnapps.
What lent an additional charm to this festivity was the
fact that you could not be arrested for debt while the Fair
was on. That was an ever-present contingency in old Amsterdam, and any moment you might suddenly find your-
self in a debtor's jail for an installment on something or
other that you had been temporarily unable to meet. So
for the two weeks of the Fair you could live tranquilly and
with an easy mind. Market Street today, which runs off
Whitehall, is a reminder of this old section, and Petticoat
Lane is also suggestive of its frills and furbelows. There
are still many street markets in New York, the best known,
perhaps, being "Paddy's Market" under the darkened
shadows of the elevated on Ninth Avenue near Thirty-
ninth Street, and the Jews' Market under the New York
Central tracks on Park Avenue near 130th Street. There
are dozens on the East Side and other parts of town. They
all descend from the Dutch market in front of old Fort
Amsterdam in Bowling Green.

The next and probably the most widely known structure was the Windmill. That is shown in all the drawings
of that period which have come down to us. As this building provided all the flour for bread-making, it naturally
was of universal interest. The business of bolting flour was
conferred on New York exclusively and was one of its most
valuable trade possessions, while it lasted. This monopoly
was ended by Royal Decree some years later, as the rest of
the Provinces objected, but not before New York had
gained considerable prestige and trade as a result.

A little further along, about where Peck Slip begins, was
a boat moored to a tree growing on the bank of the shore.
A horn hung upon this tree and if you took it down and
blew a long blast upon it, a ferryman in his house close by
would emerge and ferry you over to Brooklyn for the trifling sum of about six cents. This was a journey, by no

means to be lightly undertaken in winter, with the water filled with huge cakes of heavy ice.

It was against the law to use the Ferry crossing to Brooklyn "when the sails of the Windmill are taken in." In other words, that was a storm warning. When the wind was too high for the sails of a windmill it was dangerous for craft on the waters. And this weather forecast seldom went unheeded. When the ferryman started for Brooklyn, several loud blasts of a trumpet notified the opposite shore that a passenger was coming. The ferryman appeared only when required. He was usually at work in the fields when the blast from the trumpet would summon him to his duty. It was at this location that Robert Fulton afterwards established his steam ferry to Brooklyn which enjoyed a profitable career till the opening of the East River bridge which marked the second step in transportation to Brooklyn.

The buildings were mainly of brick, brought from Holland, and had the characteristic high front stoop needed in the old country to protect the lower floor from water. This afterwards became a dominating feature of all New York houses and persisted until a comparatively recent period. Thousands of them still survive in the old brownstone fronts of our residential streets. The steep gable roofs and small dormer windows were features also largely copied. The influence of this early Dutch architecture was long apparent in New York.

A little further north we come to a bright green marshy valley opening on the river bank, down which a stream flowed. To this stream came the young women of the town on wash day to rinse the clothes with Dutch thoroughness in the limpid water of this little brook. You can see similar scenes almost anywhere today in rural Holland. The stream has long ago vanished, and for years the present generation has known this little green valley—Maiden

At the foot of Maiden Lane, 1634, on East River.

Lane—as the headquarters of the jewelry trade. Only the name remains to remind us of its former romantic existence.

The Stadt House, which stood at the juncture of Pearl Street and Coenties Slip, was the headquarters for the Burgomaster, Schepen, etc. It is perhaps more importantly remembered, however, not for the governmental activities of the local magistrates, but because it was the scene of the introduction of our present gigantic Post Office business. Governor Lovelace dispatched from this old building the first postman on horseback who carried the mail from New York to Boston.

Retracing our steps to the waters opposite Governors Island, we find that a short narrow arm of the sea made an inroad from Pearl Street to the stockaded wall. It was a

veritable replica of a street in Holland, and the Dutch
further heightened the illusion by walling its sides with
stout planking, spanning its width at intervals with several
wooden bridges. There was one at where Exchange Place
now enters Broad Street, which became, by natural selection, a meeting place for merchants who stopped here on
the way home for lunch. Quite a little business was here
transacted, and in time the little bridge became a recognized exchange in a modest way; and from this circumstance the short street I have spoken of, running to Broadway, received its name. This little bridge exchange is the
father of all the great exchanges in New York. At a later
date when the canal was filled in, the exchange moved to
a buttonwood tree in Wall Street. In its present development, it now occupies the imposing Ionic-columned marble building known the world over as the New York Stock
Exchange, which overlooks the old canal in Broad Street
that was bordered on both sides by a waving green sheep
pasture. Lambs graze elsewhere these days.

The sheep pastures were later occupied by ill-smelling
tanneries, which were banished first to Shoemakers' Land
and then to what we now know as "the Swamp" at Cliff
and Beekman Streets. The leather trade has ever since
made this section its headquarters.

That queer little church, which occupies a room in the
building at the corner of Fulton and Nassau Streets, is a
relic of the sheep-herding days of Broad Street. After ex-
pulsion from Broad Street, the tanners bought the land
now bounded by Broadway, Ann, Gold and John Streets,
which was known as Shoemakers' Land, where they tanned
hides and made boots. John Harpendinger, one of their
number, left to the Dutch Reformed Church certain land
for a church in which divine service must be held daily.
The church was built on this lot at the corner of Fulton
and Nassau Streets (the old Middle Dutch). This building

burned down many years ago, but the church was never restored. A palatial office building rose on the site, in which a room was reserved for daily divine service. Promptly at noon certain persons repair to this "church" (the Fulton Street Daily Prayer meeting) in this office building daily between twelve and one. This complies with the stipulation in the will of shoemaker Harpendinger. It is open to the public.

There were the usual jail, a few taverns, a rather large tobacco house owned by Isaac Allerton. That name is perpetuated in our day by the Allerton hotels, a semi-philanthropic hotel chain for young men or women at moderate rates. The rest of the settlement was composed of little one- and two-storied low gable-roofed brick houses with high stoops—possibly a hundred or so.

Outside the City wall, conditions were still largely in a primeval state. Cow paths and dirt roads indicated future streets. One such roadway—now Broadway—leading north from the Fort, made a straight line to where St. Paul's Church now stands; there it deflected to the east along what is now Park Row. The open land facing is the "Common Lands," now our City Hall Park. The turn of the road at this point cut off a considerable corner of the land originally set aside for common use. The triangle formed by Ann, Nassau, and Spruce Streets is the part thus inadvertently lost to the public. For Governor Dongan, seeing that it belonged to nobody in particular, thoughtfully appropriated it to his own personal use. The real southern boundary of the Common Lands was Ann Street to Nassau. He performed a similar operation on Wall Street, shaving off a considerable slice for himself on some pretext or other, which is why Wall Street is one of the narrowest streets in the city till it reaches Pearl Street: at this juncture it suddenly widens out. That, however, is artificial ground and before being filled in was a sort of general

public dock. Murray's Wharf, where Washington landed
from Mount Vernon to become our first President, and
where the first tea party was held, was located here. That
New York Tea Party considerably antedated the Boston
Tea Party. The latter, however, has received such vocifer-
ous advertising as to dwarf all reference to any other similar performance, if not to blot it out altogether.

This curious indifference to credit she should receive
for this and many other instances of great public service, is
characteristic of New York. Few people in it know anything of her history, and most of them care less. You rarely
meet a man who was born on the Island, or has been here
more than a few years at most. Civic pride is an emotion
which they have never experienced, and a national spirit
would die of malnutrition.

The Common Lands (City Hall Park) in a short time
superseded Bowling Green as a place for great open-air
meetings and was the scene of many exciting episodes during the Stamp Act agitation, and later as the chief rallying
spot for the Sons of Liberty just prior to the Revolution.
Young Alexander Hamilton, a student at King's College,
now Columbia University, sprang into notice here by a
fiery harangue delivered to a mob at one of these impromptu meetings. The Liberty Pole, that stood here and
was cut down by British soldiers, has been restored within
the past few years. The base of the present pole consists of
stones brought from a Revolutionary battlefield in each of
the Original Thirteen States. It rises on the exact site of the
original, which was cut down by British soldiers six times.
Iron bands at the bottom preserved the last one from the
fate of the others.

Just north of the Common Lands stood a pump which
gained great celebrity on the Island for the purity of its
water. Generally speaking, the water, while abundant, was
brackish. This particular pump was an exception, and its

Collect Pond. Site of French settlement, Norumbega, 1525; now site of new County Court House building.

water was peddled in barrel carts all through the city. It was known as the "Tea Pump" and it retained its famous reputation till late in the nineteenth century.

Beyond the Tea Pump was a charming little inland lake called the Collect Pond and sometimes Fresh Water. It was a very deep and limpid lake. For Indians, Dutch, and English it was a generous reservoir of dainty fish, and in the winter it was the scene of gay skating parties. William IV, when a midshipman, was nearly drowned as the result of breaking thin ice one winter. Around the shore of this bright and sparkling sheet of water, stood a village of Manhattan Indians before the white men came. And it was the site of Norumbega, the little French trading post of which we have spoken. The old Tombs prison and the new

County Court House and other units of our new Civic Center occupy the site of Collect Pond, drained and filled in a hundred years ago.

Continuing north along what is now the Bowery, we would pass the old Kissing Bridge near Chatham Square. This was a popular stroll at all times because of a very ancient privilege conferred on all travelers, that of kissing your fair companion as you crossed the bridge walking or driving. Moonlight nights in the vicinity of the Kissing Bridge rivaled in popularity the back seats of our modern motor cars.

Passing the ancient milestone at Rivington Street which marked two miles to City Hall, we soon came upon Bowery Village—a cluster of settlements founded by Governor Stuyvesant on his own territory. There was a church, a smithy, and an inn which provided excellent fare for both man and beast. When we include the farm of Jacobus Kip at 33d Street and Third Avenue, we have practically exhausted the main features of the Island at about the time the English took possession.

Chapter VI

Broadway

The Great Wagon Road Leading to the Fort

The Londoner, sweltering under the tropic sun of India or Africa, consoles himself with the thought that some day he will again revel in the delights of the Strand and Piccadilly Circus. The Frenchman thinks of his beloved Champs Élysées, the Italian of the Corso, and the New Yorker of Old Broadway; the discomfort and loneliness of the present moment is forgotten in fragrant memories of the past and the coming pleasures of the future.

Broadway has a charm all her own. Of all the streets on Manhattan Island, it, alone, has its roots deep in the past.

It was there before the white man came. The prowling savage, hunting or hunted, skulked along this backbone of the Island. From its commanding heights, he could look to the north, to the south, to the east, and to the west. Naught could escape his vigilant eye. Over hill and dale, across streams, and by the side of still waters, it crept the length of the Island, and finally to the mainland. Then along the shores of the beautiful Hudson, to its confluence with the Mohawk; there to branch off westward to the Great Lakes, northward to Champlain and the waters of St. Lawrence. Great iron bands now cover this trail and concrete roads lead past the once populous haunts of the powerful Five Nations. It is now policed and lamplighted from the Battery to Buffalo and from Ticonderoga to Quebec. More

A bit of Broadway, England, which gave its name to the Main Street in our village, and where our May Anderson now lives.

people have walked on Broadway than on all our other
streets together. The Dutch called it *"Der Heere Straat,"*
the High Wagon Road; the English called it the Broadway after the old English village where our own May
Anderson now lives and where Edwin E. Abbey made his
English home. It has marked the growth of New York step
by step, and has changed its raiment and companions to
suit the changing eras. It is the one American street known
the world over from Liverpool to Mandalay, from Calcutta
to Singapore, from the Straits Settlements to the Antip-
odes. To the New Yorker, it is the belle of the Western
World.

A very haunting and lilting legend still lingers around
the hallowed spot which marks the beginning of old
Broadway. For here at one time stood the modest little
tavern of one Paul Koch—a name which is ever recalled by
old New Yorkers with feelings of sincere, unashamed affection, and lasting gratitude. Although a prosaic and massive
structure of steel and concrete now covers the site of the
old tavern at No. 1 Broadway, time cannot destroy nor
custom stale the glory of old Koch's Tavern. For it was
here (and I have it upon the authority of a descendant of
an officer on Washington's staff) that the divine concoction
known as the Martini Cocktail was born. Some second Lo-
renzo the Magnificent will yet arise and seize immortality
by depicting, in colors of living fire, this greatest moment
in history; and some mute and inglorious Milton may
strike anew the lyre that shall direct again the feet of the
adoring multitude to this hallowed site.

Certain other envious persons, undoubtedly of the lower
orders, would rob old Broadway of this immortal distinction and ascribe its origin elsewhere—notably the Tavern
kept by one Mrs. Betsy Flanagan on the road between
Tarrytown and White Plains. Nay, Mrs. Flanagan herself
goes so far as to embellish her tale with many flounces and

furbelows in the true Rabelaisian manner, so that we have Yankee and French soldiers belonging to Washington and Rochambeau foregathered in her hospitable mansion many a time and oft; that the Yank brought Gin and Johnny Crapeau, Vermouth. These royal beverages were blended together and the resulting concoction stirred with the tail feathers of Mrs. Flanagan's pet rooster—"A b-u-r-r-d of high degree," as Mrs. F. remarked grandiloquently.

Yet another claimant appeared in the captivating Peggy, Mistress of Van Eyck's Cock's Tail Tavern in Yonkers, which bailiwick is at the north end of old Broadway—just beyond the city limits. Learned and scientific antiquarians, however, prefer to believe the Paul Koch legend. Did not Hawthorne in his *Blythedale Romance,* Fenimore Cooper in his *Spy,* and the gentle Thackeray in that rare Virginia tale, *The Newcomes,* pay tribute to the magic of the nectar of Paul Koch of old Broadway? Nor must we omit the sad fate that befell poor Rip Van Winkle who "switched" from the frisky cocktail to the heady rum, and who slept for twenty years in consequence.

No. Our story is authentic.

It also has the authority cited above and no gentleman, entrusted with the responsibility of passing along a sacred family tradition of this immense social importance, would be guilty of adding to or detracting from the original story one iota, as handed down from father to son for many, many generations.

With the exception of Broadway, all the Dutch streets below Wall, are narrow, tortuous paths surveyed and laid out originally by bovine instinct. Broadway, however, was destined to be great from the first. It has always possessed a peculiar individuality, arising from no other source than its own dignity and impressiveness. Pearl Street, Wall Street, Pine Street, Greenwich Street and many other streets seemed destined at one time or another to become

A view of New York, 1790, showing the high lands bordering the river before later improvements added Washington and West Streets. Trinity Church at left.

New York's most famous thoroughfare, but Broadway heeded not. The shores along the East River front, in those days, were populous and busy. The commerce of the growing City clustered thick around the waterfronts, East and West, and Broadway seemed far away. It was in the middle of the town, people said, too remote from either shore to be ever of any particular importance.

In the old days, the waters of the Bay came up to the foot of Broadway. A rocky promontory projected a slight distance from the shore, forming a sort of natural break-water and a well-protected cove. It made a sheltered landing place and was the resort to which many Indians came in their canoes. Small bands were constantly arriving at this quiet corner. Here they would chat, exchange the gossip of the day, do a little trading among themselves, and depart in peace. So this little cove under the rocks became a well-known rendezvous among the adjacent tribes of the Pavonias, Raritans, Manhadoes, Canarsies, and all the various affiliates of the vicinity. It had somewhat the combined social and business atmosphere of the market places of the whites. This bowlder, projecting in the water, afterwards formed part of the ramparts of Fort Amsterdam, which was built around it. All the city south of the present Custom House, from river to river, is built on land filled in since the days of the Dutch.

Even before the Fort was built, some of the earliest traders occasionally stopped here for a few weeks at a time and they built a few huts on Broadway. When Adrian Block was here in 1613, his vessel, *The Tiger,* burned to the water's edge, and he selected Broadway for his company's winter quarters. There is a tablet on the building, No. 39, telling of his visit and of the fact that he contrived to build a new ship while here which he called the *Restless.* Broadway was, therefore, the scene of the first ship-yard ever erected in the city, and that was more than a dozen years before the Dutch finally decided to settle here permanently.

For nearly two centuries a fort always stood here. Under the Dutch it was called Fort Amsterdam. When the English took it in 1664, they changed the name to Fort James, after the Duke of York. When it again came into the hands of the Dutch in 1673, they renamed it Fort William Hendrik after the Prince of Nassau. When it finally passed into the hands of the English to be retained by them till the Revolution, it was called, successively, Fort William, Fort Ann, and finally Fort George. During the Revolution, the British added a redoubt to the Fort and erected thereon a battery of guns for defense against an attack by sea. And this gave the name "Battery" to the site, which, strangely, has endured long after the Fort has been forgotten.

During this long period, it was the headquarters of the social and political life of the city. When the Revolution was over, the Fort was finally razed to the ground, and on its site was erected an imposing structure designed to house the President of the United States and the Congress, for New York was the Federal Capital. Washington never occupied the building, however, as the Capital was changed the next year to Philadelphia. This building, which was known as Government House, was taken down in 1815 and the land sold to private parties for $80,000. The City Chamberlain, Mr. Mercier, was rapturously dined by the citizens for his superb business acumen in obtaining such a stupendous sum for the land. No reference to this transaction, however, was made by the Government when it repurchased this same site in 1900 from the heirs for the insignificant sum of three millions! This new block was called Battery Place. It became a very fashionable street. Many New Yorkers can recall these houses now, in the days of their adversity, as "Steamship Row." They were removed not many years ago to make room for the present Custom House. And so it is rather interesting to note that this historic spot of ground, which was the people's property at the beginning, has once again come into the possession of the people and is once more used for Government purposes.

Broadway grew naturally. A fort attracts people on many accounts. What little official life there was, centered about it. Visitors, distinguished or otherwise, were constantly coming and going. Soldiers on leave and without it, were always around the taverns just outside the barracks where No. 1 Broadway now is.

The ceremony of locking up the gates of the Fort in itself was a picturesque incident of more than passing interest, and always drew a group of interested spectators. At drumbeat, half an hour before sundown, the militia paraded before the Stadt House. There the Burgomaster in the robes of his office, received the municipal keys from the guard at the Fort. With an escort of six he proceeded in state to lock the gates and assign the citizens to night watch. By a similar pageant at sunrise the gates were opened and the keys restored to the Keeper of the Fort. No doubt the custom came from Amsterdam, as Rembrandt's great painting "Night Watch" clearly indicates. A similar procedure, only on a much more elaborate scale, is still in force in the Tower of London where it has been practiced since the days of Cæsar.

To the right of the Fort, past Koch's Tavern, was a pleasant shore road, where Greenwich Street now is. And toward the east, another similar path ran along the golden sands of Pearl Street. Every lass loves a sailor, and even in those days the maidens of Nieuw Amsterdam never lacked for admirers among the soldiers, town boys and the lads from across the seas. So old Broadway was the starting

point for many a pleasant stroll along the charming roads
that branched out from it and carried you to many a delightful nook and corner safe from prying eyes.

In the upper reaches of Broadway, then a region of plantations, there was one that deserves more than a passing
notice. It was owned by a planter named Dixie. This Dixie
person, while he did not exchange his mile or so of real
estate fronting on this plethoric street, as did many clever
Dutchmen, for the more fertile soil of Hoboken or Flat-
bush where cabbages grew more luxuriously, did what was
just as brilliant. It was the time of the great Mississippi
Bubble, when that charlatan of genius, the Scotchman
John Law, had undertaken with the aid of Regent Duke of
Orleans to deliver France from financial ruin through a
system of credit of which Louisiana with its imaginary
gold mines was the basis. The company's offices in Paris
were besieged day and night by crazed speculators who
fought to get their names inscribed among the stock-
holders. The glittering bubble burst, and Law, lately the
idol of France, fled for his life amid a howl of execration.

Mr. Dixie fell for the sirens who told him there was millions in sugar cane, gold mines, pearl fisheries, etc. So with
the few hundred dollars that he got for his Broadway farm
he hied him, with all his slaves, to the fever-stricken banks
of the Mississippi in the sunny Southland. The darkies
were delighted with the prospect of unlimited sunshine,
co'n pone and 'possum.

But working from sunup to sundown, with no moonlight walks along the cooling shores of the rivers or the Battery, no new faces anywhere, things began to sour. Then
the crash came. And presently these New York darkies began to hanker for the fleshpots of Egypt, and the lure of
the old Dixie plantation on Broadway. Finally this longing
found expression in a song of heartfelt yearning.

Den I wish I was in Dixie, hooray! hooray!
In Dixie land I'll take my stand,
To lib and die in Dixie,
Away, Away, Away down south in Dixie,
Away, Away, Away down south in Dixie.

Many years afterwards, Daniel Emmet, barnstorming through the South with Dan Bryant's San Francisco Minstrels, heard the tune, rearranged the words, and sang it one night. It made a tremendous hit. It is now the National Anthem south of the Mason and Dixon Line; but that's the true origin of this famous ballad—a product of old Broadway.

Broadway has seen many colorful parades in its day, but it is doubtful if it ever saw anything more picturesque, more alluring than the scene when the great chiefs and sachems of the Five Nations came to visit Governor Colden to arrange an alliance offensive and defensive against the French. Trouble in this quarter had been brewing for some time, with clashes along the borders of Lake Champlain a frequent occurrence. Upon this occasion the braves, numbering close to a thousand, came down the Hudson in their war canoes brilliant in war paint, swinging their tomahawks, and bringing with them their squaws and papooses. They landed about a mile above the Fort and soon were coming down Broadway in a riot of color. Huge crests of gorgeous feathers floated behind them.

Among their gayly painted shields and spears, were long black hickory poles on top of which long flowing scalps streamed bravely in the breeze, proof of their prowess over the French. They marched in single file, stolidly, with never a smile or a look to left or right. Reaching the open space in front of the Fort, arrangements had been made to receive them in a manner befitting their importance as England's allies, and the aim of the English was to impress them with the might and power of that great Empire.

So the Fort was gay with flags and streamers. Drums beat, trumpets blared, bands played, and with great pride and circumstance, the Great White Father set the stage to receive the principal chiefs and sachems in a style befitting their high estate among the Council of the Five Nations. Elaborate ceremonies marked the presentation of each individual warrior; deep and profound salutations accompanied the greeting of the Governor and his gold-braided staff. A royal salute boomed from the guns of the Fort and the King's colors waved proudly in the breeze. Nothing was left undone to impress the natives with the awe and majesty of the Great Father beyond the seas. Old Broadway has seen many stirring pageants, but none to excel in tenseness and dramatic power the spectacle then before it.

Of course, Broadway had to have the first joy house in Manhattan. This was the Blue Boar Tavern that stood between Cortlandt and Dey Streets. At that time it was outside the city limits and presumably enjoyed a larger degree of license than was possible in the town. It certainly had great popularity, and to meet at the Blue Boar generally meant a party with the lid off. There have been many similar taverns on the old street since these days. The Blue Boar, however, was not disreputable and, in spite of its gay reputation, had many imitators. Similar taverns duplicating this famous Broadway resort, grew up outside of towns all through the Colonies. Aside from the Blue Boar Tavern, there were a few wooden shacks but no regular buildings beyond the Palisades.

Broadway was still in its chrysalis state. The settler, whose little clearing faced this rarely used path, often found himself robbed of the fruits of his toil from the visits of predatory animals, who destroyed his ducks, chickens, sheep, hogs, goats, and other small livestock, no small part of his most important possessions. Wolves were a particular pest. They grew so numerous and so bold one winter that Broadwayites banded together for their destruction and offered a reward for their pelts. Holes in the wall, made by the burghers' own hogs, unfortunately, afforded these marauders easy access to the town. It seems strange to read of Broadway suffering from such misadventures, but the great highway was still nothing but a dirt road leading from the Land Gate to the Fort, although it was daily becoming more and more the main traveled artery connecting the forests outside the wall with the civilized streets within. The bowling green was on the open space opposite the Fort. Its original name was the Marketfield. A path leading to it from Broad Street was called by the English "Petticoat Lane." It was down Petticoat Lane that Stuyvesant's soldiers marched after the surrender to the ships that carried them away. The green served as a parade ground for soldiers, public meetings, Maypole dances and fair grounds. Later on this plot was rented for one peppercorn a year to John and Augustus Jay, who agreed to inclose the space, make walks therein for the recreation and delight of the inhabitants and for bowling. The first Post Office was opened here and this rule announced—"N.B. No credit in future."

The West India Company had a beautiful garden just beyond Bowling Green, probably about where the Empire Building now is. It was tended by negro slaves from the Fort. It had roses of all colors, shapes and sizes; hyacinths, tulips, larkspur, narcissi and many other delightful specimens that only the garden-loving Dutch knew how to grow. With the frolics at the market place and the beauty of this garden, it was somewhat suggestive of what the street was subsequently to become—a highway of gayety with a kiss for Cinderella. Its tragedies were foreshadowed in our first public burying ground established, of all places, on frolicsome Broadway, where Morris Street now is, adjoining the Garden. During a cattle fair the animals were fastened to stakes driven for that purpose in front of this graveyard.

But the town was growing. A few houses began to make their appearance between the Fort and the Land Gate. Restrictions against quail shooting within the city limits were removed. Small boys no longer hallooed after the Indians they occasionally saw in the street. Every seventh house had to project a pole on which to hang a lantern lighted by a candle. On bright moonlight nights it was not necessary to light the candle.

Dancing, fencing, and other polite recreations were slowly being introduced, though they met with much opposition. Dancing academies were by many classed with disreputable resorts. Still the young people persisted and managed to remove, in large measure, this bigoted prejudice. A better, a pleasanter life was dawning.

Houses were now gradually rising on both sides of Broadway up to the Wall. In later years, a great fire destroyed all these Colonial structures and we now know nothing of their appearance, as every vestige of them disappeared. Fortunately, the block from No. 1 to Morris Street on the West Side was preserved, and there are still men living who can recall, as I do, the demolition of the Kennedy, Watts and Livingston houses to make way for the present huge International Mercantile Marine Building. The houses of the two sons of Governor Stuyvesant were just beyond. With the exception of Isaac Allerton's, the houses on the East Side were of a mean character and merely shacks.

A very important addition to the dignity of the street was the erection of Trinity Church just beyond the public burial ground at the head of Wall Street. This was the church home of the most important social element in town. The church was added to the Diocese of London and was under the charge of the Archbishop of Canterbury. Queen

Anne made a gift of a beautiful silver service to the new church and later on deeded to it a large tract of land belonging to the Crown, which was known as the "Queen's Farm." This land extended from the church clear up to Canal Street, its westerly border resting almost on the river. It is now one of the most valuable church holdings in all the world. Part of this land, a small section lying on what is now College Place and Murray Street, was subsequently given by Trinity as a site for a proposed new college. That college, originally called King's College, is now Columbia University.

The establishment of a branch of the Great Church of England on Broadway—Old Trinity—had, naturally, a great effect on the desirability of the street as a residential section. It also imparted to the whole neighborhood an atmosphere of refinement possessed by no other thoroughfare. Families of the first rank socially gradually moved to Broadway, deserting Wall, Pearl, Pine and Greenwich Streets, the former fashionable quarters. At a later date, a roll call from No. 1 up to Rector Street, on Broadway, would embrace practically every family of any social standing whatever. As if to emphasize its aristocratic connection, the street beyond Vesey Street was changed, to honor England's King, to Great George's Street, but the old name —Broadway—was restored after the Revolution.

About this time an event occurred which was destined to have a great effect on Broadway's future. The great Wall, which had hitherto restricted the growth of the young city and had been a nuisance for a great many years, was officially removed. This seemed to give a spiritual as well as a physical relief to the confined, stifling little city. It breathed freer, and old Broadway, which already had several houses on both sides and two pumps in the middle of the street, was at last started on her amazing career. The removal of the Wall gave to Broadway an outlet to the north, which immediately invested the street with an importance hitherto lacking. It was no longer merely a cow path along which the herder drove his cattle to the Common Lands. This practice no longer prevailed, and the much greater width of the street, compared with all others except Broad, made it at once the favorite main traveled road to and from the city, and foreshadowed its coming greatness.

Soon after the Wall was removed, preparations began for the extension of the street northward. The cow path was surveyed for a wide street and opened as far as Park Row, after a fashion. This was supposed to be the "end" of Broadway. A peculiarity of this street has been that it was always "ending" somewhere. But it developed a curious habit of ignoring these "ends" and continually pushed forward. The Park Row "ending" lasted clear up to the Revolution, almost seventy-five years, and is, by far, the longest halt that Broadway ever made in deference to an "end."

A large plot of ground, extending from about Maiden Lane to Ann Street, took up a considerable portion of the vacant space between the former Wall and the Common Lands. It was known as the "Shoemakers' Pasture," and was made up of tanneries which had been expelled from their former quarters on Broad Street opposite the Stock Exchange. Beyond that and to the Common Lands, all was still open fields; no cross streets had as yet been opened.

A rapid expansion of the entire City northward followed fast on the heels of the removal of the Wall. The English had finally struck their stride and the eighteenth century was to see them secure in the saddle but riding gayly for a fall.

Transportation was still a good deal of a problem in the city, as it still is. There were no such thing as a paved street. Sidewalks were merely paths packed hard by constant usage. They were, however, a little higher than the roadbed in between, which was usually filled with mud in winter and a foot of dust in summer. Stone Street was finally paved with stones: hence its name. This was our first attempt at a paved street. It was a much frequented thoroughfare and there was consequently not so great an objection to paying for this improvement in this instance, though taxes for general benefit were as hard to raise as in our day. A few sidewalks began to be paved with brick, but it was many years ere the work was undertaken systematically. So the heavy Dutch wagons, to a great extent, carved out their own roads. Ruts were deep and gullies frequent. Some years were to elapse ere the growing transportation made the necessary improvements imperative. Wooden sidewalks were the first step in this direction and gutters were another. The hogs, and the pumps that everywhere stood in the middle of the road, made a uniform street plan impractical. Of sanitation there was none. Cholera, smallpox and other deadly diseases ran riot with no thought of their primal cause. Street cleaning was a civic operation dependent wholly upon hogs, of which thousands roamed the streets. After ten o'clock, long lines of slaves would be encountered marching single file and bearing on their heads pails of sewage on their way to disposal in the river. Their pleasantries en route were as foul as their loads.

CHAPTER VII

Governors and Oddities

To RECOUNT all the happenings under the administrations of the various Governors appointed by the King would be to weary the reader and would be more or less a repetition of what most of us learned at school. A few of the more important events are all we shall attempt to recall. The individual actions of this Governor or that are of little consequence compared with the mighty achievements of the men and women themselves who actually made New York.

For most of the Colonial period, however, a Board of Trade sat in London, the pro-British historian tells us, meeting two and even three times a week for consultation and conference. Constant reports, too, were also received from Colonial Governors who were by no means the leisurely figureheads of American tradition.

If any of these English Governors of New York, bar Nicolls, had shown himself a man of prescience or had realized the magnificent opportunity here presented for an expansion of the British Empire in keeping with their truly inherent abilities as colonizers, they would have written a brilliant page in history. But, no. They were largely Court favorites dominated by the single thought of feathering their own nests. Not a man among them was of statesmanship caliber. One of them—Lord Cornbury, an uncle of Queen Anne—was actually so impressed by his connection with the Queen and his undoubted close family resemblance to her, that he thought to heighten this illusion by dressing himself in a female costume similar to that worn by the Queen, including high false hair and transformers. Thus attired, he would adorn the front porch of the Governor's house with a knitting bag and sit tatting all day long, or parade the most conspicuous part of the city. This chap should have been sent to a mental hospital instead of to rule over an incipient American London even then showing signs of its coming greatness. He is described as a "spendthrift, a grafter, a bigot and a drunken vain fool."

In the case of Governor Sloughter, a most important crisis affecting vital questions of government presented itself. Two very worthy citizens, Jacob Leisler and his son-in-law, Jacob Milborne, acting, as they thought, for the best interests of the whole people, took over the reins of government during a temporary vacancy in the office of Governor owing to a war in England. This naturally brought down upon them the wrath of another faction anxious to possess the same power for themselves. When the newly appointed Royal Governor duly appeared, Leisler and Milborne at once resigned the power they had seized in favor of the designate. But the matter was not allowed to end there. Ridiculous accusations of *lese majesty,* treason, and other serious charges were lodged against the unfortunate men. They were seized, cast into prison and placed on trial. Under the circumstances, no other conclusion could be reached except that they were guilty of something or other. Their opponents said Treason. There were no grounds for such a serious charge. Even Governor Sloughter, the new appointee, stupid though he undoubtedly was, and who would have been the greatest sufferer had Leisler insisted on retaining power, could not be brought to view the verdict in that light, and refused to sign the bill which would have consigned Leisler to the scaffold.

Leisler's enemies bided their time. It came on an evening when Sloughter attended a festive gathering. When he was thoroughly potted, they prevailed upon him to sign the bill and the two men were hanged. It is one of the foulest deeds in the early history of the city, and the end of these two men was pathetic in the extreme.

When Sloughter sobered up and realized what he had done, his remorse was pitiful. But he lacked the moral courage to proclaim his fault and redress the wrong. The result of the whole thing was that the Governor killed himself shortly after. To avoid further scandal, it was given out that his demise was from natural causes. The property of Leisler, forfeited under this treason conviction, was later on restored to the family; but the useful and valuable lives thus sacrificed were lost forever. No one knows where Leisler is buried. A beautiful monument erected to his memory stands in New Rochelle. Upon the revocation of the Edict of Nantes, Leisler purchased a large tract of land there as an abiding place for the distressed Huguenots forced to leave their native land. And this is their kindly remembrance of him.

This statue of Leisler, erected by the Huguenot Society of New Rochelle, also commemorates the fact that Leisler was the real founder of this now flourishing suburb. It appears that all the arrangements for the reception of the Huguenots were made by Leisler in New York and that the emigrants first landed in our city and then proceeded to their final destination. Whether Leisler's connection with the enterprise was wholly speculative, or whether, as one of their own faith and kin, he was in sympathy with the Huguenots, depends largely upon whether he himself was a German or a Walloon. As to his ancestry, authorities differ, but from his sympathy with these refugees it is more than likely he was a Walloon. At all events, he evidently was highly esteemed, as may be judged from the fact that on one of his voyages when he was captured by the Turks, money was raised by his friends in New York to pay the needed ransom and collected by Governor Andros himself, "from well disposed persons." His was a worth-while life and it was a tragedy that it should have ended on a scaffold.

But perhaps the strangest, yet withal one of the wisest, appointments was that of Governor Dongan. In a community where Catholicism was looked upon as synonymous with all that was abominable, and where in the New England section of the Colonies to be a Papist was equivalent to invoking an early death, the selection of Dongan is all the more mysterious. Despite the fact that he became the first of that long line of grafters for which New York is famous, his administration was marked by the first definite recognition on the part of the Crown that New York was entitled to manage her own affairs in her own way. Accordingly, a Charter, the first of the many since, was granted to the city in Dongan's administration, and for the first time in the history of the city, its people were accorded the privilege of electing those whom they would put over them and the right of taxation by the Government clearly restricted and definitely stated. Life and property were thus secured to each inhabitant in a measure hitherto denied. Popular government became a substance and not a shadow. It was a distinct departure from the traditional policy of the Crown and under the new dispensation New York prospered mightily.

Dongan did another remarkable thing. He actually had the courage to establish a Catholic church. That is old St. Peter's, now at the corner of Barclay and Church Streets. In New England such an act would have created civil war at once. But New York was indifferent to the rabid ranters who fulminated against the innovation. The slow

growth of Catholicism in this period can best be realized
from the fact that this little parish church of St. Peter's was
enough for all the demands made by this religion for almost two hundred years! Up to almost 1820, the services of
two priests were all that were required to supply the spiritual needs of Catholics not only in New York but for the
neighboring towns as well.

Dongan was the type of Irishman of which so many
splendid prototypes were afterwards to make their homes
in New York. He afterwards returned to Ireland where he
became a member of the bloated aristocracy as the Earl of
Limerick. He was a good man and deserves well of New
Yorkers.

In sending Dongan to rule New York, England but followed her classic and inimitable policy in dealing with her
former seditious and belligerent Irish subjects. "When you
boys are through scrapping with me," she would say, "I
want a lot of you to go out there and lick the Sepoys." And
Cardogan went. "And you, Arthur Wellesley, I want you
to make a mess of Napoleon," and Wellington did. When
New York, Boston and other cities were threatened with
attack by the French, it was Admiral Richard Howe, an
Irishman, who kept our coasts inviolate. And the only
tomb in Westminster Abbey paid for and erected by Americans is in loving memory of Lord Howe's brother, Viscount Howe, who fell in a skirmish before Ticonderoga.

Another Governor Nicolls—not the same family—should
be remembered for one thing. He established horse racing
as an industry at Hempstead, Long Island "for improvement of the breed," and offered a cup to be awarded each
year. After a similar race course in England he named this
one "Newmarket." And the races at Newmarket were
famous for many years. It doubtless did improve the breed
of horses at that time. The bookies of our day should ever

be grateful to that New York Governor who supplied them with that specious argument about improving the breed whenever it is proposed to abolish this sport of kings.

Of Fletcher, Hunter, Burnet, Lovelace, Danvers and Andros, who complete the list of English Governors, not much can be said. None of them left any particular impress on the young city over which they ruled. The only reason why they have not sunk into complete oblivion is because of the fact that they were at one time connected with our city. Lovelace, however, should be remembered for establishing our Post Office.

The tendency of the Old World in matters political was ever in the direction of autocracy. In Europe that policy created less public resentment than it did in the New World. Here, the divine right of Kings to rule was treated more in a spirit of levity than of reverence. In a country three thousand miles distant from Court and Palace, that would be only a logical result. Royal vengeance was not so easily put in motion and the demand for a larger measure of public responsibility in the hands of all the people was insistent and endless. Attempts to extend kingly authority, to curtail what little privilege the common people had already achieved, met with instant and determined resistance. The granting of a charter to the City of New York with extraordinary political privileges was one result of these contentions and the right to criticize the Government in the Press was another. The latter event was really important. The attempt to stifle free speech was a dramatic incident in the political life of New York. We shall dwell at length upon this incident further on.

The city's history does not really become exciting till we approach the great conflict of the Revolution. This really begins with the second French and Indian War which ended French dominion in America. It was the expenses of that war and the attempt by Great Britain to

*What the well dressed man and woman wore in
New York two hundred years ago.*

indemnify herself for that expense by levying an unjust
tax on the Colonies, that ultimately brought on the War
for Independence. So our story will be considerably skele-
tonized through the eighteenth century, becoming more
extended as we approach the dark clouds of the Revolution
and the stirring events that brought it about.

Perhaps no more sinister page blackens the history of
New York than the horrible experience that befell the colored people in what was called the Negroes' Plot. Ever
since the West India Company introduced slavery into
New York, the traffic in human flesh had been continued
and constantly increased. Nearly half the population of
New York in 1712, about six thousand, was colored. Most
of the wealthy families owned from forty to fifty of them,
while those of moderate means had from three to half a
dozen. They were considered as necessary as chairs or
tables.

They were as a rule ignorant and stupid, but on the

whole rather good-natured as Negroes usually are. In anger, however, their natural ferocity blazed out in all its primeval wickedness. A few who had been harshly treated by their masters suddenly resolved to seek revenge by killing as many whites as they could, regardless of whether they were the offenders or not. So a small group armed themselves with butcher-knives, hatchets and whatever other deadly weapon they could seize and set fire to an outhouse. When the flames brought persons running to the scene, they were mercilessly attacked and murdered in the most brutal and fiendish manner. Nine men were thus ruthlessly killed and six terribly injured. Those who escaped gave the alarm and soldiers from the Fort were hurriedly dispatched to the scene. They captured all but six who committed suicide to escape a worse fate. Twenty-one were condemned and executed. Most of them were burned at the stake, others were hanged, one was broken on wheels, another was hung in chains to die of starvation. A few who were arrested were later discharged for want of evidence. It was a sickening affair and brought much hardship on the slaves who were left. If three Negroes were thereafter seen together at one time the penalty was forty lashes on the bare back. If a Negro happened to be seen carrying a stick of wood in his hand or anything that could be construed as a weapon, he was sure to receive a like punishment. This harsh treatment on the part of the whites made matters worse.

Negroes were constantly pilfering small articles from their employers. Ordinarily these things were of small value and if the Negro had any sense he could have learned to leave them alone. But his sense of morality was not highly developed at that period, and petty thieving never occurred to him as anything particularly horrible. So he continued to fall from grace from time to time to the rising irritation of his employer.

Finally the house of one Robert Hogg at the corner of Broad and South William Streets was entered one night and robbed. Suspicion immediately fell upon the Negroes and two were arrested. In the meantime, several fires occurred which seemed to be of incendiary origin—the Governor's house in the Fort, together with the secretary's office, the little chapel, and several adjoining structures, and were totally consumed. Then a chimney caught fire in the house of Admiral Sir Peter Warren, the storehouse of another citizen was discovered in flames; the next morning coals were found under a haystack near a coach house on Broadway. Three more fires broke out in the course of the same afternoon.

It looked like a plot to burn the city and a feeling of panic spread through the town. Fear is the most unreasoning thing on earth and this time it had direful results. Recalling the tragedies of thirty years before, the suspicion at once fell upon the poor slaves. A wave of hysteria swept over the town similar to the diabolical mania that afflicted the people of Salem during the witchcraft delusions. And it followed practically the same course. Negroes were arrested indiscriminately and convicted on the flimsiest evidence and frequently on no evidence at all. As usual in these cases, one person, a woman, Mary Burton, in this case, was the principal accuser. Emboldened by her success and the prominence she achieved, she began to accuse important white persons, which finally led to her undoing. But before the end was reached, New York had put to death in the most cruel and horrible manner thirty-odd Negroes, four whites, and imprisoned or transported almost a hundred and fifty others. It was a frightful chapter in her history, and this reign of terror is still spoken of as "the Negroes' Plot."

Although slavery was supposed to cease when the Revolution declared all men free and equal, the practice continued in New York a full half-century later. It was not until 1826 that it was legally abolished in this city and State.

We now record a most interesting event in the city's history—the establishment of its first newspaper, by William Bradford.

Bradford's office was an unpretentious affair. Its location on Broad Street is now marked by a bronze tablet. It must have been much like the modest shop of Caxton's in the Almonry at Westminster, where the first book ever printed in English was produced—a little inclosure, containing a chapel and almshouses, near the west front of the old church where the alms of the Abbey were distributed to the poor.

Bradford left no alluring comments on the emotions which must have been his on printing the first newspaper in the great city of New York. Caxton tells his story simply in a few touching words—how "his pen is worn, his hands are weary, his eyes dimmed with over much looking on the white paper, by the exhausting labor involved in copying books by hand. Therefore," he says, "I have practiced and learned at my great charge and dispense to ordain this said book in print, after the manner and form as ye may see, and it is not written with pen and ink as other books be, to the end that every man may have them at once, for all the books of this story here emprynted as ye see, were begun in one day and also finished in one day."

Nevertheless, Bradford was not insensible of the importance of the work on which he was engaged. He was dimly conscious of the fact that his was a great enterprise. His mind may have instinctively turned back to that first Venetian newspaper which sold for a farthing—a *"gazza"*—and was called *The Gazette*. For that was the name he chose for his paper. He could not, however, see the spiritual side of it, and deliberately sacrificed a priceless opportunity to be of incalculable service to mankind, in order that his coffers might be constantly replenished. He was a practical man and sold his birthright for a mess of pottage, by accepting a subsidy from the British Government, thereby placing a muzzle on his tongue. The honor and glory of founding the Freedom of the Press in a new world, accordingly, passed into other hands. His *Gazette* could have been a mighty fortress to the Colonists in their hour of need, but he preferred the ducats.

John Peter Zenger's *Journal* was the medium by which a Free Press was eventually established, and this undertaking forms one of the most exciting and dramatic stories of early New York.

Young Zenger was a German who had worked in Bradford's printing shop and learned the business. He knew the mechanical side of newspaper-making, which was very essential, as men with practical experience of this nature were scarce. Of the great principles involved in a Free Press, he knew little and cared less. He understood, which was enough for him, on which side his bread was buttered. To credit him with a heaven-born love of liberty for which he was prepared to sacrifice even life itself, is something that would cause Zenger to laugh himself sick. He was printing a paper for profit, and the people who desired to use him saw that he got his profit. They were a determined patriotic group of men ready to do and dare. There were certain abuses in the Government which they would tolerate no longer, and the Government's decision to permit no public criticism of these abuses in the public Press produced the clash.

Ably written articles of the well known "scathing" kind suddenly appeared in Zenger's *Journal*, bitterly attacking the Royal Governor and scoring relentlessly some of his acts. Zenger was clapped in jail and his paper confiscated. The offending numbers were ordered burned at the whipping post, and arrangements were made to carry out this decree with all the fuss and feathers possible. A whole platoon of soldiers headed by a noisy drum corps were ordered to attend the ceremonies. The soldiers and their noise were supposed to attract a huge crowd so that the burning of the papers would properly impress the populace with a realization of the Governor's power and the vengeance which would overtake any infringement upon it.

Unfortunately, for the plans of the Governor, the burning part of the program turned out a miserable fizzle. The crowd showed their sympathy with the imprisoned editor by enthusiastically declining to be present. The streets around the jail were completely deserted. The papers were burned in silence and the militia looked and felt foolish. It was a stinging rebuke, but the worst was to follow. A trial by jury was demanded by the men behind Zenger. To refuse such a reasonable request would not only be exceedingly dangerous but suicidal. News of such a course was sure to cause wild alarm throughout all the Colonies and create a disturbance in England as well. The Governor had sense enough to see this and proceeded to prosecute Zenger in the courts.

News of the coming event spread rapidly through all the country and all eyes were turned toward New York. The testimony was everywhere followed by the keenest interest. Andrew Hamilton (not Alexander) of Philadelphia, the most renowned leader of the bar in his day, was retained by the Zenger men and the battle was on.

When the verdict "Not guilty" was rendered, the joy and enthusiasm of the Zenger party was boundless. In spite of the remonstrance of the Court, wild cheers rang in the court room; Lawyer Hamilton was borne in triumph from the room and a deafening roar greeted his appearance on the street. He was presented with the freedom of the city, a great banquet and ball were given him in the evening and a large procession of citizens accompanied him to his barge when it sailed for Philadelphia.

It was a signal victory for popular rights won against tremendous odds and the people were deeply moved. The principle of a Free Press was something very close to the hearts of Englishmen.

At St. Paul's East Chester Church at Mount Vernon, where in 1733 the election was held that led to the famous trial of Editor Peter Zenger, the 200th anniversary of the establishment by Andrew Hamilton of the principle of freedom for the Press was observed on October 28, 1933.

Col. Robert R. McCormick, publisher of *The Chicago Tribune,* was the principal speaker and honorary chairman for the celebration. Others on the committee were: Adolph Ochs of the *New York Times,* William Randolph Hearst of the *New York American,* William T. Dewart of

The celebrated Tea Water pump at Chatham and Pearl Streets, 1750.

the *New York Sun,* J. Noel Macy, Westchester Newspapers, Inc., Myron C. Taylor, President, U. S. Steel Corporation, Frank D. Noyes, Associated Press.

Another paper which enjoyed a rather long life and enviable popularity was the *Weekly Museum,* which was something of a society journal. Its column of Marriage notices, however, was evidently a frequent cause of trouble. In one issue it announced the nuptials of "Mr. Levy Phillips to the amiable Miss Hetty Hays, daughter of Mr. Michael Hays of this city," but on the following week was obliged to print a correction, which it did in these vigorous words:

The marriage of Miss Hetty Hays handed in by Aaron Henry is false. . . . The Printer begs the parties will pardon the insertion as it was imposed on him by an infamous LIAR.

The matter did not end here, however, and the poor printer merely jumped from the frying pan into the fire. His next issue contained further details.

The following paragraph was handed in on Thursday the 12th inst.

Here he repeats the notice but adds—

In justice to Mr. A. Henry, the Printer declares that he was not the person who handed in the notice, but it was imposed upon him by a person who called himself Aaron Henry and who has added to the infamy of lying, that of counterfeiting. For which, unless satisfactory concessions are made to Mr. Henry and the Printer, the law against counterfeiting, will be put vigorously in force against him.

Evidently this was not the only time a bad half hour resulted from errors in the matrimonial column, as we find in his issue of April 5th of the same year he was again compelled to apologize—this time to a Capt. Moses Toulon for announcing his marriage to Miss Anna Mott. The doughty Captain was evidently real rude and, as befitted a warrior, demanded immediate satisfaction. As a result of these two disturbing experiences, we find the printer reaching this mournful conclusion:

The difficulty of such impositions, compels the printer to refuse the insertion of marriage notices in future.

But this good resolution did not last long. Evidently the value of these items as news outweighed the occasional shindies which inevitably followed mistakes, as we find their publication resumed and permanently continued thereafter.

Other difficulties which he encountered may be judged from the following:

Mr. Low aged 25, married Thursday Evening, to Mrs. Rachel Bryan aged 69.

Next week, a Mr. William Low, of Hanover Square, objects to the notice as not being sufficiently distinctive and compels the printer to insert a notice that—

The Mr. William Low married to Mrs. Bryan is NOT the Mr. Low of Hanover Square.

The enterprising editor of the *Museum* apparently led the strenuous life at times, but he seemed able to keep smiling no matter what befell.

But let us read a few more of the Marriage notices. There is a charm in these little intimate items, that far exceeds their academic value; they now have for us something of the atmosphere of Pepys' appealing *Diary*. In no other way can we so clearly visualize social life and mannerisms in Old New York.

The young men of that day evidently believed literally, that "all the world loves a lover" and were not at all backward in publicly proclaiming their ecstatic joy and the charms of their fair partners. Judging from their enthusiasm, one would imagine that no one had ever been in love before. However, their willingness to share their happiness with "the world and his wife" is commendable. This example is only one chosen from many:

On Monday evening June 7th 1792, by the Rev. Mr. Beach, JOHN BUCHANAN Esq., to the amiable, adorable, incomparable, inflexible, invincible, and non-pareil of her sex NANCY LUCY TURNER, both of this city.

Occasionally it appears that mere humdrum prose cannot do justice to the exuberance of the emotions and the sighing swain must perforce drop into poetry.

On March 30th, 1786, married in New Jersey, Mr. James Walker, merchant, to the amiable Miss Anne Vanderbeck, daughter of Isaac Vanderbeck, Jun'r. Esq.

If worldly happiness is e'er complete,
It is when two fond lovers meet.

We regret to add to these idyllic symposiums one or two that smack of a worldliness that is simply shocking.

On Monday the 31st of July 1786, in Washington Co., Maryland, Major General Horatio Gates to Miss Mary Vallance; a lady distinguished most deservedly for her good sense, liberal education and amiable disposition, with a handsome fortune.

On Wednesday evening 24th of May, was married Samuel Osgood Commissioner of the Treasury Board, to Mrs. Franklin, widow of Walter Franklin, an opulent merchant of this city. The lady is possessed of every amiable accomplishment, added to a very large fortune.

Most of these little papers are filled with intelligence from London, together with learned essays and sermons on the whole duty of man. Latin quotations abound in almost every article. If you didn't know Latin in those days you

were slightly lower than the animals. De Witt Clinton at
the opening of Columbia College delivered his thesis entirely in Latin, and the few pioneers who moved up-State
evidently took along with them Gibbon's *Decline and Fall
of the Roman Empire,* for they promptly began to dis-
card all our lovely native Indian names and substitute
such unnatural and illogical high-sounding titles as Troy,
Syracuse, Ithaca, Rome, Carthage, Alexandria, etc., etc.
A slight eminence near Troy is also called Mt. Ida after a
similar hill near ancient Troy, from which the gods
watched the Trojan War. This was also the scene of the
rape of Ganymede—that beauteous youth who, whilst tend-
ing his father's flocks on Mt. Ida, was carried up to Heaven
by an eagle. The counterfeit presentment of this person-
able young man now adorns the street car ads to proclaim
the excellence of the shirts and collars made by this enterprising city.

Yet as the town grew older, the papers became more
human and printed small items of local news that are today of absorbing interest.

But perhaps the best evidence we have of the coming
commercial greatness of New York is also shown in these
little business announcements. It gives us an idea of the
hustle and bustle even then noticeable in the city. It was
evidently a busy maritime port too by this time. Most of
these notices state that they have just received "by this
ship or that, the following choice items."

It is interesting here to note the first appearanc of John
Jacob Astor. At that time he was plain Jacob Astor, the
John being a later acquisition. Whether John or Jacob, he
showed even then that if trade wouldn't come to him he
would go to it. The descendants of most of these adver-
tisers are prominent in society today and evidently have
money. "It pays to advertise."

Jacob Astor, No. 81 Queen St. two doors from the Friends Meeting House, has just imported from London an elegant assortment of musical instruments such as piano fortes, spinets, piano forte guitars, guitars, hautboys, fifes, and every other article in the musical line, which he will dispose of on very low terms for cash.

Peter Goelet at the Golden Key, No. 48 Hanover Square, has imported in the last vessel from London a very large and general assortment of ironmongery, Cutlery, Sadlery, and Hardware, all kind of tools and material for clock and watch makers, gold and silver smiths, joiners, carpenters, black and gun smiths, saddlers, shoemakers, etc. . . . also great variety of pewter spoons, coat, vest and sleeve buttons, leather and hair trunks, boot legs and vamps, bind leather soles, etc. etc. And a consignment of playing cards.

Mr. Goelet was evidently an enterprising fellow. Mr. Archibald Gracie, Mr. Leonard Kip, Mr. Abraham Brevoort, Mr. Nicholas Hoffman, Mr. Hugh Gaine, and dozens of other now well-known old family names figure in the list. A reminder of the long residence in New York of our President's family may be gained from this—

Isaac Roosevelt, having repaired his Sugar House, is now carrying on his business of refining as formerly and has for sale (by himself and son) at his house, 159 Queen Street opposite the Bank, Loaf, Lump, and strained Muscaroda Sugars and Sugar house treacle. The new Emission Money will be received in full value as payment.

The reference to Emission Money recalls to mind one of our early inflation experiences. Apparently Mr. Roosevelt approved and had faith in the new coinage.

Here are two items of a rather unusual nature:

A person lately from London now stopping at 29 Little Dock Street has a composition for sale that will destroy the very troublesome vermin commonly called Bugs.

A variety of Muffs, Tippets and Fur trimmings among which are a *few black Fox Muffs for gentlemen* may be had on reasonable terms at 89 William Street.

Black Fox Muffs for gentlemen is certainly something new. But our Old New York merchants were nothing if not enterprising and always on the lookout for a novelty.

One of the charming divertissements provided by the British during their occupation of New York was the printing of counterfeit Continental money. As the genuine article ultimately sold as low as a dollar a carload in silver (at which price Hamilton's friends were charged with buying several tons), there could not have been much profit in the business at that time. Nevertheless, it is interesting to reproduce the following from the *Mercury* of April 14, 1777, as a curious war measure, as it was designed to hurt the American cause:

Persons going into other colonies may be supplied with any number of counterfeited Congress notes for the price of paper per ream. They are so neatly and exactly executed, that there is no risk in getting them off, it being almost impossible to discover that they are not genuine. This has been proven by bills to a very large amount which have already been successfully circulated.

Inquire of Q. E. D., at the Coffee-house, from 11 A.M. to 4 P.M., during the present month.

Some of the Real Estate announcements are particularly interesting.

Here is one from the *Weekly Post Boy*, 1765, offering the farm on Harlem Heights which was purchased by Captain Roger Morris, and is now Washington's Headquarters, a corporation founded by the Daughters of the American Revolution of New York City, who care for this house which was purchased by the City under Seth Low's administration in 1903. Further reference to this historical mansion will be found elsewhere.

To be Sold

A pleasant situated farm on the Road leading to King's Bridge, in the Township of Harlem of York Island, containing about 100 acres: about 30 acres of which is Wood land, a fine piece of Meadow Ground, and more may easily be made; and commands the finest Prospect in the whole country; the Land runs from River to River; there is Fishing, Oystering and Claming at either end. There is a good House, a fine Barn, 44 feet long and 42 feet wide, or thereabouts; an Orchard of good Fruit, with plenty of Quince Trees that bear extraordinarily well; three good gardens the Produce of which are sent to the York Markets daily, as it suits. An indisputable Title to be given to the Purchaser. Inquire of James Carroll, living on the Premises, who will agree on reasonable Terms.

To be sold The "Dog and Duck" Tavern in the Bowery Lane at the two mile stone. The house has eight rooms with a large garden and the best bed of asparagus on this island. Enquire at 44 Gold Street opposite the Baptist Meeting House.

Samuel and Josiah Blackwell offer for sale the well known farm of Jacob Blackwell, deceased, about six miles from New York on the East River. It contains 160 acres and 25 acres of salt meadow.

This was the famous Blackwell's Island, since acquired by the city for Correctional buildings. A few years ago some sentimentalists had the name changed to Welfare Island, thus disposing of an historic name by which it was known for over a century.

A fine lot of ground on the West side of Broadway near the old Lutheran Church, is for sale. Enquire of Alexander Hamilton in Wall Street No. 58.

Four or five stables in Wall Street to let opposite Col. William Livingston's with stalls for from two to four horses, room for carriages and large lofts for hay.

Evidently Wall Street was not always the proud financial center it is today.

To be sold, Mount Pitt, the place where the subscriber now lives, situated near Corlears Hook, one mile from City Hall, containing a handsome dwelling house, our kitchen, containing several rooms, a large stable, a new carriage house, a complete ice house. There are about eleven acres of land, between three and four hundred bearing fruit trees and a handsome garden. The place being so well known needs no further description.

This was the home of Morgan Lewis, one of the "Signers" and a very prominent New Yorker at the time. The house stood somewhere about where Grand Street crosses the Bowery and was one of the show places in town. A contemporary print of it is in the Public Library. It was named after the famous English statesman, a friend of the owner. The site is now covered with hundreds of the best paying tenement properties in the city. Any single block is worth many times more than the whole eleven acres including the five buildings brought at that time.

There is nothing so exasperating as to hear a man tell you that his forefathers owned such and such a farm. "If he had only kept it he would now be worth millions, etc. etc." That's an old story and its recital simply a waste of time. But lots of people like to torture themselves that way.

We now shall conclude our survey of our early newspapers by a few quotations describing the current fashions.

These fashion items are of the vintage of 1800. There seems a possibility that our present-day styles will swing back a little in their direction. The waist line of the Directoire and Empire periods is constantly striving to reassert itself. The meaning of some of these names today is not very clear, but perhaps our women readers will understand.

Double soles on satin slippers, though introduced, are quite an exception and as for leather footwear no lady of condition would dream of putting on anything so coarse. They are quite Gothic, and appropriate to none but the lower orders.

Bird of Paradise Yellow is a favorite color for Satin gowns a l'Empire.

The mania for classic attire has completely metamorphosed feminine costume. The waist is now a lost quantity, for the gown is drawn in but slightly under the arms, like an infant's robe and thence the skirt falls quite straight trailing on the floor at the back from a double pleat that falls from a low open neck, the edges occasionally draped with a silk kerchief or finished with a high standing lace ruff.

Parasols are made on the same principle as the "surprise fans" lately invented—i.e. with a joint which makes them appear to be broken. A sliding cylinder-like fixture holds the joints firmly in place when the parasol is raised.

Except in morning dress, ladies invariably carry their reticules (vulgarly called ridicules) with them. A reticule contains the handkerchief, fan, card money and essence bottle. They are made of figured sarcenet, plain satin, velvet, or silver tissue, with strings and tassels to match. It is necessary that they be of the same color as the wrap or pelisse.

The conversation bonnet is a nicely modified coal scuttle shape that is greatly favored. The most fashionable styles in straw are the conversation cottage models which are distinguished for their negligent neatness. At the back the hair is cropped or tightly braided and has somewhat dishevelled curls in front. Necklace and earrings are of Mocha-stones, linked with burnished gold.

Muslin dresses are worn unlined and skirts are short enough to display the ankle through them. Flowers and loops of ribbon are worn over the left side of the coiffure and face, so placed as to almost conceal the left eye. Fugitive coats made of exile cloth are worn this season and the name is a tribute paid by fashion to the sufferings of the exiled house of Braganza.

The fashion of tight lacing has revived with a degree of fury which posterity will not credit. Stays are now made of bands of steel and iron from two to four inches broad and many of them not less than eighteen inches in length.

Grand masterpieces of Psyche has brought pallor into fashion. It is so much the rage to look ethereal and delicate that a pot of rouge can now be purchased for half a crown and lotions, instead, are used to promote the interesting shade of the lily which has of late subdued the rose. *Poudre de riz* is universally selected and all fashionable women in these days of the Empire endeavor to render themselves still more interesting by making up their lovely faces *a la Psyche*.

The art of dressing a woman's hair is nearly allied to genius, and in order to exercise it nobly, one should be a poet, a painter or a sculptor. It is necessary to understand shades of color, chiaroscure and the proper distribution of shadows, so as to confer animation on the complexion and render other native charms more expressive.

A very fashionable article of jewelry is a gold neckchain and heart with a patent spring which when pressed opens and reveals the eye of friend, relative or lover, beautifully executed on ivory and finished with an enamelled border.

Styles have changed since the eighteenth century closed, and when one thinks of the dainty footwear of today it seems a far cry from the day when leather shoes were fit only for the "lower orders." In all these fashion notes there is to be detected the strong European influence which still prevailed. The rage of violets in honor of Napoleon's return from Elba and the "Hundred Days" seems rather strained from today's point of view, but many costumes were designed to compliment this or that reigning family. Jaconet gowns were worn in honor of Louis XVIII and the Directoire and Empire gowns also reflected the politics of the hour.

With our present boyish bobs, short skirts, sports clothes and athletic tastes, these old-time modes and fabrics seem strangely out of place. But it reflects high society at the very threshold of the nineteenth century in our great city. We passed Philadelphia in population that year, making ours the leading city in the New World. We then had about 60,000 inhabitants.

One cannot deny the charm of some of these old styles as portrayed in these quaint old engravings. The women of New York have ever been noted for their exquisite taste in dress, and there is no city in the Union that can begin to turn out such a smartly dressed throng as one sees any day on Fifth Avenue. New York women are lovely.

The usual amount of domestic infelicity seemed to prevail in those days as in our own, except that there is a touch of candid belligerency in their recital, which seems to indicate that the state of harmony which formerly existed has gone completely haywire, and there is none of that Hollywood blah about being "just as good pals as ever," etc., etc. No, they were not chiselers. They took it standing up.

Benjamin Jacobs notifies the public that his wife, Elizabeth, has eloped from his bed and board and that he will pay no debts of her contracting.

Elizabeth sees this, dips her pen in vitriol and pens the following little note:

Elizabeth Jacobs, who was advertised by her husband on the 5th inst., informs the public that she was compelled by his cruel treatment to leave him, that no person who knows him would trust him with a shilling and is happy that the law protects her from paying his debts.

This undoubtedly held Mr. Jacobs for a while, as he made no response.

Here is an item that is unconsciously very funny. A certain Mr. William Smith moves to New York from a little country town, Red Hook, in Dutchess County. To his great surprise and indignation, he finds that there are many other Bill Smiths in town, which is, of course, in Mr. Smith's opinion, simply intolerable. So he inserts this little card in the paper:

Col. William Smith late of Dutchess County informs his friends and the public that having moved to New York and finding so many of his name, to distinguish himself from them, has added between his names the letter M.

Mr. Smith's natural desire to be distinguished from the common herd of Bills is not at all hard to understand.

Apparently the Society of the Cincinnati has just been organized as we find this advertisement:

Members of the Society of the Cincinnati are informed that their Diplomas are ready for delivery at 27 Water Street.

Here is an item that requires explanation these days.

A few German Redemptioners are landed from the ship *Union*, Capt. Hazard from Hamburgh, and are for sale on reasonable terms: One mill wright, one weaver, one baker, several women suitable for house servants and maids, with some few boys and girls. The terms of sale and time of servitude may be known by applying to Murray, Munsford and Brown.

"Redemptioners" were the passengers who had no money to pay their passage, but agreed to pay it out of their first earnings. Their wages were consequently paid to the shipowners till their claim was satisfied. The same arrangement applied to many other shipments. Occasionally some were sold outright as slaves. Mary Johnston has woven a very pretty romance out of an instance in Virginia, where the victim was a young, high-spirited English girl, exceedingly pretty, who was bought outright by a rather upstanding young tobacco planter.

Apparently there was some risk in hiring these Redemptioners as we frequently find such ads as this:

Run away: two indented German servant men, who came last year, named Peter Sweine and Jacob Ronk. Neither of them speak English, they were seen near Kings Bridge and it is supposed intend for Albany. Eight dollars reward for each will be paid by Isaac Roosevelt or Thomas Pearsall.

Slavery in the city was well-nigh universal. Almost every family had one or two. They were the frequent cause of such notices as these:

Augustus Van Horne, of 58 South Street, offers a Half Joe reward for the capture of his negro slave George. He is a very talkative, saucy, impertinent fellow.

A negro boy named Harry about 14 years of age ran away from William Cammayer of No. 59 Broad Street.

Ran away from her place at No. 55 William Street, a mulatto wench named Diana. She is good looking, about 20 years old, middle sized, had on a blue stuff short gown, a yellow calico petticoat, spriged, a new pair of leather shoes and solid silver buckles, a black silk bonnet and mixed coloured cloth greatcoat. She took with her a variety of articles and may appear in a chintz bedgown and quilted stuff petticoat. Whoever apprehends the said Wench shall have Two Dollars Reward.

Two dollars doesn't seem adequate for the return of such a valuable cargo.

There was a gallery set apart for slaves in many of our churches in those days. Now only one of these old slave galleries remains—in the Church of All Saints, at the corner of Henry and Scammel Streets, the third oldest Protestant Episcopal Church edifice in New York.

A news item is headed:

Cow Kills Man on Beekman Street

Yesterday afternoon as a respectable looking citizen was walking across the Commons [City Hall Park] he was attacked by a vicious cow which pursued him to the corner of Beekman Street where it gride him to death.

The small news items reflect the current life of the city more accurately than all the learned essays we have ever read. Here we have history in the making; the men and women at their daily occupations. They are buying, selling, moving—and above all, working. In a sense it is a kaleido-

scopic view of the little city in action that is vastly instruc-
tive and tremendously informative. Nothing in our opinion reflects so graphically or so accurately the progress of
the city and shows so clearly the everyday lives of the people as do these little announcements—summing up as they
do the whole gamut of everyday needs. Historically they
are priceless.

CHAPTER VIII

George Washington Comes to New York

WE NOW welcome to our city for the first time George Washington, Lieutenant Colonel in His Majesty's Army in Virginia. He stopped with his friend Beverly Robinson, whose father was Speaker of the Virginia Assembly. The family occupied the De Lancey Mansion, corner of Broad and Pearl Streets, now Fraunces' Tavern. Perhaps some remembrance of this first visit influenced Washington when he became President, to select the old Tavern as our first State Department, with Jefferson as his Secretary of State. His office was in the Long Room and Jefferson himself lived at 57 Maiden Lane.

Washington was just twenty-two years old, stood six feet, four inches in his stockings, and as straight as an Indian. His strength was that of a dozen men. His hands were the largest ever seen, and very powerful. He could bend a horseshoe with no apparent effort and could sit an hour after dinner cracking all kinds of nuts wtih his fingers. His grasp on a man's shoulders was like the clamping down of a steel trap. He walked with the tread of Mars in a 13 boot. He rode his horse like a centaur. He was well educated according to the standards of his day. Yet he spelled "cat" with two "t's" and spelling was ever the bane of his life.

Among his books at home, the one that showed the most signs of wear and tear was a volume entitled *The Gentle Art of Polite Behavior.*

He arrived in New York accompanied by two aides and

two servants, all riding horseback. The journey was a
rather gorgeous affair, and he traveled in the grand manner. He and his people were dressed in the most elegant
fashion. He wore a buff and blue uniform. His stockings
were of white silk, with silver knee buckles, and there were
silver buckles on his shoes. A "jabot" was pinned to the
white linen stock around his neck, an affair of lace ruffles,
so that it fell over his bosom like a flowing modern neck-
tie. His hair was worn long, and drawn tightly back in a
queue, which was inclosed in a silk bag. On his shoulders
a cloak, one side white, and the other scarlet, and a sword
at his side with a golden hilt. Over his enormous hands fell
cuffs of lace. His aides were dressed in similar fashion, and
the servants were decked out in white and scarlet livery.

The young Virginian tarried a week in town. It was an
amazing experience. He had never before been in so huge
a city. The population at that time was over ten thousand.

He spent much time at The Microcosm, in the Royal Exchange on Broad St. near Pearl, at that time displaying a
miniature Roman Temple filled with mechanical figures
who sawed wood, played music, beating exact time to each
tune, and fired guns. There was an illusion of a pond—a me-
tallic pond on which ducks swam, reaching back with their
bills to pluck their wings. One would hardly call this a wild
time, but one must remember that it was his first experience
in a gay metropolis. No doubt, he had heard something of
the dangers that lurked within her bosom for pure young
men from the country, and was taking no chances.

It was on this visit that he met the fascinating belle of
Phillipse Manor, Miss Mary Phillipse. Young Beverly
Robinson had married Mary's sister, Susan. It is a legend
along the Hudson that the young lady rejected him in favor
of young Captain Morris, a dashing young red-coated officer
in the British Army. Years afterward, General Washington was to make Mary's old home, the Morris Mansion,

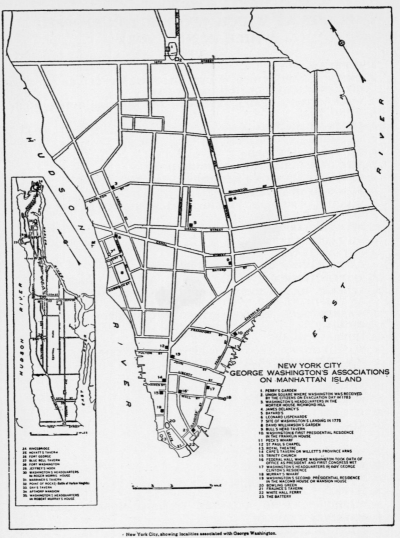

Places at which Washington stopped while in New York.
(See next page.)

PLACES AT WHICH WASHINGTON STOPPED
WHILE IN NEW YORK

1. PERRY'S GARDEN.
2. UNION SQUARE WHERE WASHINGTON WAS RECEIVED BY THE CITIZENS ON EVACUATION DAY IN 1783.
3. WASHINGTON'S HEADQUARTERS IN THE MORTIER HOUSE, RICHMOND HILL.
4. JAMES DELANCY'S.
5. BAYARD'S.
6. LEONARD LISPENARDS'.
7. SITE OF WASHINGTON'S LANDING IN 1775.
8. DAVID WILLIAMSON'S GARDEN.
9. BULL'S HEAD TAVERN.
10. WASHINGTON'S FIRST PRESIDENTIAL RESIDENCE IN THE FRANKLIN HOUSE.
11. PECK'S WHARF.
12. ST. PAUL'S CHAPEL.
13. ROYAL THEATRE.
14. CAPE'S TAVERN OR WILLETT'S PROVINCE ARMS.
15. TRINITY CHURCH.
16. FEDERAL HALL WHERE WASHINGTON TOOK OATH OF OFFICE AS PRESIDENT AND FIRST CONGRESS MET.
17. WASHINGTON'S HEADQUARTERS IN GOV. GEORGE CLINTON'S RESIDENCE.
18. MURRAYS WHARF.
19. WASHINGTON'S SECOND PRESIDENTIAL RESIDENCE IN THE MACOMB HOUSE OR MANSION HOUSE.
20. BOWLING GREEN.
21. FRAUNCES' TAVERN.
22. WHITE HALL FERRY.
23. THE BATTERY.
24. KINGSBRIDGE.
25. HOYATT'S TAVERN.
26. FORT GEORGE.
27. BLUE BELL TAVERN.
28. FORT WASHINGTON.
29. JEFFREY'S HOOK.
30. WASHINGTON'S HEADQUARTERS IN ROGER MORRIS HOUSE.
31. MARRINER'S TAVERN.
32. POINT OF ROCKS (Battle of Harlem Heights).
33. DAY'S TAVERN.
34. APTHORP MANSION.
35. WASHINGTON'S HEADQUARTERS IN ROBERT MURRAY'S HOUSE.

his headquarters in New York during the battle of Harlem. Unlike Sally Fairfax, Mary Phillipse did not see in the young Virginian soldier, the builder of a new Empire.

Washington at this time was fond of pretty girls. He was said to have been in love several times, and particularly with a certain "Lowland Beauty," as he calls her in one of his letters. This "Lowland Beauty" has become as mysterious to historians as the "Man in the Iron Mask." She has been variously identified as this, that, or the other reigning belle of the day. But the consensus of opinion is that she was a Miss Lucy Grymes, who afterwards married Richard Henry Lee and became the grandmother of General Robert E. Lee. Her husband led Virginia into the Union and her grandson led it out.

Washington was to be again in New York. Once on his way to take command of the Army in Boston, and again to take the oath as first President of the newly formed Republic.

Little did he think that some day the city in which he walked almost unknown, would mark reverently, with imposing tablets, almost every place his feet had trod.

CHAPTER IX

England and France—Enemies in America

THE age-long rivalry between England and France quite
naturally extended to the New World. This deadly ill
feeling between these two great powers had its roots deep
in the past. We in New York are apt to forget that England
at one time owned the larger part of France till she was
finally expelled by Joan of Arc. Our own State of Maine
is named after an English province in old France and those
two beautiful ocean liners, the *Aquitania* and *Mauretania,*
are also the names of other French provinces of England's,
and the *Berengaria* recalls an early French Queen of an
English King. So their ancient rivalries and hatreds were
as a matter of course transferred to the New World.

The French declined to admit the claims of England
regarding her rights of discovery by reason of the Cabot
voyages, and set up a counter-claim of her own.

New York City had a very direct and vital interest in
these wars. It was the main source of supplies for the army,
and for more than twelve years it did a huge business with
the British and Colonial Governments in supplying food-
stuffs and other war material.

A great contest, such as the Seven Years War, which
lasted nearly ten, brought also a huge floating as well as
permanent population. It added immensely to the city's
material prosperity. So when we describe briefly part of
this thrilling drama, we are still recording the local history

173

of the people of New York, who even then were making the country.

The French were continually starting trouble. They were determined to confine the English to the narrow strip along the Atlantic. The boundless West was to be for them.

With the aid of her Indian allies, France soon began to make things decidedly uncomfortable for the English. All along the western and northern frontiers and on the Great Lakes, there were constant clashes. Finally the French captured Oswego and Ontario and leveled the two forts to the ground. They proceeded further south, taking Ticonderoga, Fort William Henry and Crown Point on the way, and finally reached the Ohio.

New York was thrown into a state of intense excitement by this news. The way was now open for a drive down the fertile Mohawk Valley and the Hudson to New York. British power in America was vitally menaced and the devastating massacre by the Indian allies of the French at Schenectady, spread terror throughout that region. The Indians, unused to civilized warfare, paid little or no heed to such trifling details as terms of capitulation, and promptly proceeded to butcher all who surrendered. Montcalm, to his credit, put an end to this by ordering a file of soldiers to shoot down the savages who disregarded his orders. The rest sulkily put up their tomahawks and knives and retired.

As usual, the incompetency of the British Governor Loudon led to this deplorable state of affairs, but a kind Providence came to the rescue just in time and removed Loudon from command. A meeting was called to be held in our city in the City Hall in Wall Street to consider the whole situation and New York was to behold in her streets some of the great romantic figures that loomed large in the Indian fighting days of New York.

The room in which the meeting was held was devoid of
ornate furnishing. The roof of plain rafters does not suggest the beautiful Gothic carvings in the London Guildhall. A long table takes up most of the space. Around this
table are some oaken chairs, wide and with arms. The pre-
siding officer's has a higher back and some ornamentation.
A canopy is over it. Some flags are draped on the walls.

As a result of this conference it was decided to make
three attacks: One on the Great Lakes beginning at Lake
George; a second on Louisburg in Quebec; a third on Fort
Duquesne on the Ohio River. In a week the captains had
departed each to his appointed post and active operations
began.

The Assembly, sitting in our City Hall, put heart in the
movement by promptly voting a huge sum for the sinews
of war, thus placing New York in the forefront of the
movement to end French dominion in America and to
sow the seed of the coming new Republic.

In order to supply the troops with all the necessary supplies needed for this campaign, a special market was
opened on Broadway between Liberty and Maiden Lane.
It was a very large market for its day, and a busy one. As
it sent most of its stores to Oswego, it took its name from
that fact and was called The Oswego Market.

After the war was over the market continued to operate,
not as a depot of military supplies, but as a regular house-
keepers' everyday market.

But residential houses were fast locating in this neighborhood and the pungent odors from this institution were
not calculated to enhance real estate values in the vicinity. So after repeated complaints, the authorities
finally decided to order its removal to a site near the
North River; and that is how our present Washington
Market came into being. It changed its name to conform
to the street on which it was located. For more than

a century it did a flourishing business and does to this day; but you now never see women of good social position going to the market, basket on arm, for the day's supplies, as was the custom till well into the '80's of the last century. Another street was also opened connecting Broadway with the ferry to Brooklyn on the East River where a fish market was opened. This was called Fair Street. Years afterwards, when Fulton selected this street from which to operate his new steam ferry, the name was changed to Fulton in his honor and the market followed suit.

New York had an additional interest in this war from the fact that out of it we acquired one of our most distinguished citizens of the time, Admiral Sir Peter Warren. As Commodore in the British Navy, he headed the attack on Louisburg in 1745, the most formidable defense of the French in America, and in coöperation with Governor Shirley and Sir William Pepperell captured the town. His four ships of the line were essential to the success of the great New England Expedition. He took the French Frigate *Vigilant* with all her valuable stores, and in addition took heavy toll from the enemy in the way of rich prizes composing the rest of the fleet.

Commodore Warren was immediately promoted to be Admiral and raised to Knighthood and was soon domiciled in New York. He was most fortunate in the matter of prizes and was rated an extremely wealthy man.

Incredible though it may seem, Louisburg, the Dunkirk of America, was given back to the French two years later by the Treaty of 1748, ending King George's War, and this work had to be done all over again ten years later at an enormous additional expenditure of blood and treasure.

Sir Peter returned to England several years before the Revolution and became a noted member of Parliament. Like many of his close friends in America—the De Lanceys,

De Peysters, Livingstons, Phillipses, he remained loyal to the Crown, and so lost his valuable estate in the city. But Greenwich Village, which was his estate, is enough to keep his memory green in Old New York.

Warren Street was named after him and he was highly esteemed in the city: he married a sister of Chief Justice Oliver De Lancey, and lived in splendor in a noble mansion which he had named after the well-known city in England where his boyhood was spent and which furnishes time to the rest of the world.

In this fine old home many of his old comrades-in-arms gathered—young Captain Jeffrey (afterwards Lord) Amherst, General Abercrombie, "Billy" Howe (later General William F. Howe, who hanged Nathan Hale), Admiral Richard Lord Howe, "Dick" Montgomery, who fell at Quebec, and Captain Cook, who was with him in the attack on Louisburg, and afterwards became the celebrated explorer and navigator who discovered Australia, New Zealand, etc., Captain Cornwallis, who was to surrender at Yorktown and end the Revolution, General Robert Moncton, who was badly wounded at Quebec and who was later appointed Governor of New York, and Field Marshal Townsend, another officer at Quebec.

Two of Sir Peter's daughters married into the British aristocracy—one the Baron Southampton and the other Lord Fitzroy. These two names are pleasantly recalled in Fitzroy Place and Abingdon Square—ancestral home of the Southamptons in our present Greenwich Village.

Nor should we omit General Schuyler, Governor Shirley, or General Pepperell. The famous Indian Chief, Joseph Brant, deserves a page all to himself. He visited England and was received by the King and many of the nobles. He was a great sensation in London, and was entertained everywhere. He was also brother-in-law to Sir William

Johnson. Even in those far-away days New York maintained its reputation for attracting the biggest and best from all the rest of the country.

It is extremely doubtful if the greatest figure of them all in the last Canadian expedition, General Wolfe, was ever in New York. There was, however, a monument erected to his memory by his friend Oliver De Lancey. It stood on De Lancey's country place at about where Eighth Avenue and 40th Street now is. The street adjoining it is called on Ratzer's map of the time, Monument Lane. The statue disappeared during the Revolution and its fate is unknown.

Brigadier General John Nixon, who was at Louisburg, Lexington, Bunker Hill, commanded Governors Island in 1776, and was wounded at Saratoga, was also a visitor.

Sir William Pepperell used to tell a good story anent the fall of Louisburg. It was about the chaplain of his regiment, an excellent fellow, but woefully afflicted with abnormal prolixity. Pepperell, on the night of the capitulation of the great fortress, gave a dinner to Admiral Warren and other high officers of the army and fleet. Knowing the failing of the pious Dr. Moody, Chaplain of his Regiment, he was embarrassed by the thought that the good parson's long-winded grace would put his guests *hors de combat*. Imagine his relief and amazement when the dominie addressed the throne of Grace in this wise:

"O Lord, we have so many things to thank Thee for, that time will be infinitely too short for it; we must therefore leave it to eternity"—and sat down. When the guests recovered from their astonishment they rose in their places and showed their appreciation of the good parson's magnanimity by three rousing cheers and a tiger.

The start of this final war began at what is now one of the most beautiful and charming regions in all our State. To many thousands of New Yorkers, beautiful Lake

George is known only as a summer resort of unsurpassed charm and restfulness. The magic lure of her forest-clad hills, the exquisite clearness of her waters, the peaceful solitude of her mountain-sides, all combine to make it a favored spot beckoning men to leave care behind and enjoy her repose. Few of us recall, however, that this same sylvan scene resounded to the tramp of armed hosts and upon the placid bosom of this lovely sheet of water once floated the mightiest armada ever gathered at one time upon the inland waters of our country.

More than fifteen thousand fighting men on nine hundred small boats; one hundred and thirty-five whale boats with their horses and heavy artillery mounted on rafts, embarked from the shores of Lake George in the lovely autumn of 1755 to decide once and forever which nation should rule the New World, France or England. Looking backward through the mists of two centuries, it seems incredible that this idyllic region should have been the theater of the most spectacular and romantic combat ever waged upon our soil; that its restful silence should have been shattered by the hoarse commands of the captains and the loud roar of cannon. The summer cottager of to-day will be amazed at the recollection, and many will think the story is such stuff as dreams are made of, so strange and unreal it seems. Yet here began the great French and Indian War which resulted in the fall of Louisburg, the capture of Quebec, and the end of French dominion in America.

The great flotilla was now ready to embark. A foreign legion of more than six thousand, three hundred soldiers were in the first division. They had come from all parts of the British Empire and had campaigned in Flanders, in France, in Spain, in Italy and in India. They were the flower of the English Army with their red coats, their high busbies and shakoes, their swords and their guns. They were veterans all. Supporting them was a still larger body of American soldiers—backwoodsmen, Indian fighters, hunters, rangers, settlers and farmers. These were dressed in striking contrast to their allies from across the seas. They wore no gaudy uniforms nor did they march in files. They were dressed in the hunting shirt and leggings of the woodsman, they carried firelocks and tomahawks as side arms. Under the right arm was a powderhorn, a leather bag for home-made bullets at their waist. Each officer carried a pocket compass for a guide through the primeval forests through which they marched, not in companies but singly and in two's and three's, ready to seek shelter behind rocks and trees in case of attack. The fiery Stark was among them. Later at Monmouth he was to say, "By night they must be ours or Molly Stark will be a widow." The intrepid Israel Putnam, also. He was to be captured on this expedition, to have his cheek gashed by a tomahawk, then bound to a forest tree and a crackling fire lighted around him. A humane French officer happened by and rescued him from his appalling situation. Anthony Wayne—Mad Anthony—was there, too.

While Capt. Jeffrey Amherst was breaking through the line of forts, an expedition under Wolfe entered the St. Lawrence and anchored below Quebec. Pitt had discerned the genius and heroism which lay hidden under the rather backward manner of the little red head, Wolfe, who was but thirty-three years of age. But for a while, his sagacity seemed to have failed. No efforts could draw Montcalm from his long line of inaccessible cliffs which at this point borders the river, and for six weeks Wolfe saw his men wasting away in inactivity and himself prostrate with sickness and despair.

With a quick eye, Wolfe had discovered an almost hidden footpath leading up the cliffside to the summit. He resolved to seize this forlorn hope. At one o'clock in the morning of September 13th about half the force set off in boats and using neither sail nor oars, glided down the stream. Not a voice broke the silence of the night save that of Wolfe himself, as he quietly repeated the stanzas of Gray's "Elegy in a Country Churchyard":

> The boast of heraldry, the pomp of power,
> And all that beauty, all that wealth e'er gave,
> Awaits alike the inevitable hour:
> The paths of glory lead but to the grave.

"I would rather," he remarked as the boats neared the shore, "be the author of that poem, than capture Quebec tomorrow."

He was the first to leap ashore and to scale the narrow path where no two men could go abreast. His troops followed, pulling themselves to the top by the help of bushes, roots and boughs. At daybreak his whole army stood in orderly formation on the Plains of Abraham, and Quebec was doomed. Wolfe fell in the moment of victory. He is buried in St. Alfage Church, Greenwich, England. The coat which he wore when he fell is still preserved in the Tower of London.

Louisburg was defended by a garrison numbering upwards of five thousand men. It took more than twenty-five years to build, and cost many millions. It had been greatly strengthened since its first capture. Its capitulation was one of the most spectacular and brilliant military achievements of its time. News of this important victory filled America with joy and Europe with astonishment.

It is pleasant to record that in spite of the exigencies of war, the spirit of chivalry even in the wilds of an unknown wilderness was not dead. During a lull in the fierce fighting, Drucour, the French Commander, under a flag of truce sent word to Amherst that there was a surgeon of uncommon skill in Louisburg, whose services were at the command of any English officer who needed them. Not to be outdone in courtesy, Amherst sent back messages and letters from wounded Frenchmen in his hands, adding his compliments to Madame Drucour, with an expression of regret for the disquiet to which she was exposed, begging her at the same time to accept a gift of pineapples from the West Indies. She returned his courtesy by sending him a basket of wine; after which they commenced to murder each other again. This energetic lady was on the ramparts every day, where her presence roused the soldiers to enthusiasm; and every day she fired three cannon to encourage them.

When the prizes of war were distributed, Sir Jeffrey Amherst, who had nothing to do with the founding of the college which bears his name, became a baronet and is probably better known to Americans by the popular glee club ballad sung wherever Amherst students gather: "Lord Jeffrey Amherst was a soldier of the King." There were, of course, any number of sons, brothers, lovers and husbands who got nothing but six feet of earth in an unknown grave; for they are a necessary, but entirely detestable, background to every famous victory.

During one of Amherst's visits to New York by sloop from Albany, a small shack on the shore was pointed out to him and a curious story in connection with it was told him. "Ah!" remarked His Lordship, "very interestin', very interestin'; I shall make a note of it." And here it is—from his "Journal."

Oct 11th 1758. We were opposite Kinderhook this morning. The wind came fair & we sailed very fast. Got at night beyond Livingston House & to the Highlands. Passed a house where the boatmen told us that the woman had allways lived with two Husbands, one an Irishman & the other a Scotchman; the children were from both Fathers. Some resembled one & some the other, the woman bedded with them night about, and they never quarrelled or had disputes.

The second expedition against Fort Duquesne in 1758 on the Ohio was a complete success. Washington, overcoming the objections of his commanding officer who wished to postpone the attack, led his column till it came in sight of the French forces now thoroughly disheartened. Surmounting the formidable defenses, he was about to give the order to charge when the garrison set fire to the fort and by the light of the flames sailed down the Ohio. As the banners of England were raised over the ruined bastions of the fortress, the place was with one voice called Pittsburgh in honor of America's great friend and England's first citizen.

Braddock's field near by was visited the next day where the slaughtered comrades of the former expedition still lay unburied. Where the havoc had been fiercest, bones, whitened and dismembered, lay in the utmost confusion.

None could be recognized save two—Sir Peter Halket and his son, who fell together. The great tree, near which they had been seen to fall, still stood like a sentinel over their remains. The shrill cry of a savage who stumbled upon them, brought the son of Sir Peter and a small group, among whom was Washington and his comrade-in-arms, Benjamin West, who was afterwards to become President of the Royal Academy and one of England's best-known portrait painters.

The remains of the two dead heroes were wrapped in a Highland plaid and reverently interred where they had fallen. A beautiful monument to commemorate this forest tragedy was erected only last year by the descendants of the soldiers who fell here.

In the drama now unfolding, we see the first pangs of the birth of a new Nation. Many of the actors were to reappear in other but not more heroic rôles than were then assigned to them. Some who fought for the Union Jack were later on to fight for the Stars and Stripes. Many, like Wolfe, were to find that the "path of glory leads but to the grave."

Young Lord Howe, who was the heart and soul of the expedition, was the first to fall. In England's most famous of all her famous cathedrals—Westminster Abbey—there stands a monument to this fine young soldier—a monument erected by the people of the Province of Massachusetts Bay in New England by order of the Great and General Court "in loving memory of Brigadier General George Augustus Lord Howe who was slain July 6th, 1758, on the march to Ticonderoga in the 34th year of his age in testimony of the sense they had of his virtues and of the affection his officers and soldiers bore to his command." The body of this fine soldier, said by Wolfe to be one of the finest in the British Army, was found in a tangle of underbrush and fallen timbers, shot through the heart. A random bullet found a shining mark. It was a hopeless task to attempt its removal in the scorching July sun through the trackless forest to Boston. His comrade-in-arms and warm friend, Philip Schuyler, whose house guest he had been but a few days before, took charge of the body and with solemn services placed it beneath the high altar in the old Cathedral of St. Peter's in Albany, where the last resting place of this gallant young English nobleman may be seen to this day. The memorial stone is thus inscribed:

BENEATH THIS
PAVEMENT
LIES THE BODY OF

GEORGE AUGUSTUS
VISCOUNT HOWE

A DISTINGUISHED MAN & SOLDIER.
A FRIEND OF THE COLONIES.
KILLED ON THE MARCH TO TICONDEROGA
JULY 6, 1758

Captain Richard Montgomery, just twenty-one years, who was afterwards to fall into the arms of Aaron Burr in the American attack on Quebec during the war of the Revolution while fighting under the Stars and Stripes, was in the command; with Captain James Cook, who was afterwards to reap imperishable fame by his discoveries of Australia, New Zealand, most of the South Sea Islands, and who was eventually killed by cannibals in the Philippine Islands.

Captain William F. Howe, brother of Viscount Howe, was in the attack at Louisburg. He afterwards became General-in-Chief of His Majesty's forces in America with headquarters in New York during the Revolution, and in that capacity sentenced that sterling young Connecticut schoolmaster, Nathan Hale, to execution.

A third brother, Captain Richard Howe, defended the Coast against the attacks of the French Fleet sent to assist the beleaguered fortress, and scattered them.

Captain Isaac Barre, Wolfe's devoted friend, followed him in his dash on the shores of Louisburg. In the struggle which followed he was severely wounded by a ball which destroyed the sight of one eye. The terrible sufferings he endured in this combat lent superb eloquence to his tongue when in the House of Parliament at a later date he rose to defend the Americans.

In that charming and beautiful city of Bath in England one may see the modest little home where General Wolfe spent his boyhood.

Colonel Edward Cornwallis founded the first English city in the Canadian wilds, and named it in honor of his friend, the Earl of Halifax. The young Colonel was later succeeded by his nephew, Lord Charles Cornwallis, who took part in the first major combat of the Revolution— the Battle of Long Island and the capture of New York. It was his sad fate to be in command of the British Army when it fought its last fight and surrendered at Yorktown. No censure, however, was placed upon Cornwallis. The cause of his failure was well understood in England.

He returned home to take charge of England's newly acquired empire in the East—India, and, as Viceroy, ruled for many years. It was there that he formed his great friendship with Captain Arthur Wellesley, afterwards the great Duke of Wellington. He served with him through the hundred days in the Peninsular Campaign and was with him on that memorable day at Waterloo when the power of Napoleon fell before the might of England. The Cornwallis countryseat—home of the Cornwallises for more than six hundred years—has many mementoes of the Viceroy. A beautiful avenue of trees in Minton Park is named Wellington Road in memory of his friend and comrade-in-arms for many years.

At the time of the attack on Louisburg, young Wellesley was an unknown private in the ranks of an Irish regiment, the same which numbered among its members our great Revolutionary soldier, Richard Montgomery. His departure to India removed him from further action in the Western World.

Montgomery, fighting as an American soldier in the Revolution, was later to die on the same Plains of Abraham and to be tenderly buried by a former British comrade-in-arms—Sir Guy Carleton, whom he was now opposing.

Dan Morgan, the scourge of Tarleton in the Carolinas and the hero of the battle of Cowpens; Benedict Arnold of Saratoga fame; and Morcer all received their education in arms for the Revolution in this French and Indian War. But what was more important, the skill and bravery of these untried backwoodsmen in action, was so superior to that of the red coats that their hitherto invincible reputation, not as fighters, but as tacticians, suffered severely. In traditional British style, they stood in their famous "hollow square," or company front, and took it on the chin. They never saw the savages who picked them off in bunches, and whole companies were decimated without a return shot. It was a fine exhibition of physical courage, but a foolish performance just the same.

By the treaty of Paris, France ceded all her territory in America east of the Mississippi, to the English. While this was for the moment a great victory for England, it proved in the end a colossal catastrophe. Had France retained her American Empire when the Revolution broke out, it is doubtful if even her hatred of England would have induced her to draw the sword in aid of the Colonies. Her interests would have been all the other way. But her dream of an Empire having forever vanished, she had nothing to lose and much to gain. The Colonies could, no doubt, have won without the French alliance. Even so, they would have been confined to the narrow strip along the Atlantic Coast and the boundless prairies of the great West would still have belonged to another nation. The red coats who were fighting for King George, under Wolfe and Amherst, were, in reality, fighting for an unborn Republic. The monument erected on the Plains of Abraham to commemorate this battle is in honor of both commanders—General Wolfe, the conqueror, and General Montcalm, the vanquished. Both names appear on the column.

In these wars for control, the story of Arcadia is interesting. Echoes of this tragedy were printed in New York papers for many years.

An English expedition attacked Cape Breton, Arcadia (Nova Scotia), and conquered it completely. Perhaps no chapter in all history is sadder than the fate that befell these unfortunate victims of a war about which they knew nothing and cared less. They were simple peasants, tilled the fields for a meager living, and knew naught of the great world outside. Even the Treaty of Utrecht, which had ceded their territory to Great Britain, meant nothing to them. For nearly forty years the world had passed them by and they had built up a little community of their own in their precious seclusion. The fruits of industry were theirs in moderate abundance. No courts or law officers were needed in their simple lives and the tax gatherer was unknown to the land. The parish curé was their mentor and guide. It was an ideal existence.

Into this peaceful valley came the horrors of war. Some panicky fear must have seized the invader to convince him that so large a body of homeless settlers of alien blood must of necessity be dangerous. And so, an order in Council decreed the banishment of these poor people, and their colony was sent adrift to the far winds. For many, many months the New York papers contained anguished appeals for news of loved and lost ones. The heart sickens at the mere recollection of the wanton cruelty. The story is best told in Longfellow's *Evangeline*.

This incident produced a profound and lasting impression upon the red man. Heretofore, he had fondly imagined himself to possess a monopoly in the art of revolting cruelty and fiendish deviltry; but after Grand Pre, he hid his diminished head in shame, and sorrowfully admitted that he was but a bungling amateur compared with the whites.

The cold, dispassionate historian, however, cannot utterly condemn the English. This wholesale measure of expatriation was not put into effect till every resource of patience and persuasion had been tried in vain. The agents of the French Court, civil, military and ecclesiastical, had made some act of force a necessity by obnoxious practices which produced a state of affairs impossible of continuance. And when the storm they provoked, burst on these unhappy people, they quietly, in the characteristic French manner, left them to take the consequences.

Curiously, a similar fate had been decreed for the whole Protestant population of the Colony of New York by Louis XIV. All of them—some eighteen thousand—were to be seized, despoiled of their property, and dispersed among other British Colonies in such a way that they would be permanently scattered. Want of power alone prevented the execution of this plan.

Of the men who figured most prominently in this war, several are worth recalling. They were familiar figures in our streets and had their homes here. Few more romantic characters were ever seen in Old New York than those of Sir William Johnson, the great Over-lord of the Six Nations; Joseph Brant, the famous Indian Chief, whose sister Molly was the mother of several of Sir William's more than a hundred children; Philip Schuyler; General Abercrombie; and last but not least, Admiral Sir Peter Warren, uncle of Sir William Johnson and patron saint of our own Greenwich Village.

Sir William's frequent appearances in our city arose from the fact that he and Sir Peter were business partners, Sir William as a youth, having come out to look after the large land holdings held by his uncle in the Mohawk Valley, bestowed upon him as a reward for his brilliant naval services to England. He made his New York home with the Admiral in Greenwich Village.

But it was in the wilds of the Indian country that Johnson showed to the best advantage. In the center of the rich Mohawk Valley, where the thriving town of Johnson now stands, Johnson Hall was the feudal home of the last of the great English barons in America. Here Sir William reigned in savage splendor after the manner of the ancient barons of the Middle Ages. He was monarch of all he surveyed. His lordly acres stretched as far as the eye could reach. To the red man he was the Great White Father; and in far-off England his power and prestige was known and respected. His influence among the fierce warriors of the Six Nations was supreme. But for Sir William and his power over the red men bordering on the Great Lakes, there would have been a different ending to the struggle between the French and the British for supremacy in the New World.

Sir William's first meeting with Molly Brant was typical of his other romantic experiences. She was just sweet sixteen, tall, exquisitely formed, with all the charm that goes with youth and beauty. The scene is a militia muster in the wilds of Northern New York. One of Johnson's field officers, riding a mettlesome horse, comes near her and Molly shoots a quick glance at him. Nothing like that ever happened at Ascot, but this was America. "I'd like to mount behind," Molly remarked to a companion in a whisper not loud enough to be heard more than a mile.

Never dreaming she would attempt such a foolhardy feat, the young officer said, "Come ahead."

At the word, she leaped lightly upon the crupper with all the grace of a young fawn. The horse sprang off at top speed with Molly gracefully at ease. Her many-hued blanket and her long black hair streamed in the wind.

As they flew around the parade ground Sir William, who was never known to pass up anything good, was captivated by the enchanting picture. He promptly ordered the young officer back to his quarters and calmly appropriated Molly for himself—which was just exactly what this simple little trusting child of the forest hoped would happen.

As a rule, Johnson's matrimonial alliances were without benefit of clergy; but he married Molly just before she died, and her descendants are today among the best people in Upper Canada.

Part of his duty involved the performance of his *"droit*

du seigneur" obligations. It was considered a great honor to have the dusky bride pass her nuptial night with the Great White Father, and right nobly did Sir William respond to the call of duty, without in the least neglecting a rather large and constantly growing list of more or less permanent brides of his own.

Although sent out to look after the lands of Admiral Warren, he soon began to acquire land on his own account. One rather large piece—some say a hundred thousand acres—came into his possession as the result of a dream, and together they were rulers over a vast domain. Among the Six Nations, Sir William was virtually a feudal lord. His great manor house was a marvel for its time, and many rich and racy tales of his career in this capacity are still remembered. One that bears retelling is his experience with one of the great chiefs in a neighboring tribe.

This old chief was fond of anything gay and colorful and took a great fancy to a beautifully embroidered and bejeweled silk scarlet coat which Sir William had just received from London. The General was very proud of this coat and winced inwardly when this Indian began telling him of a dream he had just had. He dreamed that Sir William had made him a present of that identical coat. There was nothing to do but hand over that coat or suffer a loss of prestige which he could not afford. So the old chief got his coat.

Meeting him a day or so later, Sir William stopped him long enough to tell him that he, too, had had a dream. He dreamt that the Indian and his council had made him a present of a large tract of land. In fact, so vivid had been this dream, that Sir William could remember the exact boundaries of the land and indeed had been able to draw a map with scientific exactness showing the distances from such a river to such a tree, etc., etc.

The gift was accordingly given by the old Indian. He

was afterwards heard to remark ruefully, "I no dream any more. White chief dream heap much better than Indian."

Sir William eventually became a Brigadier General in the British Army. All through his long and arduous life he was a stanch friend of the young Colony of New York. His interest in our city was keen. He saw in it a London of the future. Although his forest home claimed most of his time he considered himself a New Yorker. He died, it is said, from a stroke, caused by the final break with the Mother Country just before the Revolution began, and thus was spared the pang of breaking old friendships; for in all probability he would have remained a partisan of the King's, along with his uncle, Admiral Warren, and the De Lanceys.

Colonel Ephraim Williams was one of Johnson's trusted lieutenants, but fell while leading his men near Lake George. By his will he bequeathed his property to a township west of Fort Massachusetts, upon condition that it be called Williamstown, and the money to be used for the maintenance of a free school. The school was afterward incorporated as a college. Such was the origin of that now famous institution known as Williams College.

CHAPTER X

The American Revolution Smolders

WITH the triumph of Wolfe on the Heights of Abraham
began the first steps of New York on its march to the leadership of the cities in the New World and for its brilliant
part in the great struggle soon to commence with the
Mother Country. By removing an enemy whose dread
had knit the Colonists to England, Pitt inadvertently laid
the foundations of the great Republic of the West. He
had truly exclaimed when news of the victory at Plassey,
India, reached him the same day that news came that Quebec fell: "This day England has gained an Empire in the
East and lost an Empire in the West."

England was no longer a mere European power. Mistress of Northern America, soon to be ruler of India,
claiming as her own the Empire of the Seas, Britain suddenly towered high above the nations whose position in a
single continent doomed them to comparative insignifi-
cance in the after-history of the world. A consciousness
showed itself in the restlessness with which their adventurers penetrated into far-off seas. The Atlantic was dwindling
into a mere strait within the British Empire, but beyond
it to the westward lay a reach of waters where the British
flag was almost unknown. In the year which followed the
fall of Quebec, two English ships were sent on a cruise of
discovery to the Strait of Magellan; three years later Captain Cook, whom we have just mentioned, traversed the
Pacific from end to end and wherever he touched in New

Zealand or Australia, he claimed the soil for the English Crown and opened up another world for the expansion of the British Empire. Its people saw in the growth of their vast possessions, the monopoly of whose trade was reserved for the Mother Country, a source of boundless wealth. To guard and preserve so vast and lucrative a dominion became from this moment not only the aim of English statesmen but the resolve also of the people.

How completely these ambitions, these lofty dreams of power, were to be shattered by the rascality, incompetence and soul-destroying egotism of George the Third, will be revealed as our story unfolds.

When George III mounted the throne in 1760, there was as yet nothing to cloud the good will which the Colonist felt toward the Mother Country. Even in matters of trade, the supremacy of the homeland was far from being a galling one. The restriction of trade to Great Britain was more than compensated by the commercial privileges which the Colonists enjoyed as British subjects. But strong as the attachment of the Americans to Britain seemed at the close of the conquest of Canada, keen lookers-on saw, in the very completeness of this victory, a danger to their future union. The menace of the French in Canada, their designs in the West, had thrown America for protection on the Mother Country. With this danger removed, all need of this protection vanished. If questions of trade and taxation awoke murmurings and disputes, a more serious undercurrent of thought was ever behind these grievances. The English Government dreaded the growth of the democratic spirit which the government and society of the Colonies had taken on, and increasing uneasiness greeted each successive gesture in that direction. It was to the task of curbing, at once, further tendencies of this nature that the young King devoted himself, with an enthusiasm worthy of a better cause. For the first time since the accession of the house of Hanover, England had a King determined to play the part of an autocratic ruler. So well did he play the part that in ten years he had reduced government to a shadow and lost the loyalty and affection of his subjects at home; a decade later he had forced the Colonies into revolt and brought England almost to the brink of ruin.

Such results usually are the work of very great men or very wicked men. George accomplished his amazing achievements without the aid of either. He had a smaller mind than any English King that had preceded him except James II, prince of bunglers as well as King. In addition to having the smallest brain, it was also tainted with *dementia præcox*. He could brook no counselors. Unlike Elizabeth, he could not endure greatness in others. He longed for the time when "death or decrepitude" would put an end to Pitt, his incomparable minister, and even when death had freed him from his "trumpet of sedition," he denounced the proposal for a public monument to the great statesman as "an affront to me personally."

Having made up his mind to follow his mother's oft-repeated admonition in his adolescent days: "George, be *King*"—George started out to be as absolute a monarch as circumstances permitted and even when they didn't. The traits that now stand out most prominently in his character are his monumental egotism and his unrivaled obstinacy. His education had been neglected, his natural abilities were of the feeblest kind, and his great ambition was to govern free from the dictation of parties, ministers, or the limits of the Constitution. Quite an undertaking, but he approached his task blithely and with a sublime confidence in the rectitude of his own desires.

How perilously near he came to wrecking the British

Empire, history records, and the shame of the darkest hours in English history lies wholly at his door. His attitude toward the growing disaffection in his American Colonies was summed up in a letter to one of his ministers. "They would only be lions while we are lambs; if we take the resolute part, they will undoubtedly be very weak."

In order to recoup themselves for the expenses of the war just ended, a generous part of which had already been defrayed by the Colonies, George III decided to tax them still further and without consulting them at all.

Looking back upon the events which led up to the Revolution, it is now conceded that this measure finally caused the smoldering embers to burst into flame. It is known as the Stamp Act. Aside from its manifest injustice, the provisions of this Act included by long odds the most objectionable and irritating features ever devised in a bill to raise money from a free people. Crass stupidity could go no farther. You could do nothing without affixing one of those odious stamps. If you neglected to put one on your marriage certificate, you might just as well have mated without benefit of clergy. It is easier to think of things that were included than those which were omitted. It had, however, one all-embracing and righteous effect. It finally convinced even the thick-witted King that he had gone too far; that it must be repealed or armed conflict would inevitably follow.

The moment the stamps arrived and were ready for distribution, New York blossomed out into a riot of posters. They were put up everywhere; they stared at you from every vacant wall, shop window or building. The Governor passed dozens of them on his short walk to the Fort. None saw them put up. They sprang out of nothingness. This was the warning conveyed:

The able Doctor; or America Swallowing the Bitter Draught.

Political Cartoon during excitement of the Stamp Act.

PRO PATRIA

The first Man that either distributes or makes use of Stampt
Paper, let him take care of his House, Person, & Effects.

Vox Populi

Such was the situation when, on the 31st of October, the
Governors of the several Colonies took the required oath
to carry the Act into effect. Yet there was not one who
dared make the attempt. Cadwallader Colden, Governor of
New York, retired within the Fort, fully persuaded that he
could over-awe the people with his loaded guns and strong
guard. "He was fortified as if he had been at Bergen-op-
Zoom, when the French besieged it with a hundred thousand men," wrote John Watts, "which gave more offense
and made people's blood run higher than any one thing
that happened." The date set for putting the Act into effect, November first, was termed the "last day of liberty,"
and numbers of people were flocking into the town; "They
came," so said Gage, "by thousands."

They uttered terrifying threats. They sang ballads as
they wandered through the streets. The favorite was one
of thirteen verses, with a chorus, which had been produced
by no indifferent versifier, and printed and scattered broad-
cast a short time previously. A few specimen lines will
suffice:

> With the beasts of the wood, we will ramble for food,
> And lodge in wild deserts and caves,
> And live poor as Job on the skirts of the globe,
> Before we'll submit to be slaves, brave boys,
> Before we'll submit to be slaves. etc.

In the evening the important merchants of the city met
at Burns's Coffee House to consummate the first blow
which was to be struck in retaliation at the trade and industry of Great Britain. Over two hundred names were

signed to an agreement to cease the purchase of further
goods from England.

That never-to-be-forgotten first of November was ushered in by the tolling of muffled bells, and pennants
hoisted at half-mast. During the day letters were sent as
usual, and large placards were put up all over town, threatening destruction to every person and his property, who
should in any way touch a stamp, or delay business for
the want of one. An open letter addressed to the Lieutenant Governor which had been posted in the Merchants'
Coffee House all day, was delivered at the Fort towards
evening by an unknown hand. It assured Colden that his
life would be forfeit if he did not that night make oath
solemnly before a magistrate, and publish it to the people,
that he would not execute the Stamp Act.

About seven o'clock an organized band of the Sons of
Liberty appeared in the streets, led by Isaac Sears, and,
proceeding to the Common, erected a movable gallows,
upon which they hung an effigy of Colden, and one of the
Devil whispering in his ear. His Satanic Majesty held a
boot in his hand, designed as a satire upon the Earl of
Bute, prominent in passing the hated measure. One party
of citizens marched down Broadway to the Fort, attended
by a most formidable mob, carrying candles and torches.
Another party, meanwhile, had placed an effigy of Colden
upon the gallows with which they were parading through
the streets, now and then firing a pistol at the effigy. In
front of the house of James McEvers on lower Wall Street
they halted and gave three cheers. They continued the
march to the Fort where they placed the gallows, with the
effigy swinging thereon, within ten feet of the Fort gate.
The mob derided the soldiers in the Fort, clambered to
the top of the ramparts and defied the guards to fire upon
them. They then threw bricks and stones against the Fort,
and used the most offensive language. Not a word was re-

turned, General Gage having prudently given orders to that effect. The mob then broke into the Lieutenant Governor's coach-house, and taking out his chariot, dragged it through the streets to the Common and back again. The Fort fence facing Broadway had been taken down by the soldiers, in order to expose the assailants to the fire of the Fort, which was another cause of wrath. Hence the boards were gathered into a pile, and the chariot, chair, gallows, effigies, and everything movable which could be found in the stables, placed upon them, and the whole set on fire. Affairs had reached a serious stage when a message finally came from the Fort, in the form of a placard, announcing that the Lieutenant Governor would distribute no stamp papers, but "leave the matter to be regulated by Sir Henry More; and was willing to put them aboard a man-of-war, if Captain Kennedy would receive them," which he, unwilling to offend the people, declined.

A deputation of merchants waited upon the Governor and urged him to deliver the stamps to the corporation. He pleaded his oath to the King, and the great contempt into which the government would fall by concession. His counselors advised him to yield. Still he hesitated. At 4 P.M. a large crowd collected about the City Hall to learn the results. The Mayor, attended by the aldermen, visited the Fort and warned Colden of the imminent danger of further delay. He was in great distress, and appealed to General Gage for counsel. The latter avowed the belief, that a fire from the Fort would be the signal for "an insurrection" and the commencement of civil war. "So," says Bancroft, "the head of the Province, and the military chief of all America, confessing his inability to stop the anarchy, capitulated to the municipal body which represented the people." It was agreed that the stamps should be surrendered to the corporation. Accordingly, the Mayor and aldermen, attended "by a prodigious concourse of people of all

ranks," proceeded to the Fort gate, and received the
stamps; the crowd gave three cheers, and after seeing the
packages carried to the City Hall, dispersed. Civil war was
for the moment averted.

When the matter was brought before Sir Henry More
for further action, one of the first questions he put to the
Council was, whether it would be practicable to issue the
stamps. They replied unanimously, "No." And that ended
the matter for the time being.

The scene now changes to England. The King and his
committee had just received what, to their benighted in-
tellects, seemed astounding news. Says a contemporary:

The news which came across the water distressed the King.
The surrender of the stamps at New York to the municipal
government of the city, he regarded as "extremely humiliat-
ing." "This is undoubtedly the most serious matter that ever
came before Parliament," he said, and was impatient to receive
a minute report of all that occurred.

*Home of Clement C. Moore, Chelsea Village, author of
"The Night Before Christmas."*

Nothing could exceed the crass stupidity of the King at this critical juncture. Instead of seeking a plan of honorable adjustment, he was determined to enforce the Act. All England was excited over the news from their distant friends in America, but the great majority of the people were clearly in favor of the Colonists. The matter was the main subject of discussion by the Crown in the House of Commons on the day appointed for its consideration, January fourteenth. It was upon this occasion that Captain Barre made his memorable speech.

Captain Barre's terrible sufferings with Wolfe before Quebec enabled him to make a speech against this Act which was one of the most inspired, most dramatic ever heard in the ancient Hall of Rufus in defense of an oppressed people.

Townshend, the reputed master of American affairs, had closed his speech with these words: "Will these American children, planted by our care, nourished by our indulgence to strength and opulence, and protected by our arms, grudge to contribute their mite to relieve us from the heavy burden under which we lie?"

Barre's answer deserves to rank with Antony's oration over the body of Cæsar.

They planted by YOUR care! No; your oppression planted them in America. They fled from your tyranny to a then uncultivated, inhospitable country; where they exposed themselves to almost all the hardships to which human nature is liable, and among others to the cruelties of a savage foe, the most subtle, and I will take it upon me to say, the most formidable, of any people upon the face of God's earth; and yet, actuated by principles of true English liberty, they met such hardships with pleasure, compared with those they suffered in their own country, from the hands of those who should be their friends. *They nourished by YOUR indulgence!* They grew by your neglect of them. As soon as you began to care about them, that care was exercised in sending persons to rule them in one department and another, who were, perhaps the deputies of deputies to some members of this house, sent to spy out their liberties, to misrepresent their actions, and to prey upon them,—men whose behavior on many occasions has caused the blood of those SONS OF LIBERTY to recoil within them; men promoted to the highest seats of justice; some who, to my knowledge, were glad, by going to a foreign country, to escape being brought to the bar of the court of justice in their own. *They protected by YOUR arms!* They have nobly taken up arms in your defense; have exerted a valor, amidst constant and laborious industry, for the defense of a country whose frontier was drenched in blood, while its interior parts yielded all its little savings to your emolument. And believe me,—remember I this day told you so,—the same spirit of freedom which actuated that people at first will accompany them still. But prudence forbids me to explain myself further. God knows I do not at this time speak from motives of party heat; what I deliver are the genuine sentiments of my heart. However superior to me in general knowledge and experience the respectable body of this house may be, yet I claim to know more of America than most of you, having seen and been conversant in that country. The people, I believe, are as truly loyal as any subject the King has; but a people jealous of their liberties, and who will vindicate them, if ever they should be violated. But the subject is too delicate; I will say no more.

After an extra-strenuous session lasting until four o'clock in the morning, a resolution was passed for England's right to do what the Treasury pleased with three millions of freemen in America. The Colonists were henceforward excisable and taxable at the mercy of Parliament, according to this measure; but the end was not yet.

Springs days were on the wane and yet the Lords of England were still discussing the Repeal Bill. Pitt hobbled into the house on crutches, swathed in flannels, such was his zeal to defend America. Edmund Burke won undying fame for his assistance to Pitt and the House was won for repeal.

History tells us that on the morning of March 18, 1766, the King went in state to Westminster and gave his reluctant assent, to what he ever after stupidly referred to as "the wellspring of all his sorrows—the fatal repeal of the Stamp Act." He returned amid the shouts and huzzas of the applauding multitude. As a matter of fact, the King was temporarily insane at the time and his signature was secured by a commission. There was a public dinner of the friends of America in honor of the event; Bow bells were set ringing, and on the Thames the ships displayed their colors. At night a bonfire was kindled and houses illuminated in many parts of the city.

Swift vessels hurried across the Atlantic with the tidings. On the 20th of May, the news was announced in New York, and the city "ran mad" with gladness. On the 4th of June, the anniversary of the birth of the King, an ox was roasted in City Hall Park, twenty-five barrels of strong beer was provided, and a hogshead of rum, with the necessary ingredients for making it into punch. A pole was erected at the top of which waved a flag inscribed "Liberty"; twenty-five cannon were ranged near by, and amid the thunder of artillery, and the music of the band playing "God Save the King" the standard of England was displayed, greeted by deafening shouts. The jubilee was attended by Sir Henry More, by the gentlemen of the council, by the Mayor and aldermen of the city, and by the military officers then in New York.

Such was the gratitude and good feeling, that at a large gathering shortly after, at the coffee-house, it was resolved to petition the Assembly to cause a statue to be erected to Pitt. John Cruger brought the matter before the House and it was received with favor. Money was appropriated; but provision was first made for the erection of an equestrian statue of King George III in metal, because of his benignity and condescension; the one of Pitt to be in marble.

Both were subsequently erected; the King's in Bowling Green. It was pulled down during the Revolution and melted into bullets to fire at his soldiers. Pitt's was erected in Wall Street at the corner of William. It was destroyed during the occupancy of New York by the British, but the city of Pittsburgh still endures. A new Liberty Pole has recently been erected in City Hall Park on the same site as the one that stood there on this historic occasion. Each year "Flag Day" is celebrated by the Sons of the Revolution at the foot of this new Liberty Pole to whose care this shrine has been committed.

Notwithstanding the significance of this incident, George III and his ministers continued to harass and annoy the Colonists. "Whom Jupiter would destroy he first drives mad." In the present case, this was literally true. How long George was secretly insane can only be surmised. It is only charitable to suppose that if he had been in possession of a sound mind, his policy toward his Colonies might have been vastly different.

Long after a regency had been appointed, the old King would be frequently encountered walking round his grounds. Tears would stream down his face and he would be heard ceaselessly moaning, "Oh, my poor Colonies, my poor Colonies."

His mind, never good, was irreparably wrecked by his stupid war with his American Colonies. He bequeathed to George IV an enormous amount of memorabilia concerning New York City collected by the Duke of York. George IV gave it to the nation and it now reposes in many volumes in the British Museum.

Many of the speeches delivered on both sides of the Atlantic during the various debates have since become classics in English oratory, Patrick Henry, Edmund Burke, William Pitt and Isaac Barre being the most frequently quoted.

During the next half-dozen years there was constant friction upon one ground or another between the King and the Colonies. After ten years of fruitless effort and marvelous patience on the part of Benjamin Franklin, he came to the conclusion that it was absolutely useless to look for any justice, let alone generosity, from the British Government. An excellent judge of human character was the old philosopher, and his decision was reached only after many and bitter disappointments. He finally turned thumbs down on George and his ministers and betook himself to France to accomplish by the sword what he couldn't by the pen.

Thomas Paine undoubtedly seized the psychological moment in which to launch his powerful argument in favor of absolute and unqualified separation from and total independence of Great Britain. His pamphlet *Common Sense* spread like wildfire. His arguments, his logic was unanswerable. Franklin saw to it that it reached the widest possible circulation and his official position as Postmaster enabled him to be a valuable ally.

The effect of Paine's pamphlet was remarkable. Instantaneously, it seemed, a new national spirit was born. Paine undoubtedly gave expression to a thought that was dormant in many minds, but few would have been able to clothe the idea in such powerful and convincing language. There was no appeal from Cæsar. He set forth the situation in such lurid, unanswerable terms that it set the Colonies ablaze from one end to the other. From that moment public opinion was aroused to the wonderful possibilities of a nation free from all foreign entanglements of every kind whatsoever, and converts grew with prodigious rapidity.

The Colonies now had a definite and worth-while purpose to achieve.

Paine came to New York in 1774. His coming here is another star in Benjamin Franklin's diadem of American achievement. Franklin saw his ability while at London and furnishing him with letters of introduction to friends, induced him to go to America. Although Franklin was in London at that time on a peace mission, he probably could have done nothing more likely to provoke war than to turn Thomas Paine loose in the Colonies. For within a year he wrote *Common Sense*.

Undoubtedly, the fact that the English government had bitterly prosecuted Paine for his outspoken criticism of their stupidity in political matters at home, and had shut him up in Newgate for a year or two, added vitriol to his pen and spurred him on to do his utmost. All these mealy-mouthed petitions which the Colonists were fond of sending to their dear King, assuring him of their love and loyalty, caused him to froth at the mouth. Yet he was sincere in his belief and his personal resentment was merely an unavoidable accessory.

Paine lived in Grove Street, in the Ninth Ward for many years where he finally died. His body, buried in New Rochelle and then dug up by despoilers, was taken to England by his friend William Cobbett, where it underwent many vicissitudes; its present whereabouts is unknown. Moncure D. Conway is said to have purchased the skull for five dollars. It was brought to America and buried here. Cobbett himself was a picturesque character who had a book shop in Philadelphia and was at one time quite wealthy. No more charming book than his *Rural Rides* can be had for a leisurely tour through England. He explains his theft of the body by saying: "These bones will effect the Reformation of England in Church and State." The little town of New Rochelle where Paine lived for a while on some land given him by the Government has converted his little house into a museum and the grounds are carefully kept by the Huguenot Society of that town. There are now quite a number of such societies that honor him, the principal one having its headquarters in Greenwich Village not far from where Paine breathed his last.

When the war broke out, Paine enlisted as a private soldier. He served under Greene at Fort Lee and Fort Washington and in the retreat to the Delaware. After being cited for bravery on the battlefield, Paine was made a member of the Foreign Affairs Committee. While clerk of the Pennsylvania Assembly in 1779, he subscribed £500 toward the continental treasury; and by sending an appeal to others succeeded in raising £300,000. He received the honorary degree of M.A. from the University of Pennsylvania in 1780.

Washington was among the last to become converted to the idea of complete independence. For that, there were good reasons. His older brother had been educated in England and he himself would have matriculated at Oxford or Cambridge but for the change in the family fortunes. His early life had been spent with Lord Fairfax to whom he owed much, and he was a Virginian of the Virginians. The Washingtons were still living at Sulgrave Manor when the first permanent English settlement on American soil was planted at Jamestown, Virginia.

Both Franklin's and Washington's ancestors came from the same section in England. Washington's ancestral home in Sulgrave Manor is a modest little stone house at one time attached to the Priory of St. Andrew, Northampton, probably one of the smaller religious houses dissolved by Henry VIII. Except for the American Embassy, Sulgrave is the only building in England where the American flag constantly flies.

Appropriately enough, it was Washington Irving, another New Yorker, who first pointed out the historical importance of Sulgrave. It was when a little boy of six that Irving first made the acquaintance of the Father of His Country. His nurse maid seeing him approach while perambulating with her charge near the President's home in Cherry Street (the Irvings then lived in William Street where young Washington was born) could not resist a curtsey and the remark that her little charge was a namesake of his. Washington smiled, patted the little fellow's head and passed on. It is pleasant to know that on Irving's grave in Sleepy Hollow, a sprig of ivy from Sulgrave Manor has been planted by the Sulgrave Institution.

After the Revolution it was often said in England that Washington fought as much for English liberty as he did for American. The Manor is now a Washington Museum, lovingly cared for by both English and American admirers and is one of the most largely visited American Shrines in England. It is almost an uncanny coincidence that the Washington coat of arms at Sulgrave shows the stars and bars which now form the basic design of the Stars and Stripes of our National Emblem. The crest of the design shows an eagle rising from a ducal coronet. Washington himself used two crests—one a griffin and the other an eagle. It is not at all impossible that the Betsy Ross flag with its thirteen stars and stripes had no connection whatever with Washington's coat of arms, and was a wholly original conception by her. If this is so, it is certainly one of the most marvelous coincidences on record and might well justify the claim of the righteous that Heaven itself from its starry domain smiled on the banners of the Revolutionists from the beginning.

The home of Franklin was not far from Sulgrave in the little farming village of Ecton. The Ecton Franklins were small freeholders or yeomen cultivating about thirty acres of ground and making little or no change in their habits for centuries. It was the immemorial custom for the eldest son to act as the village blacksmith and it is not at all unlikely that an ancestor of Franklin's may have made the acquaintance of an ancestor of Washington's in the pursuit of his professional duties. There were no other farriers between Ecton, Bridgeton and Sulgrave, and it is not at all unlikely that an ancestor of Washington's may have had his horse shod by an ancestor of Franklin's. No other contact between the two families would be apt to occur until that greater intimacy commenced when Postmaster Franklin met Colonel Washington at Madam Esmond's hospitable mansion at Castlewood; or—if we accept the more exact though less entertaining version—at General Braddock's camp in the Wilderness. Possibly some "throw-back" to these horseshoeing days may have unconsciously prompted Franklin's caustic comment on Washington's acceptance of the presidency of the Cincinnati Society.

Benjamin was the youngest son of his father. His four immediate progenitors were the youngest sons of youngest sons. Benjamin's grandfather was once imprisoned for a political lampoon. This literary talent, however, passed by the second generation completely, only to reappear with increased power in the grandson.

Franklin in later life met Hogarth either at the Ecton Rectory or the great Manor House. If at the latter, he was doubtless the first to enter the baronial mansion as a guest.

Old home of the New York Historical Society, Second Avenue and 11th Street. This is the oldest and the first Historical Society organized in this country—1804.

CHAPTER XI

The Declaration of Independence Is Born

IN VIEW of the march of events which we have just nar-
rated it need not come as a great surprise to our readers
that the seeds containing the germ that was afterward to
blossom into that most magnificent of all human documents—the Declaration of Independence—was born in this
fine old city of ours in the month of April, 1765. It is in
all humility and in meekness of spirit that we make known
New York's claim to this proud distinction. The garments
of sackcloth and ashes which have been assigned to us as
proper raiment by Boston and Philadelphia while discussing Revolutionary subjects may now be joyfully discarded.

The reason why this interesting story has not hitherto
been included in the memorabilia of this important document is, no doubt, due to the fact that Cæsar Rodney, one
of the delegates to this first Colonial Congress, or "Stamp
Act Congress," as it subsequently became known, took
along with him the original minutes of the meeting and
they remained among his private papers unknown for more
than half a century.

Upon his death in 1812, his nephew, Cæsar A. Rodney,
discovered the document; it is signed with the name of
John Cotton who acted as Clerk of this Congress. He sent
them to his friend the editor of the *Baltimore Weekly Re-
porter,* who gave to the world this interesting Revolutionary item, calling attention at the same time to the fact that
no less than four members of this early Congress were sub-

sequently signers of the Declaration; viz. Cæsar Rodney, Robt. R. Livingston, Thomas Lynch and James Otis.

The reader has now of course, a good idea of the troublous times that existed just before the Revolution. While disaffection was widespread, it was not always wise to be too outspoken. The Crown officers were amply provided with means to punish seditious utterances.

So in 1765, disaffected New York men issued a call for a meeting to be attended by representatives from all the Colonies. That was the first gathering of what we might call a National character. This meeting, as we have just said, became popularly known as the Stamp Act Congress, since it was mainly occupied with a consideration of that measure. Its proper name however was First *Colonial* Congress. The subsequent congresses were called Continental Congress and Provincial Congress. None of them, however, appeared until nine years after the one held in New York.

At this Congress, a Resolution or "Declaration of Rights and Grievances," written by John Cruger, a New York man, was adopted. And if you read that resolution, you will find in it the germ of the immortal Declaration of Independence.

A second similar "Declaration of Rights" was made at a town meeting in Providence, Rhode Island, 1774, and the idea rapidly spread through all the Colonies. Before the year was out, all the Colonies except Georgia had passed similar resolutions and arranged to send delegates to a general meeting to be held in Philadelphia. This was the First *Continental* Congress. The very name is significant. It denotes a departure in thought from the dependent state of a Colony and a new *National* life is suggested.

It was in the Second Continental Congress that the Declaration matter was brought up again. On June 7th, Richard Henry Lee of Virginia moved "That these United Colonies are and of right, ought to be free and independent states; that they are absolved from all allegiance to the British Crown; and that all political connexion between them and the State of Great Britain is, and ought to be, totally dissolved."

No action was taken at the moment; but the next day it was: "*Resolved,* that the resolutions respecting independency be referred to a committee of the whole Congress."

Congress then resolved itself into a committee of the whole, but did not reach a conclusion. The matter was put over for further consideration on the 10th. On that day Congress decided that "consideration of Mr. Lee's original motion be postponed till Monday, the first of July next," and in the meanwhile, that no time should be lost, appointed a committee to prepare a declaration to the effect of the first resolution, which is in these words—"That these United Colonies are, and of right ought to be free and independent States; that they are absolved from all allegiance to the British Crown; and that all political connexion between them and the State of Great Britain is and ought to be totally dissolved."

On June 11th, Congress "Resolved, that the Committee for preparing the Declaration should consist of five members"; the following names were then selected: Thomas Jefferson, Chairman; John Adams, Benjamin Franklin, Roger Sherman and Robert R. Livingston.

On July 1st, it was "Resolved, that this Congress will resolve itself into a committee of the whole to take into consideration the resolution respecting independency."

Upon request of a colony, the word "tomorrow" was inserted. So the matter went over another day.

On July 2nd, as agreed, the Congress resumed consideration of the subject. The Committee of the Whole, reported that they had agreed upon adoption of Lee's motion in his exact language. On resolution, Congress moved "to meet tomorrow to take into further consideration the declaration respecting Independence."

On July 3rd, further consideration was given the measure, and later in the day it was decided to go again into a committee of the whole for still further debate. These frequent delays and postponements show clearly that Congress fully understood the serious nature of the legislation proposed.

On Thursday, July 4, 1776, however, debate ended. The Declaration of Independence, as amended, was adopted unanimously by the votes of the *Colonies* present, but not the unanimity of all the *delegates*.

With the exception of Maryland and New York the delegates from all the Colonies were free to act as they chose. Maryland forbade her delegates to vote for Independence, but her delegates disregarded their instructions. New York was instructed not to vote on it at all. Their delegates sent a copy to their Assembly sitting in White Plains. This body then ordered them to sign.

The Declaration was the composition almost wholly of Thomas Jefferson who wrote it at his lodging house, kept by Mrs. Clymer, at the southwest corner of Seventh and High Streets, Philadelphia. He, however, undoubtedly adopted some suggestions by others; but in the main it is his work.

There are many details now almost forgotten regarding this great document but which possess absorbing interest.

For example, it was not adopted unanimously. On the contrary, it very nearly failed of adoption and was saved by only *one vote*—that of John Morton of Pennsylvania. There were six Colonies in favor and the same number against. The Pennsylvania delegation, itself, was divided. Two members were absent. Franklin and Wilson were in favor, while Willing and Humphrey were opposed. Morton cast the deciding vote "in favor," and the great deed was done. His signature, as a writer afterwards nicely expressed it, "formed the Keystone of the Arch of Liberty"; hence, Pennsylvania's popular nickname, "the Keystone State."

It was arranged that the bell in the steeple of the State House was to ring out in case of the successful passing of the measure. By a singular coincidence the bell bore this inscription: "Proclaim Liberty throughout all the land unto all the inhabitants thereof." The joyful pealing of the bell was echoed by tremendous cheering by the crowd on the streets.

Curiously enough, this great document was first given to the world with only the two signatures that were customarily attached to all bills passed by the House, just as they are today. John Hancock as President of the Congress, signed it first; and then came the signature of Chas. Thompson, who was really a clerk though called "secretary" of Congress. It was in this shape that copies by direction of Congress were sent to the several assemblies, conventions, committees or councils of safety, to the several commanding officers of the Continental troops, etc., with the request that it be proclaimed in each of the United States at the head of the army. It was a copy of this kind that Washington read to his troops in City Hall Park, New York, a few days later. It bore the date of July 4, 1776.

Almost at once a "fair copy" written on paper was signed by John Hancock, Pres., Chas. Thompson, as secretary, and by all the delegates who had voted in favor of the resolution. This original or "fair copy," to the lasting regret of all Americans, was lost or probably destroyed. In the meantime, Congress ordered that the measure be engrossed on parchment for permanent preservation, so no value was apparently placed on the priceless original.

The parchment copy was completed on August 2nd, and only then was it signed by fifty-four delegates. Two others, Thos. McKean signed later in October and M. Thornton in November. Morris, Rush, Clymer, Smith, Taylor, Ross of Pennsylvania and Thornton of New Hampshire were not even members of Congress when the Declaration was passed. In fact, several other signers occupied the same nebulous state. They were permitted to sign as an act of fealty. So many new members were elected to the new Congress that their sympathies were not known to a certainty. Some might be Tories in disguise. So the signing of the Declaration was in those cases an oath of loyalty. Each of the new members, before taking his seat, was required to fix his signature to the document and was thus unconsciously rescued from the oblivion into which many of them would have fallen.

Another effect the Declaration had, was to efface the words "United Colonies" from all future public documents and to substitute in its place the words "United States."

All the signers had smooth faces, wore periwigs and short clothes. The oldest was Franklin, seventy-one; the youngest Edward Rutledge (ancestor of Anne Rutledge, sweetheart of Lincoln's), who was only twenty-seven.

John Morton was the first to die; Charles Carroll the last. At death, five signers were over ninety years of age, eight over eighty, ten over seventy, fourteen over sixty, eleven over fifty, seven over forty and one under forty. The youngest was Thos. Lynch, only thirty, who was lost at sea the same year he signed.

A rather convincing and corroborative sidelight is thrown upon New York as the origin of the seed that ultimately blossomed forth as the Declaration, in her continued interest in the early history of this great document.

In 1826, after all save one of the band of signers had descended to the tomb, the venerable Carroll alone remained among the living. The Government of the city of New York, recalling the meeting of the first Colonial Congress in this city and its Declaration of Rights, deputed a committee to wait on the illustrious survivor and obtain from him, for deposit in the public hall of our city, a copy of the Declaration of 1776, graced and authenticated anew with his sign manual. The aged patriot yielded to the request, and affixed with his own hand, to a copy of that instrument, the grateful, solemn, and pious supplemental declaration which follows:

Grateful to Almighty God for the blessings which through Jesus Christ our Lord, he has conferred on my beloved country in her emancipation, and on myself in permitting me under circumstances of mercy to live to the age of eighty-nine years, and to survive the fiftieth year of American Independence, and certify by my present signature my approbation of the Declaration of Independence adopted by Congress on the Fourth of July, 1776, which I originally subscribed on the second day of August of the same year, and of which I am now the last surviving signer; I do hereby recommend to the present and future generations the principles of that important document as the best earthly inheritance their ancestors could bequeath to them and pray that the civil and religious liberties they have secured to my country may be perpetuated to remotest posterity and extended to the whole family of man.

CHARLES CARROLL of Carrollton

August 2, 1826.

There were some expressions in the original draft of the Declaration, omitted in the text as finally adopted, that are quite touching as showing the real affection which the Colonies had for the motherland and which she so brutally ignored:

We might have been a free and great people together; but a communication of grandeur and of freedom, it seems, is below their dignity. Be it so, since they will have it. The road to happiness and to glory is open to us too; we will climb it apart from them, and acquiesce in the necessity which denounces our eternal separation.

We must endeavor to forget our former love for them; we must, therefore, hold them, as we hold the rest of mankind, enemies in war; in peace, friends.

There are a great many other passages of singular power and beauty in the original draft that are well worth reading. But perhaps the paragraph referring to slavery is the most important.

Slavery in those days was not confined to the South by any means. It flourished in all the Colonies. Its importance in the labor market in the North, however, was negligible compared with the South. So the sentiment voicing the detestation of the Colonies to this practice shows that slavery was not wanted and would have been prohibited by law but for the veto power exercised by the Crown.

If this paragraph had been allowed to stand, we would, no doubt, have escaped the horrors of the Civil War that came a century later. It refers to George III and his attitude toward slavery:

He has waged cruel war against human nature itself, violating its most sacred rights of life and liberty in the persons of a distant people, who never offended him, captivating and carrying them into slavery in another hemisphere or to incur miserable death in their transportation thither. This piratical warfare, the opprobrium of infidel powers, is the warfare of the CHRISTIAN King of Great Britain. Determined to keep open a market where MEN should be bought and sold, he has prostituted his negative for suppressing every legislative attempt to prohibit or to restrain this execrable commerce.

New York is so modest in claiming her just proportion of credit for National service, that it is a pleasure to place this record before her people. By a curious coincidence, Thomas Jefferson who wrote the Declaration, and John Adams who quickly seconded the proposal of Richard

Henry Lee's, both died on the 50th Anniversary of the signing of the document and on the same date, July 4th.

The excitement caused in England by the news from America must have astonished even the friends of the Colonists. To produce such a profound commotion in the councils of the greatest Empire on earth must have been a source of great satisfaction. The debates in the House produced some of the finest oratory ever heard in that ancient hall. On Pitt's first appearance he was in the very zenith of his virulent manhood. At the end he was carried in on a litter and fell back in a faint at the close of an impassioned plea for the Colonists. He spoke in reply to the men who were glorifying Howe's successes. "You cannot conquer America. If I were an American as I am an Englishman, while a foreign troop was landed in my country, I never would lay down my arms. Never, never, never!"

Then in an outburst of indignant eloquence, he thundered against the use of the Indian and his scalping-knife as allies of England against her children.

The proposals which Chatham advanced even at this late hour might, perhaps, have drawn America and England together. His plan was one of absolute conciliation and of a Federal union between the Colonies and Great Britain, which would have left the Colonies absolutely their own masters, in all matters of internal government, and linked only by ties of affection and loyalty to the general body of the Empire.

Pitt's last appearance was touching in the extreme. In a last despairing effort to save America, the people of England recalled the aged minister to power. But on the eve of his return to office this last chance was shattered by the hand of death. Broken with age and disease, the Earl was borne to the House of Lords to utter in a few broken words his protest against the war in America. He listened impatiently to the reply of the Duke of Richmond and again

To the PUBLIC.

THE Senfe of the City relative to the Landing the India Company's Tea, being fignified to Captain Lockyer, by the Committee, neverthelefs, it is the Defire of a Number of the Citizens, that at his Departure from hence, he fhould fee, with his own Eyes, their Deteftation of the Meafures purfued by the Miniftry and the India Company, to enflave this Country. This will be declared by the Convention of the People at his Departure from this City; which will be on next Saturday Morning, about nine o'Clock, when no Doubt, every Friend to this Country will attend. The Bells will give the Notice about an Hour before he embarks from Murray's Wharf.

By Order of the COMMITTEE.

NEW-YORK, April 21ft, 1774.

rose to his feet. But he had hardly risen when he pressed his hand upon his heart and sank to the floor. He was carried from the hall and borne home to die.

Another matter which greatly aggravated the Colonies, and which does not get the prominence which it deserves, was the persistent attempt of the British Government to establish the Church of England on this continent with all its obligatory rules and regulations. By this time the old-time bigoted Puritan had well-nigh disappeared. There was a deep religious feeling through the Colonies, but an equally deep feeling to have their religious life a thing wholly apart from State control. The Church was regarded as something pertaining to a man's spiritual life, and to be exercised according to the dictates of his own conscience. Feeling was strong on many secular questions, but nothing in comparison to that which existed on the religious one. It was one of the most vital questions of the time, and men who cared little for other differences were very keen on this. Its importance is not generally touched upon by the casual commentator; but it was nevertheless a burning question if ever there was one. Something of the old Cromwellian spirit was aroused and the feeling grew more bitter as time wore on. If every other difference had been adjusted, this one would have eventually caused a break, had it been left to fester. The bishops of the Church were singularly short-sighted and were headed for destruction. In the constantly growing numbers of "dissenters," they failed to see the handwriting on the wall. The struggle had commenced with the opening of Old Trinity and had never ceased. The beginning of the family quarrel can rightly be placed at this point. It was a sore spot long before the Stamp Act was ever thought of. It should be remembered that all the original settlers who came here from England did not come to escape religious persecution solely, but also because of the material advantages offered. The prospect of improving their condition in life, of acquiring a competence, were the prime considerations except in a comparatively few cases.

The great majority, however, much as they may have differed among themselves in religious beliefs, were united in one respect—they would not consent to the establishment of the Church of England with its connection with the State, its system of "holdings" and special privileges of the clergy. On this point they were adamant. Although the people may have been unreasonably prejudiced against the Episcopal Church, they had abundant reasons for it in a general way. The Church promoted and protected the acts of the Royal Government whenever they conflicted with the interests of the people, so the Dissenters insisted on a complete separation of Church from State.

The Bishops of the Church of England insisted that their Church was the one and only true Church of Christ; that no one could become a Christian or be ordained a minister outside its fold; that legitimate marriages could be performed only by Anglican clergymen; that the King ruled by Divine Right; that obedience to the King and Government were Christian duties; and that an Established Church was essential to the life and security of every nation.

It is difficult for us today to realize the vital interest religion then had for the ordinary person nor the bitter feeling aroused by religious controversy. And the Dissenters, as they were called, who opposed the Church and State idea, were a powerful and independent group of unsurpassed and dauntless courage. Their attitude on this question was far more belligerent, far more aggressive, than on matters more political and possibly more important to the State than was recognized. When you have added to the tax troubles, the far more emotional and tremendously moving one of religion, you have here a cause of irritation far more disturbing than a secular one capable of compromise and adjustment in a dozen directions.

This trouble had been brewing since as far back as 1693. An Act passed by the Colonial Assembly provided for the establishment of Protestant churches in each of the five counties surrounding New York City. This act provided for the selection of a minister in each parish by a majority vote of the freeholders.

This permission would have resulted in placing dissenting ministers in each parish church. So Governor Fletcher promptly proceeded under instruction of the King to nullify the Act. With such a spirit on the part of the Crown, the end was a foregone conclusion.

CHAPTER XII

Bunker Hill—and the Fight Is On

WHEN the details of the battle of Bunker Hill reached England, the news created great astonishment. The loss of so many officers in so small an engagement was staggering. It seems that a shift in the position of the forces had brought General Howe and his staff directly in the line of fire and nearly all of his personal aides were killed, the General himself being badly spattered with blood from one of his staff officers who fell at his side. His vacillating tactics, his reluctance to attack the Americans at White Plains a few months later, has been ascribed to the shock received on this occasion.

The King remarked petulantly that he would have twenty thousand soldiers in America before Spring. Whether this was an indication of the approaching permanent insanity that was to affect the rest of his life, we do not know. At all events, there was no such number to be had in his realm. The war was not at all popular. So George was obliged to scour Europe for recruits, most of whom were obtained from petty German princes who needed the money.

Franklin, who was in France at the time, very cleverly contrived to have an imaginary letter printed in many of the Continental newspapers, which was a master stroke. It purported to be a private communication from the Count de Schaumbergh to his friend the Baron Hohendorf commanding the foreign troops with the British in America.

As the British Government was paying thirty guineas for each soldier killed and only ten guineas for those who came back unharmed, the delicious sarcasm of Franklin's letter is the more appreciated. It obtained wide circulation where it would do the most harm, and recruiting was sadly interfered with as a result. Here is the letter. Franklin adroitly laments, in an apparent burst of candor, that the Prince needs the money to pay for his last trip to Italy and for his coming season at the opera.

Dear Baron Hohendorf:

I am about to send you some new recruits. Don't economize them. Remember glory before all things. Glory is true wealth. There is nothing so degrading to a soldier as the love of money. He must care only for honor and reputation must be acquired in the midst of dangers. A battle gained without costing the conqueror any blood is an inglorious success while the conquered cover themselves with glory by perishing with their arms in their hands. Do you remember that of the Lacedaemonians who defended the defile at Thermopylae, not one returned? How happy should I be if I could say the same of my brave Hessians!

Most of the Hessians who fought in the Battle of Long Island, the site of which is now covered by flats and stores, as well as those who fought at Harlem Heights, evidently remained there, judging by the population which now inhabits these two sections of our city. The old headquarters of Knyperson on Washington Heights is covered by a delicatessen shop, and General Howe's headquarters in Brooklyn is marked by a dainty lingerie shop, with rayon silk *robes de nuit* in the window.

The Cortelyou house, so valiantly defended by the Maryland troops, is buried under twenty feet of rubbish deposited there by patriotic Brooklynites in the process of grading a new street. A commemorative monument has been erected in Prospect Park, part of the scene of this battlefield, by no less a personage than nature herself. It is a massive granite bowlder, upon which has been placed a small bronze tablet informing the passer-by that here was fought the Battle of Long Island, which was England's courteous response to our somewhat tardy Declaration of Independence.

One of the most dramatic and spectacular incidents of the Revolution was the ill-fated expedition to Canada. After Ethan Allen's sensational capture of Ticonderoga, the American forces under Montgomery, proceeded north with the intention of attacking Quebec. Montgomery's force was known to have been greatly weakened. Arnold, in charge of the New England troops and Montgomery's greatest friend (Montgomery's will bears, as witness, the signature of "B. Arnold") headed a detachment of reën-forcements to go to his relief. Montgomery was marooned in Montreal. Arnold's relief columns marched through three hundred miles of the trackless forests in New England in midwinter; they encountered almost unendurable hardships. For more than a month they never saw a human face and were at the point of starvation when they finally reached the St. Lawrence at Quebec, only to find that Montgomery was one hundred and twenty miles distant. Word of their arrival must reach Arnold's friend at all costs and Aaron Burr volunteered for the dangerous journey.

Disguised as a priest and making use of his French and Latin, Burr borrowed a local wagon and guide and essayed the task of reaching Montgomery. Passing from one pious family to another, he finally reached Montreal. Montgomery, delighted with his daring courage and brilliant resourcefulness, immediately attached him to his staff as aide-de-camp. In the attack on Quebec he was in the thickest of the fight, and when Montgomery fell, fatally wounded, it was Burr who carried him off the field.

Burr lost the Presidency in succession to Washington by only one vote. This vote was cast by Mathew Lyon who was elected to Congress, *while in jail.* Burr escaped all the dangers of armed conflict; the moving accidents by flood and field; only to die a thousand deaths from an unfired bullet in the pistol of Alexander Hamilton.

Montgomery was buried where he fell and received all the honors and respect which his former comrades-in-arms could give. Fifty years later the Canadian Government courteously surrendered his body to the United States where it now reposes in the churchyard of Old St. Paul's. The inscription on his memorial reads:

This monument is erected by order of CONGRESS, 25th Janry, 1776, to transmit to Posterity a grateful remembrance of the patriotic conduct, enterprise and perseverance of MAJOR GENERAL RICHARD MONTGOMERY, who after a series of successes amidst the most discouraging Difficulties Fell in the attack on QUEBEC 31st Decbr. 1775. Aged 37 years.

The State of New York caused the remains of Majr. Genl. Richard Montgomery to be conveyed from Quebec and deposited beneath this monument the 8th day of July, 1818.

At that time Mrs. Montgomery, in the forty-third year of her widowhood, was living near Tarrytown on the Hudson. Governor Clinton had told her of the day when the steamboat *Richmond* bearing her husband's remains, would pass down the river; and sitting alone on the piazza of her home, she watched for its coming. With what emotions she saw the pageant is told in a letter written to her niece:

At length they came by with all that remained of a beloved husband, who left me in the bloom of manhood, a perfect being. Alas! how did he return? However gratifying to my heart, yet to my feelings every pang I felt was renewed. The pomp with which it was conducted added to my woe; when the steamboat passed with slow and solemn movement, stopping before my house, the troops under arms, the Dead March from the muffled drums, the mournful music, the splendid coffin canopied with crepe and crowned with plumes, you may conceive my anguish. I cannot describe it.

If the Battle of Bunker Hill proved a surprise to the British, the fate of Burgoyne's army produced consternation. Here was the flower of England's fighting forces reduced to utter helplessness and completely destroyed. Military men knew the significance of this reverse, and wise ones saw in Burgoyne's defeat the beginning of the end. Those who had seen service in America, were filled with dismay. They saw at once that if such a redoubtable army could be cut to pieces so easily, there was little hope that future engagements would result differently. The effect in Europe was similar and the enemies of England began to consider what advantage the situation held for them. Franklin lost no time in calling upon Vergennes. When the French minister saw that there was no danger in now helping the Colonies, he finally agreed to make a little advance in case that would enable the Revolutionists to do still more damage to his ancient foe, and pave the way for the restoration of the lost Colonies of France.

There is no monument to Burgoyne in that Valhalla of England's mighty dead, Westminster. After his surrender he was allowed to return to England, where he entered Parliament and advocated peace with America. From the conclusion of peace until his death, he devoted his time to the production of light comedies in which he was successful: *The Maid of Oaks, Bon Ton* and *The Heiress*, yielding an income that largely made up what he lost when he gave up his various public emoluments, which were considerable.

He was a natural son of Lord Bingly. He was also at Bunker Hill, and had enjoyed a rather successful military career in Europe before coming to America.

It was on the private yacht of Sir John Burgoyne, a descendant of General Burgoyne, that the Empress Eugenie escaped from Paris when Napoleon III was deposed.

This battle of Saratoga produced the first in a series of misadventures that were to curse the warring nations in the years to come.

Just as the campaign was about to be launched, Sir Guy Carleton was removed as Commander-in-Chief of the British forces in America in favor of Burgoyne, by Lord Germaine, then at the head of the British Government. Germaine failed to pursue the French at the Battle of Minden and was convicted of cowardice by court-martial, was dismissed from the service and declared unfit to serve in any military capacity whatever. His name was erased from the Privy Council. Yet this was the man that George III chose to put at the head of his Government, with unlimited power, at the most critical moment in her history. It was by such performances that Royal George destroyed what would have been the mightiest Empire the world has ever known.

Carleton had, with a soldier's bluntness, expressed his opinion of this coward; so when Germaine came to power Carleton was naturally removed. Burgoyne had never seen America and knew absolutely nothing of the conditions he would face. Carleton had already successfully driven back an American attack under Montgomery. He saved Canada to the British Empire. They finally recognized his services by making him a peer (Lord Dorchester) and appointing him Governor of Quebec. He was retired on a liberal grant of money.

But for Arnold, Saratoga would have been lost. General Philip Schuyler, who had planned the campaign to meet Burgoyne, was, at the last minute, relieved of command in favor of wire-pulling, incompetent Gates. They have left a blank space in one of the panels on the monument that now marks the Battlefield; Gates left two blank spaces in his report of the battle to Congress. Gallant Phil Schuyler is ignored, and Arnold is not even mentioned.

In my schooldays I was taught to look upon Arnold as the arch sum of all human wickedness. There was no crime in the category of human iniquity equal to his betrayal of West Point. And we were incessantly fed with dreadful tales about how he was everywhere shunned in England, even by his brother-officers. Finally I read that a man lay dying alone in a miserable garret in London, where he was found by a kindly English woman. "My good man," she said, "is there nothing I can do for you? Have you no relatives, no friends, who can help you? Tell me, and I'll send for them."

"Alas, madam," says the dying man, while the tears coursed down his cheeks, "I am the only man in the whole wide, wide, world who has not a single friend—I am Benedict Arnold, the Traitor." So saying he expired.

The best biographies of Arnold give the lie to this. In England, Arnold was regarded as one of the two best generals in the British Army and he rendered distinguished service in the West Indies in the wars with France and Spain. Dr. Schroeder, in his *Life and Times of Washington*, wrote:

Benedict Arnold's country and the world owe him more than they will ever liquidate; and his defection can never obliterate the solid services and the ample abuse which preceded it.

During the Battle of Saratoga, and at the most critical moment—when it was all but certain he would be victorious—he was peremptorily relieved of his command. Had not his officers and men sent word to Gates that they would not fight, except under Arnold, he would have been removed then and there. He was sorely wounded in the fight.

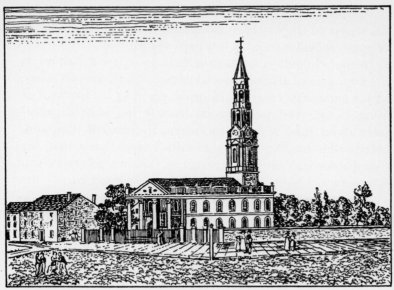

From contemporary drawing by Strickland. Courtesy of New York Historical Society.

St. Paul's Chapel 1820. Broadway and Fulton Street.

Gates never saw or smelled powder in that battle. Yet he took all the credit for it and never mentioned Arnold's name once in his reports, nor Schuyler's.

Instead of promoting him, Congress treated Arnold shamefully. While Gates was doing what he could to destroy Arnold, Schuyler and Washington, he sought and obtained a General's commission for his twenty-year-old office boy, James Wilkinson, and got it. These two worthies later almost succeeded in poisoning the mind of Congress against Washington, and came within an ace of having him removed from command. To add insult to injury, Congress deliberately violated the terms of Burgoyne's capitulation, agreed to by Arnold, which distinctly provided for the shipment to England of the troops captured at Saratoga. Instead, the poor fellows were condemned to wander for four long years among the hills of Virginia, without money, food or shelter, despised and hated. It was an unspeakable act of barbarity.

While Arnold lay alone with a shattered hip on a narrow cot in an improvised hospital in Albany, in a small cheerless room, smelling of drugs, soap and raw lumber, Gates was entertaining gaudy British soldiers in his comfortable tent in Saratoga and receiving the homage and acclaim of all the countryside. According to Gates, Arnold wasn't even at the battle.

On the morning of August 22, 1775, the British Army in New York was stunned by the news of the capture of Major André and the discovery of Arnold's treason. Curiously enough, this act of treachery recoiled most severely on those who counted upon it to achieve great honors. General Clinton was severely criticized for the part he played in the dastardly enterprise and the whole affair was viewed with disgust by the British public. Lord Germaine all but lost his leadership in the ministry and the war increased in unpopularity throughout England.

The fate of young André was deeply regretted by the British Army who were ordered into mourning for thirty days. When taken prisoner, he wrote that he had been "stripped of everything except the picture of Honora which I concealed in my mouth. Preserving this, I yet think myself fortunate."

Alas! for this touching romance, the lovely Honora soon after consoled herself with a mature widower, Richard Lovell Edgeworth, and thus renounced the leading rôle in what would have been one of the most beautiful love stories in all history. She passed her life instead, in the reflected glory of her famous stepdaughter—the well-known Maria. Fifty years later the body of André was transferred to England where it now reposes in her famous Valhalla—

Westminster Abbey. As a mark of respect and kindliness
on our part, the bier was decorated with garlands and
flowers as it was transported to the ship. When the coffin
was exhumed, it was found that the roots of a cypress tree
had lovingly entwined themselves around his body. Upon
the arrival of the flag-draped and garlanded cortège in
London, the roots were taken out and planted by request
of the King, in his private garden at Carleton House. Every
honor was done to his memory, and it was a reverent and
dignified procession that conveyed the body amid much
pomp and circumstance from the warship to the Abbey.
Seldom has London witnessed a more impressive ceremony.

That a little backwoods, sparsely populated country like
the Colonies could emerge victorious from a contest with
the richest empire then on earth is one of the most extraordinary events in history. Perhaps France came to our
assistance from altruistic motives and a genuine affection
for downtrodden humanity. At the same time, it was an
opportune moment to inflict injury on her ancient foe and
to make an effort to regain her lost empire in America.

But even then she acted with her customary caution.
Not a penny did she advance till the news of the destruction of Burgoyne's splendidly equipped army at Saratoga
reached Europe. This disaster was everywhere conceded by
military strategists competent to judge, to mean that England could not possibly win the war.

The money France hesitatingly advanced was not to be
repaid and it was so understood. Letter of Louis XVI: "I
do not speak of success of money and other kinds which
we have given her [U. S.] ostensibly on the score of trade."
To rob England of her Colonies was compensation enough.
Later on, Louis and his ministers hoped to annex the ex-
Colonies for *la belle France* and be as supreme in the
New World as she once was in the Old.

She collected the loan just the same. The entire debt to France, amounting to $2,024,900, was paid out of his own private pocket by James Swan, a wealthy merchant of Boston. In after years he was imprisoned for debt by the French Government and spent twenty-two years in Ste. Pelagie Prison. He died three days after he was released from jail.

CHAPTER XIII

The First Experiments with Independence

THE great Revolution was now at an end. Everywhere the arms of the defenders of human liberty in the New World had been victorious. A new nation had been born, dedicated to the proposition that all men are born equal, that every man is entitled to life, liberty and the pursuit of happiness. We then further resolved that Government for the people, by the people and of the people should not perish from the earth.

With the signing of the Peace Treaty, the new nation was an accomplished fact. France and Spain began their schemes, first to curb, then to swallow the young republic.

Our territory nowhere touched the Gulf of Mexico, nor was our flag seen beyond the Mississippi River. Spain owned the great West and the ground on which stands New Orleans, Florida and all the territory below 31 degrees north latitude. She also held by force of arms what are now the States of Alabama and Mississippi. She had also garrisoned all the important heights and bluffs along the river as far up as Tennessee, and had closed the Father of Waters to navigation by a friendly power who owned the east bank. Not until 1795 did we succeed in getting Spain to recognize our southern boundary, to withdraw her garrisons north of 31 degrees and to concede a right whereby we were allowed to deposit goods at New Orleans for exportation only, and to use the river commercially.

These reasonable concessions nevertheless alarmed

France greatly. Talleyrand saw at once that Spain should never have given up these forts if she meant to stop the progress of the Americans, who were determined that they, and not France, were to rule America.

But Spain was in no position to do this. So Talleyrand induced her to cede to France the Floridas and Louisiana. "From that moment," he wrote the French minister at the Court of Madrid, "the power of America is bounded by such limits as it may suit the interests of France and Spain to assign her."

But ere the scheme was carried out, Talleyrand fell from power. The Directoire was overthrown; Napoleon returned from Egypt and made himself master of France. Luckily for Talleyrand, the great First Consul recalled him to power and negotiations for the cession of Louisiana went rapidly forward—so rapidly that on the first of October, 1800, Charles of Spain signed a secret treaty, which bound him to return to Napoleon the Louisiana which, in 1763, France had given to Spain. Talleyrand had triumphed, and the country in which he had found employment as a real estater in New York during his exile from France in the days of the "Terror," was one step nearer the rapacious maw of *la belle France*. America was now to be shut up within the narrow confines of the Atlantic coast; her ambition was to be checked, and her future was to be only what it pleased France and Spain to permit till they were ready for the next move.

But Talleyrand reckoned without Old New York. News of the secret treaty leaked out; Spain suddenly, and in direct violation of the agreement of 1795, took away our right to land goods at New Orleans and closed the Mississippi completely to our commerce.

Congress instructed John Jay of New York, our Minister to Spain at the time, to surrender the free navigation of the Mississippi outright, and to assent to anything that

France proposed, to avoid war. To his everlasting credit, Jay calmly repudiated these instructions.

Matters dragged along, when suddenly Jefferson sent Robert R. Livingston, another New York man, to see what it was all about. He was one of our cleverest statesmen. He wasted no time with Talleyrand. He wasn't afraid, and went to Napoleon himself. When he finished, he had Louisiana safely tucked away in his inside pocket.

New York also played a dramatic part in the matter of pre-revolutionary land grants. All the Original Thirteen States had claims on vast stretches of land west of the Alleghenies. Connecticut, for instance, owned the northern half of what is now Ohio, Indiana, Illinois including Chicago; Virginia held the southern half of these same States, North Carolina, all of Kentucky (originally named Franklin, after the great Benjamin) as well. New York claimed most of the great Northwest territory stretching to North Dakota. Several of the States refused to come into the Union until their rights to this land were admitted. The whole scheme of a united country hung fire.

New York led the way to a solution of this problem by surrendering her claims and investing her title in the Federal Government, thus giving proof of the growth of the national spirit among her people. Congress used this surrender as an argument by which to move the other States to similar action. In the same National spirit, she gave up the capital in order to get the necessary two votes to pass the great financial measure of Hamilton's which placed the Nation's credit above question and forever ended all talk of repudiation.

Strange as it may seem, the average person takes it for granted that our Nation came into existence completely equipped and fully prepared to assume the enormous responsibilities that were to be hers. As a matter of fact, the birth of our country was attended with the same labor

pains that accompany such an event on every occasion. And
the waiting time was the hardest time of all. Nearly seven
years elapsed between signing the Peace Treaty and the
installation of Washington as President. Actual hostilities
ceased in 1781, but two years were spent arranging the exact terms. France had to be considered, also Spain which
had joined forces against England. France proposed that
England give up all her Indian Empire save Bengal. Spain
stubbornly insisted upon the cession to her of Gibraltar—
England's Key to the Mediterranean. These were preposterous terms. America finally decided to wait no longer for
the satisfaction of her allies and signed the preliminaries
of a peace in which Britain reserved for herself only
Canada and the Island of Newfoundland. Spain obtained
Florida and Minorca. England derived much pleasure from
the fact that France gained absolutely nothing, while she
had won ground in India and her West Indian islands were
intact.

England, however, thought less of what she had retained than of what she had lost. Her rich American Colonies were irrevocably lost and it is no wonder that in the
first shock of such a loss England looked upon herself as
on the verge of ruin or that Europe thought her position
as a world power was at an end. How utterly groundless
such a conclusion was the coming years were to show.

The treaty definitely signed, New York at once becomes
the potential capital of the New World. It was officially so
selected a few years later. Delegates from all the States met
within her hospitable borders to frame a Constitution and
create the machinery for a new government. Her streets
were thronged with all the legendary figures in the great
drama of the Revolution, and for three years our City Hall
in Wall Street was the meeting place of the Provincial
Congress called to weigh the mighty problems of state-
craft with which the new-born Republic was faced. Men,

whom we now look upon as almost supernatural beings, walked our streets, lived in our homes, exchanged greetings with passers-by, wholly unconscious of the high place in history which posterity would award to them.

Aside from the outstanding figures of Washington and his Generals, all the great actors in the recently concluded drama were in New York, even the men who had won the great battles at Louisburg, Bunker Hill, Lexington, Saratoga, Trenton, Yorktown.

Other famous men were: Captain Horatio Nelson of the *Albemarle,* afterward the hero of Trafalgar, carrying Royalists from Canada for deportation; the great Dr. Franklin; the two Adamses, John and Samuel; Jefferson, who wrote the Declaration of Independence; Tom Paine, whose pamphlet *Common Sense* first started the Colonies on the path of complete independence; Monroe, who was to give us the Monroe Doctrine; James Madison, who was to suggest the structure of government as afterwards adopted; Pickering, "Millions for defense, not a cent for tribute"; Patrick Henry, Aaron Burr, grandson of Jonathan Edwards and hero of Quebec; the Roosevelts, whose descendants were to furnish us in later years with two Presidents; Chancellor Livingston, who was soon to help Fulton produce the first steamboat; Elbridge Gerry, who was largely instrumental in having New York selected as the capital; John Jay, fresh from London, who was presented with the freedom of the city; Earl Percy, Duke of Northumberland, and his brother, James Smithson, who founded the Smithsonian Institute in Washington.

The first minister plenipotentiary from a foreign power had arrived—Don Diego Gardoqui of Spain; the consul general from Great Britain, Sir John Temple; John Rutledge, ancestor of Lincoln's Anne Rutledge; George Clinton, first Governor of New York State; Gouverneur Morris; Robert Morris, financier of the Revolution who was afterwards to spend fourteen years in jail; Richard Henry Lee, who led Virginia into the Union and whose grandson Robert E. Lee led it out; Charles Thompson, a somewhat unknown personage yet who preserved for us with his own hands and with incredible labor, the journals of Congress, through this stormy period and who was afterwards delegated by Congress to proceed on horseback to Mt. Vernon and notify General Washington of his election as first President.

Rufus King, who was afterwards to be stoned by an indignant mob after his return from a diplomatic trip to London; Samuel Bard of Kings College and creator of New York's first great public benefice, the Society of the New York Hospital; General Philip Schuyler; William Alexander Duer, president of Columbia College; Cæsar Rodney, who first suggested the Declaration; John Alsop; Theodore Sedgwick; David Ramsey, the South Carolina historian; Von Berckel, the Dutch Minister to the United States and the second of the diplomatic corps; numerous Livingstons besides the Chancellor; James Duane, first Mayor of New York; James Kent, afterwards Chancellor and for whom Kent Hall in Columbia is named; Morgan Lewis; the Van Courtlandts; Verplanks; De Peysters and one or two of the De Lanceys, cousins of General Schuyler; the Waltons whose luxurious house in Pearl Street was cited as proof of the ability of Americans to pay any tax the British Government saw fit to impose; the Beekmans to whose home in Fifty-second Street was taken captive that fine young soldier Nathan Hale, who was to die the cruel death of a spy; Melancthon Smith, leader of the bar in New York; Samuel Jones, father of the bar; John Sloss Hobart, one of the three Justices of the Supreme Court; Rutgers; Provosts; Murrays; Bayards; Ludlows; Montgomerys; John Morin Scott; even Admiral Paul Jones.

Before proceeding, it may be well to digress for a mo-

Engagement between "Phoenix and Rose" opposite about Fort Washington. 1776.

ment and look at Admiral Jones, unquestionably the most romantic and spectacular figure our Navy has ever produced. That he was allowed to shift for himself after the war, and finally to be buried in a pauper's grave in a foreign country is a blot on our history. The remains, now in Annapolis and heaped with all the honors that should have been his while living, lay neglected for over a hundred years in an obscure cemetery of a great city. Gen. Horace Porter, flushed with his success in raising money for Grant's Tomb on Riverside Drive—a project which had languished for many years and threatened to collapse from inanition—sought new fields of conquest and seized upon the neglected remains of Jones as a promising vehicle. He promptly found (?) the body in St. Louis Cemetery in Paris, and had it brought to the United States.

His real name was Paul. He added Jones while serving as a pants' presser to a tailor in Frederickstown, where lived Washington's mother and sisters. He naturally heard and saw much of the pending conflict, and undoubtedly seized upon the visits of Washington and his friends to make an early application to join the sea-going forces which he foresaw would be needed in the coming fracas. He had evidently come to this country to avoid the consequences of some escapade at home. However that may be, the tailor's pants' presser was presently the first Admiral in the new United States Navy.

Off the coast of France, in the *Bonhomme Richard*—an old rat-bitten relic that could hardly keep afloat, he boldly attacked the *Serapis* and her companions. Most of her guns could not be fired because the recoil would have sent them crashing through her decrepit decks. As a matter of fact, she sank just as the *Serapis* struck her colors. A moment more and the *Serapis* would have been the victor.

Jones sailed away in the *Serapis*. It was during this fight

that Jones accused Landis of cowardice—claiming that he
kept his ship out of the danger zone and accidentally or
otherwise sent a broadside through the *Bonhomme Richard*. This was the cause of the quarrel between the two
men when Jones met his erstwhile captain of the *Alliance*
on Wall Street. There was bad blood between the two men
due to the charge of cowardice made by Jones against
Landis; so he printed the following card in the paper a
day or two after this casual meeting:

To the P U B L I C.

HAVING yesterday, late in the afternoon, received information of a report circulating here,
that Peter Landais—(who was an officer in the squa-
dron I commanded in Europe in the late war, and
was in America, broke, and rendered incapable of
public service, by a Court Martial—for matters of a
date subsequent to, and unconnected with, the
charges I made against him in Europe, which are
of a nature to call his life in question, and of which
the most material proofs have never been published,
but are lodged in the office of Foreign Affairs—
did personally insult me in this city, on Friday last,
by spitting in my face)—I take this method to de-
clare, that the said report is an absolute falshood—
it being impossible that such an insult should have
been offered to me, with impunity, under any circumstances whatever.

                      PAUL JONES.

Monday, October 29th 1787.

The gallant Admiral was mistaken in a claim he oft repeated: that the Stars and Stripes were first saluted on his
ship *The Ranger* by the French at Quiberon Bay, February 14, 1778, by Admiral La Motte, representing his Government. As a matter of fact, the first salute was fired by a
Dutch fort on an island in the West Indies November 16,
1776, which was the flag's initial welcome on the high seas.
Incidentally, the liberty-loving Dutch Governor almost cost
Holland a war with England by this act. Yet the records
nowhere relate that the Governor was ever court-martialed
or even reprimanded.

It may not be without interest to note here that the
American flag in its present design was the conception of

a New York man—Capt. S. C. Reid, who then lived in Cherry Street. It was the same Captain Reid who fought the battle of Fayal.

After Congress had approved the new design, Captain Reid generously provided a complete flag which was flung to the breeze from the Capitol at 2 P.M., April 13, 1818, though the law named July 4 as the day of the official change. The Hon. Peter H. Wendover, another New York man, took charge of the business while the change in design was being debated in Congress, and carried the matter through.

Strange to relate, all American flags, up to February 24, 1866, were manufactured from English bunting. Not till old Ben Butler gave us one made by his new bunting mills in Lowell, Mass., was "Old Glory" made of domestic material.

The Stars and Stripes were first displayed in the Far East by a New York ship—the *Empress,* February 22—Washington's Birthday—1784. The Chinese called her the *Kaw-kee-cheum* or flower-flagship. It flew from the masthead of the first American steamer to sail around the Cape of Good Hope—the *Midas,* from New York, November 4, 1844, and on the first American propeller packetship to England, the *Massachusetts,* Captain A. H. White, September 17, 1845. It was also carried farthest south by the New York pilotboat, *Flying Fish,* lat. 70, 14., long. 100 W.

It was first unfurled at Fort Stanwix, better known as Fort Schuyler, by Colonel Peter Gansevoort. A woman's petticoat, a soldier's shirt and Gansevoort's military cloak all contributed to the making—the garrison at the time having no colors, and being under fire. That was a time of makeshifts and changes.

Many of the streets of New York changed their names after the Revolution, particularly those closely identified with Royalty, like King Street, now Liberty, and Queen

Street, now Pearl. It is, however, not without interest to
locate the exact places during and after the Revolution,
where famous people lived. The following list will no
doubt be read by New Yorkers with much satisfaction:

During the Revolution, Sir Henry Clinton occupied
No. 1 Broadway, and Sir William Howe No. 3. Toward the
close of the war, Sir Guy Carleton (Lord Dorchester) also
occupied No. 1. General Robertson resided in Hanover
Square, Knyphausen, in Verplank's house in Wall Street
near William, where also Colonel Birch of the Dragoons
resided. Admiral Digby and Prince William Henry, when
he was here as a midshipman (afterwards King William
the Fourth of England), lived in the city mansion of Ger-
ardus Beekman, at the corner of Sloat Lane and Hanover
Square. Admiral Rodney at 256 Pearl Street and Lord
Cornwallis at No. 250. Carleton's country house was Burr's
old place—Richmond Hill (Varick and Charlton Streets).
Admiral Walton still lived in his old home 326 Pearl
Street. It stood there till late in the '90's. It is said to
have been the most luxurious home in all the Colonies,
and was cited as evidence of the wealth of the city, when
the Stamp Act duties were first proposed. The French
Church, built by the Huguenots (*Du Ste. Esprit*) at the
corner of Pine and Nassau Streets. The Middle Dutch at
Nassau, Liberty and Cedar Streets; the North Dutch, at
William and Fulton. St. George's Chapel at Beekman and
Cliff Streets. Washington Irving, whose people lived in
William Street near Frankfort Street, was christened here,
and Morgan the Magnificent was married here.

Cadwallader Colden is entitled to a much larger space
than is possible here. He was born in Scotland, educated
in the University of Edinburgh and came to the city in
1716. He rapidly became one of the outstanding figures of
the community. He was very prominent in the local Government and frequently acted as Governor and chief magis-

trate. His *History of the Five Nations* is the authority on that subject. He is also credited with the invention of stereotyping, and had much to do with the first attempt to introduce running water into the city. He died just as the Revolution broke out. His was a life of achievement and his record is one of which the city is justly proud.

After the Revolution, Washington's home, the Presidential Mansion, was at 3 Cherry Street, the site of which is now covered by a pier of the Brooklyn Bridge. John Hancock's home was at 5 Cherry Street; Mr. Charles Thompson's, secretary of Congress, at 28 King Street. John Adams boarded in a house on Greenwich Road. No number is given, as there were but few houses on that street which then faced the river; it wasn't even a street—merely a path which led to Greenwich Village. There were a dozen or more little villages on the island at that time just beyond the city. Oliver Ellsworth, first Chief Justice of the United States, lived at 193 Water Street.

Pearl Street no longer faced the river. Land had been added to the ancient shore front and as the lots were sold "under water," the street was naturally named Water. Robert Morris lived at 39 Great Dock Street—now part of Broad Street. When the water came up the canal on Broad Street, there was a dock at the foot where Bridge Street now is; hence these two names—Great Dock and Bridge Streets. Charles Carroll of Carrollton was at 52 Smith Street; Richard Henry Lee at Greenwich; Richard Izard at Broadway "opposite the French Ambassador's"; William Few, 90 William Street; Samuel A. Otis, 5 Wall Street; Fisher Ames, 15 Great Dock Street; Elbridge Gerry at the corner of Broadway and Thames Street; Roger Sherman, 59 Water Street; Jonathan Trumbull, the artist, 195 Water Street; Egbert Benson, King and Nassau Streets; Elias Boudinot, 12 Wall Street; George Clymer at Mr. Andersen's on Pearl Street; Thomas Hartley, 19 Maiden Lane;

John Jay, 8 Broadway; General Knox, 15 Smith Street; James Madison, 19 Maiden Lane; William Samuel Johnson at the College; Caleb Strong, 15 Great Dock Street; Alexander Hamilton, 26 Broadway. Thomas Jefferson had just left for Paris. He then resided at 57 Maiden Lane. James Monroe, author of the Monroe Doctrine, probably lived at the same address. Admiral John Paul Jones on Wall Street; Benjamin West, afterward the great painter and Washington's comrade-in-arms at Braddock's Defeat and who taught Robert Fulton and Gilbert Stuart and then moved to London, on Wall Street. Stuart painted a portrait of the ship's master to pay his passage back to New York from London, and began his famous portraits of Washington soon after his arrival. Seignior don Diego de Gardoqui, Spanish Ambassador, 3 Broadway; Le Comte de Mountsen, Minister from France; Richard Soderstrom, Swedish Minister; Chevalier D'Avistay Chateaufort, French Consul were all at the "Court end" of town in Lower Broadway, up to Trinity Church. That might be called the aristocratic section of fashionable society. Everybody who was anybody had a house on Broadway or in the streets just off it.

Altogether New York, even at this early period, was a city of tremendous interest not only to its own people but to the world at large. It began to exhibit the traits of a world metropolis on a small scale and enlarged that cosmopolitan atmosphere which marked it at the beginning and which is still its most distinguishing characteristic.

Washington and Hamilton were easily the most noted personages. When the tall, commanding figure of our First Citizen appeared, he was followed by a respectful crowd who tried to get as near him as politeness permitted. He was frequently seen coming down the steps of Federal Hall after he became President, with the diminutive Hamilton by his side. They made a curious pair. Sometimes Washington would dismiss his rather imposing carriage with four or six horses, shining with silver harness, and walk up to Broadway with his Secretary, stopping at Hamilton's house, where the Standard Oil Building now is, for a chat and a cup of tea. At other times, he would wander round the lower part of town and rarely failed to pause a moment at the Battery. The fascinating view of the harbor possessed a strong attraction for him and the sight of a departing square-rigged beauty was always compelling. The songs of the "chanty men" as they hoisted the sails could be heard far up Broadway, and there was always something romantic in these strange songs of the deep-sea sailor. Perhaps on these occasions his thoughts would go back to the night when he almost ran away to become a midshipmite on a British frigate.

The levees which, as head of the Government, he was obliged to hold at his house in Cherry Street, were undoubtedly a tremendous bore. He was never a social soul at best, and the ordeal of shaking hands with representatives of the sovereign people was a good deal of a trial. With old friends like Generals Knox and Lafayette, for whom he had a genuine affection, it was a different matter. To them and many others, who shared with him the dangers and discomforts of battle fronts, he was a different Washington from that which Gilbert Stuart always painted. His diary often refers to strolls in Greenwich Village and other parts of the old Ninth Ward.

The General must have had a warm spot in his heart for Old New York. It was here that the crowning achievement of his life took place, and it was here that he led his ragged but exulting army down its streets at what must have been the happiest moment of his life. No man ever received a more tumultuous and enthusiastic welcome than he did when he landed at Murrays Wharf to become

Reception in the Presidential Mansion, New York, 1789.

President, and no man ever received a more affectionate farewell than he did when he left Whitehall Ferry to resign his commission to Congress. Yes; the old town had a genuine love for the great Commander, and we have since erected many enduring memorials of his presence among us.

General Knox, perhaps his really closest personal friend, had a romantic claim to his great captain's affection, apart from all others. He was in love with the daughter of a red hot Tory to whom all sympathizers with the American cause were simply anathema. They were outside the pale of common decency. Knox couldn't give up his girl nor his principles either, so when the irate old gentleman ordered him out of the front door, he went around to the back and took the girl with him. Washington always liked that story. In that terrible winter at Valley Forge, the handsome young bride of General Knox was the "life of the camp," Tobias Lear, Washington's secretary, tells us, and her constant flow of fun and nonsense endeared her to every one.

Washington's love for Hamilton was of a deep and abiding nature. Ever since the day that General Greene brought them together, the two had been inseparable. Hamilton was barely nineteen—a mere boy—and Washington could have been his father. Something of a fatherly affection undoubtedly prevailed when Hamilton, in a burst of anger, suddenly resigned his commission in the army over a fancied slight. Washington acted precisely as any father would have done in the case of sudden rebellion on the part of a son. He took him sharply to task and put him in his place with no hurt to his feelings. "My compliments to Colonel Hamilton," he remarked quietly to the orderly who had brought him the resignation, "and say that he is ordered to report at headquarters today at five o'clock."

When the aide announced Hamilton's arrival, Washington signified his willingness to receive him. He held the letter in his hand as Hamilton saluted. He looked long at the missive, then at Hamilton. He slowly tore the letter up. Neither spoke a word. Finally—"You may return to your command; good evening, sir."

His friendship with Lafayette was another beautiful thing. The young marquis was barely twenty. At a dinner party in France, he had first learned of the desperate plight of the soldiers and, with no thought of consequences, immediately placed himself at the disposal of Washington. Many soldiers of fortune were eager to join the young army, provided high commissions and large salaries were guaranteed. Lafayette made no such demands. He was fortunately in affluent circumstances and asked for nothing but a chance to serve. It was not at all to be wondered at that the young nobleman and his unselfish attitude attracted the attention of Washington. They say that the American Revolution was fought by boys. In the case of Hamilton, Burr, Knox, Lafayette and many others, it was certainly true.

A great sorrow came to Washington through his love for Lafayette. Long after the Revolution was ended and Lafayette had returned to his native land, Washington was dumfounded to learn that his brilliant young officer had been consigned to an Austrian prison. There he languished for many years despite all the efforts—and they were unceasing—to effect his release. The Royal Courts of Europe were not enamored of the young Republic in America and turned a deaf ear to Washington's entreaties. Lafayette was still in prison when Washington passed away.

New York Society had been greatly decimated by the Revolution. As in all such contests, brother fought against brother, father against son, cousin against cousin. The Schuylers, Livingstons, De Lanceys and all the other old Dutch-English families had intermarried for many generations. Many espoused the cause of the Colonies, some the

Royalist. The losers suffered huge losses of property, besides the disruption of family affection. Tremendous efforts were made to soften the vengeance of the victorious toward their defeated enemies, but the passions stirred up by the sufferings of the war could not be pacified. Extenuating conditions received no consideration as in the case of James De Lancey, for example. He was on one of his accustomed visits to England at the time the war began, and refusing to take up arms against his native country, did not return to New York. His wife was a granddaughter of the celebrated Andrew Hamilton of Philadelphia who won the Zenger case involving the freedom of the Press which we have already noted. His sister, Ann, was the wife of Governor John Penn. She lived in the Penn country-seat on the banks of the Schuylkill, Philadelphia. By a curious twist of Fate, it was this site that was chosen for the Centennial Exhibition of 1876. The daughter of his brother, James, married Henry Walton Livingston of Livingston Manor. So the ramifications of the De Lancey family spread out in every direction.

A son of Oliver De Lancey, Stephen, became a Chief Justice of the Bahamas and Governor of Tobago. Oliver, another son, succeeded André as Adjutant General of the British Army. Another De Lancey, Sir William Howe Dè Lancey, K.C.B., only son of Stephen and grandson of Oliver, was killed at Waterloo. A daughter of Stephen's, Charlotte, married Field Marshal Sir David Dund, K.C.B. The oldest daughter of Stephen, Susan De Lancey, married Sir Hudson Lowe, Governor of St. Helena during the sojourn of Napoleon. Oliver's sister, Susanna, married Admiral Sir Peter Warren of Greenwich Village fame. Her daughters married respectively, Charles Fitzroy, Baron Southampton; Charlotte married Willoughby Bertie, fourth Earl of Abingdon. Susanna married William Skinner of New Jersey, whose only child, Susan Maria, married

Major General Henry, third Viscount Gage. Abingdon
Square, Fitzroy Street, in Greenwich Village are memoirs
of old Admiral Warren's residence here, as is also Warren
Street.

The De Lanceys were, therefore, naturally adherents of
the Crown. They had enjoyed many marks of preference
(the father of James being a Lieutenant Governor) and
were of enormous wealth. Their attachment to Royalty
was the more singular inasmuch as the family had no English blood, being a mixture of French and Dutch. However, despite their powerful affiliations, their estates were
confiscated under the law and the vast property now lying
in the most densely populated section of our city—Hester,
Division and De Lancey Streets coming most readily to
mind—and with a shore front extending more than a mile
along the East River, were sold for a mere song.

Such were the fortunes of war. In fact, the plight of the
Royalists was pitiful in the extreme. It is one of the most
painful pages in the history of New York. We had, perhaps, a larger proportion of these unfortunates than any
other section of the country. The citizens of New York
were much more closely affiliated with England, both socially and commercially, than any other city in the country. So the rather large contingent of Tories who lived
here was a perfectly natural result.

A great many families suffered the loss of all they had
and were obliged to start anew in such forlorn places as
the Bahamas, Bermudas, Newfoundland and Canada.

Lord Fairfax, Washington's great friend and benefactor,
had a grant covering over five million acres—a tract larger
than many of our States. Only part of it had been re-
claimed; but negotiations were on foot to have it cleared
and settled. Every inch of it was taken away without compensation.

On the other hand, had the war resulted disastrously

for the Colonies, Washington himself, one of the largest landowners in the country (the richest man in it when he died), would not only have lost his money and his land, but he might have been hanged as well.

Undoubtedly the Loyalists were an irritating factor during the progress of the war. When the jubilant crowd that accompanied Washington and his victorious troops to New York suddenly realized what the British occupancy of the city had really meant to its inhabitants, there was a good reason for their anger. A scene of desolation met their eyes. Churches and all public buildings had been used for stables and barracks. Homes were ruthlessly ruined, and long rows of blackened ruins stood in the principal streets. Those who returned to houses, which had been kept neatly and adorned with gardens, found them neglected and in ruins. Hundreds of beautiful shade trees had been cut down; fences and barns had been destroyed for fuel; it seemed as if the sacrilege had been as unnecessary as it was cruel. It was small wonder then that a feeling of rage made itself manifest. There was cause for that, and if this sudden anger had found expression in an outbreak of physical violence, it could have been understood. All this, no doubt, had much to do with the ultimate decision which robbed them of all they had. If the Tories had been victorious, there is no telling what would have happened to the Americans. The feeling between the two was certainly very bitter.

Vigorous efforts were made by influential men in both governments to obtain a more merciful disposition of these cases; but matters dragged along without any satisfactory solution of the perplexing problem. Sir Henry Clinton delayed his departure two years trying to help some of his unfortunate countrymen, but in vain. It was finally decided to confiscate all the property of the Loyalists, leaving it for them to obtain redress from their own governments.

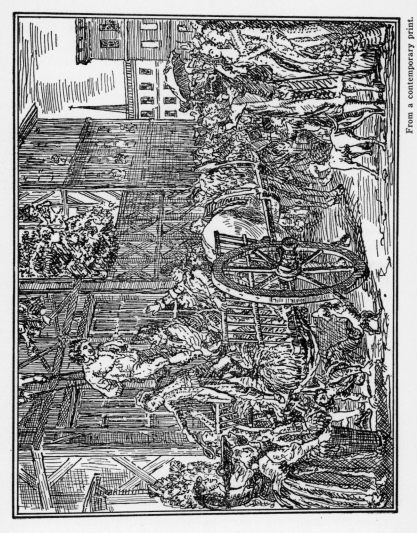

From a contemporary print.

Treating a Loyalist to a coat of Tar and Feathers, New York, 1773.

Accordingly, by Act of Attainder all the great estates like Morris's in the city and all the great manor houses in Westchester were sold under the hammer by the State.

During the exodus of the Loyalists, shocking acts of cruelty were perpetrated by the "Skinners" on these wretched people fleeing from their homes in the outlying districts, particularly in Westchester County. These were the rascals who terrorized the neutral territory between the British lines in New York and the American lines in Westchester. They robbed both sides impartially (and virtuously) in case of apprehension, in which event they were British or American, whichever served their purpose at the moment. These inhuman wretches fell upon the defenseless Tories in their region when the time came for the latter to be deported and inflicted barbarous atrocities on their helpless victims, cutting the tendons of their legs and arms, rendering them helpless for the rest of their lives. Other tortures worse if possible, were the fate of young women and girls. It is a hideous chapter and scarcely believable. It was an exhibition of pure wantonness unmatched by any other deviltry in the war. Even the savages were not more relentless and they had at least the excuse of being uncivilized.

Here is quite a different dramatic incident. New York missed by a hair's breadth the honor of providing a safe harbor for the most renowned soldier in Europe, the Little Corporal—Napoleon Bonaparte.

After his abdication, Stephen Jumel, a wealthy Frenchman who then resided in New York, having purchased the old home of Roger Morris, at one time Washington's Headquarters, invited him to make his home with him. Some years ago there could still be seen the trunk in which were many of the personal effects of Napoleon packed for the voyage. It was perhaps all for the best that Napoleon did not accept Jumel's offer of a home in New York. He said it would be suicidal, as a dozen men delegated by his French successors on the throne were ready to annihilate him on sight. Sixty had been sworn to murder him in Paris.

So instead of the Little Corporal coming to our city he went to St. Helena. After Napoleon died there, the miserable room in which he passed away, was used as a stable; and a pigsty blocked the entrance to the house. Even if assassins had killed Napoleon in New York, Jumel would assuredly have treated his memory with dignity and with profound veneration, slightly as he knew him.

Jumel went to France in his own ship, the *Eliza,* for the purpose of bringing Bonaparte to America. Although his offer was declined at the time, it resulted in a fine friendship between the two men; and a few months later, in June, 1815, Bonaparte changed his mind and returned to Rochefort with the design of embarking for the United States and accepting the hospitality of Jumel.

Unfortunately, the English had other ideas and presented Napoleon with a one-way ticket to St. Helena on the *Bellerophon.* Before leaving for his exile, Napoleon gave numerous presents to his friend, which are still preserved in the Roger Morris Mansion where there are also many pieces of furniture and paintings belonging to the Empress Josephine: a set of drawing-room furniture once the property of Charles X; an old chandelier, the property of Moreau; and relics which had belonged to various kings of France.

The African cypress trees, some of which are still standing in a semicircle around what remains of the old fish pond at the corner of 159th Street and St. Nicholas Avenue, are another relic of Napoleon's. They were presented to him by the Khedive of Egypt in the last days of 1814.

After the collapse of Napoleon's dynasty, these trees lay neglected on the ground in one of the gardens of the Tuileries, where they were secured by Jumel. The roots of each little tree were surrounded with native earth and encased in canvas bags. They were all recently sold.

Josephine Bonaparte stayed at the Jumel Mansion for a time as a guest in 1819. Although it is claimed that Madame Jumel entertained Louis Philippe, Citizen King of France, and the great Talleyrand, proof of the visit of these distinguished men is lacking. Louis Philippe was in America only from 1796 to 1800, and Talleyrand in 1794 to 1795. Both these periods antedated the Jumel occupation.

Louis Philippe was here in 1837, just before he left for France to head the movement that finally placed him on the throne. The money to finance this movement was largely advanced by Madame Jumel.

Aaron Burr was married to Madame Jumel in this house in 1833. She died in 1865 and is buried in Trinity Cemetery at 155th Street. The last distinguished guest at her festive board was the hero of that classic, "Marching Through Georgia."

That Nathan Hale volunteered as a spy from this house is likewise doubtful, although authorities agree that Hale, after accepting the duty, reported here in person to Washington and left Harlem Heights equipped with general orders from him.

The Robert Murray House and the Apthorp Mansion are both given as the meeting place of Colonel Knowlton's men to whom Washington gave the commission to procure some one as a spy. Hale who was present at the Apthorp house at once volunteered for the dangerous mission.

Undoubtedly, this old Jumel Mansion is the most noted house of the Revolutionary period still standing in New York. With the exception of Newburgh, Washington spent more time here than in any other Headquarters. His interest in this house was shown by his visit to the place in after years, as is recorded in his diary of July 10, 1790.

Having formed a party consisting of the Vice President, his lady, son, and Miss Smith, the Secretaries of State, Treasury, and War, and the ladies of the two latter, with all the gentlemen of my family, Mrs. Lear and the two children, we visited the old position of Fort Washington, and afterward dined on a dinner provided by a Mr. Mariner at the house, lately Colonel Roger Morris', but confiscated, and in the occupation of a common farmer.

The Vice-President was John Adams, and the Secretaries were Thomas Jefferson, Secretary of State, Alexander Hamilton, Secretary of the Treasury, and Henry Knox, Secretary of War.

In 1794, Colonel Roger Morris, to whom the British Government had paid rent for the house during British occupancy, died in England. John Jacob Astor then purchased the property.

Mrs. Morris died in London, July 18, 1825, at the advanced age of ninety-six years. She was Mary Phillipse of Phillipse Manor, Yonkers.

Fitz-Greene Halleck, the poet, visited this house in 1827, and here wrote his celebrated poem "Marco Bozzaris." Subsequently he became secretary to John Jacob Astor.

This historic old mansion is now the property of the City and in charge of the Daughters of the American Revolution as "Washington's Headquarters" and is open daily to the public.

CHAPTER XIV

Pageantry and Washington's Inauguration

IT SEEMED as if the troubles of the Colonies began only
when peace was signed, so widely divergent were the views
of the Federation concerning the precise nature of the next
step. We are so far removed from these troublous times
and so accustomed to our present form of government that
most of us imagine that we sprang completely formed
from the brow of Jove. We cannot visualize that there
were no less than thirteen independent States who thought
that the Federation which they had formed was merely a
temporary expedient demanded by the exigencies of war.
Now that they were victorious, each State considered itself
an independent nation with all the possibilities which that
implied. New York City, for example, was by far the
largest importer of foreign merchandise and collected all
the customs whether destined for other provinces or not.
She refused point-blank to surrender this privilege, and
would not permit the Continental Congress to encroach on
her individual rights in any way. She erected tariff barriers
against her neighbors, Connecticut, New Jersey and Long
Island. She collected impost on all exports of furs. For a
while she enjoyed the monopoly of bolting flour for all the
rest of the Provinces. In other words, the local government
exercised the powers of our present Federal Government
and of the States as well. The others all felt the same way
whenever any of their local possessions were threatened.
Nor could they be made to see that there was an absolute

necessity for a government supreme over all the individual States.

To produce a form of government based upon an entirely different set of laws; to create an instrument which would successfully meet all the needs of a newly formed nation, was a baffling task. There were no precedents to go by. Everything had to be formed out of airy nothing. But among such a resourceful body of men ideas and suggestions were not wanting. Amidst the welter of opinion, there was but one conclusion upon which all were agreed: that the Articles of Confederation which had governed the Colonies during the Revolution were unsuitable for further use. Some were strongly convinced that this old Federation agreement could be strengthened and amended so that it would answer. But the Convention called to consider this suggestion, at which Washington presided, finally decided that what was needed was a new structure entirely. So this Federal or New Jersey plan, as it was called, fell by the wayside.

James Madison of Virginia thereupon presented a document containing thirteen separate resolutions. The great point in Madison's suggestion was that in addition to the groundwork of a new Constitution designed to apply in a National and not a local sense, it was also to contain a clause creating Executive, Legislative and Judicial Departments, that would act directly on the people and be supreme within certain limits. This gave us a President, Vice-President, Supreme Court, Congress and Senate. Mr. Madison's plan appealed strongly to all the delegates, nearly every suggestion being accepted. A committee was accordingly appointed to investigate the plan more thoroughly, get all the additional information it could, and report to the Congress within a fortnight. Which they did. And their report recommended its adoption with a few slight changes, whereupon copies were made and sent to the several Legislatures in order to get the consensus of all the people. A further request was made that delegates be selected who were to be instructed to sign the Constitution on behalf of their several States, if approved.

Then the real trouble began. So careful were the framers to avoid any possible cause of contention, that the word "God" is not mentioned once. It was intentionally omitted, because it was decided that the new Republic was to be the home of all oppressed peoples, Christian or pagan; that in view of the mischief caused in other nations by union of church and state, it was decided not to put in a single thought that might possibly be construed into a recognition of any religion, creed or doctrine. Many attempts have since been made on the part of well-meaning citizens to repair what they think was merely an oversight, but without much success.

When the Constitution was finally engrossed and had been ratified by the necessary number of States, it was signed first by Washington and then by the different representatives from all the States. By this Constitution the name selected for the new nation was one suggested by Thomas Paine—The United States of America.

New York State had but one representative signature, "Hamilton." Rhode Island was the only State not represented in the Convention. On this account, Washington, when he took his famous trip through New England, made a wide detour in order to avoid entering Rhode Island. Not until measures were instituted, treating her as a foreign country, did the little State decide to be a good girl and come into the Union and play with the rest of her sisters.

Between Evacuation Day and the final adoption of the Constitution no less than four long weary years intervened. Years during which the patience, the logic and the resources of Alexander Hamilton were taxed to the utmost, creating among the indifferent States the idea of a Union,

Evacuation Day 1783. Departure of the British Fleet from the Battery.

one and inseparable, indivisible forever. The birth of a Nation was not without its pangs of travail. The oldest signer was Franklin, eighty-one, and the youngest, Nicholas Gilman, twenty-five years of age.

That Canada was not included in the new Union was due to the fact that the British Army held it in control. After its capture by the English from the French, popular legislation in all Canada was abolished and Royal Governors were appointed to make laws for the Province, which was thus deprived of any sort of representative government. This gave the British an extra firm hold on Canada and enabled them to use it to advantage against the Colonies during the Revolution. A copy of the Articles of Federation in French was presented to the people of Canada, inviting them to become part of the new nation. There being no official assembly or other public body to act upon it, the effort failed. British military officials just naturally threw the paper into the wastebasket. This separation of Canada from its national neighbors gave rise at one time to a rather serious situation.

At the time when there was a dispute regarding just where the boundary line on the northwestern section of the Louisiana Purchase should be run, it almost led to a war with Great Britain in 1849. There was a slogan which you may recall, about "54-50 or Fight." Well, it was settled at 49 and there was no fight. Great Britain proved her right to 49.

There is no fort along the whole length of this boundary line between the United States and Canada from the Atlantic to the Pacific. But from Lake Superior, West, there is a most interesting and unique set of markers, consisting of stone caissons, iron pillars, wooden pillars, earth mounds and timber posts. The stone caissons are seven and a half feet high by eight. The iron pillars are five feet high and eight feet square. Timber posts the same size. Each of them is marked "Convention of London, October 29, 1818." The British placed one every two miles and the United States one between each two British posts.

Where the line crosses lakes, huge caissons of stone have been sunk; in some places eighteen feet under water, projecting eight feet above. In forests, the line is marked by felling the timber a rod wide and clearing away the underbrush. This has been very carefully and thoughtfully done and makes a very excellent marker. The treaty also provided that no warships of either side should be allowed on the Great Lakes. For more than a hundred years we have dwelt in peace and harmony with our Lady of the Snows. There have been disputes, of course, and at times rather hard feelings. But somehow or other we have always been able to smooth out the difficulties, and it is now a settled policy on both sides that friendliness is better than enmity, and that we don't want war.

Few Americans, and hardly any Britishers, know that Canada was settled by the United Empire Loyalists—an organization that was formed in the Colonies during the Revolution, and whose members by thousands went to that part of our country which still remained loyal to the motherland at the close of the war.

So the young Government was faced with many embarrassing problems both foreign and domestic even before it had a chance to properly organize itself. Finally that point was reached and the tremendously important task of setting up the machinery for a government of the people, for the people and by the people began in earnest. It was a complicated problem with many divergent views. Five long and strenuous years were to pass ere the machinery was finally set up and in working order.

No building was available for even a semblance of a Capitol building. Our City Hall, which the Congress had already used, appealed to Alexander Hamilton as a fitting place to offer the delegates, who thought it might be the decisive factor in securing the capital for New York.

Elaborate alterations were necessary to fit the building for such an important purpose. Under Major L'Enfant, a French architect of note who was in New York at the time, a plan was submitted which was accepted. The building was therefore completely remodeled and handsomely furnished. The name was changed to Federal Hall. In its new façade, new crimson-covered balustrades and ornamented cupola, it made a striking appearance. Hamilton's prescience was justified. The beauty and commodiousness of the new structure, vastly superior to any other public building in America, took the fancy of the delegates and New York became the choice of the new nation for its capital city.

There was interminable delay in adopting the Constitution. New York was among the laggards. Session after session of its Assembly had met and postponed action. A Convention was finally called to consider the matter and settle it one way or another. It met, but seemed unable to reach a conclusion.

Meanwhile, the metropolis had grown restless while waiting for the decision, and on Monday, three days before the great event just recorded, proceeded to carry out the plan of an imposing celebration, matured by a committee, and arranged under the special supervision of Major L'Enfant. It was thought that an exhibition of the popular feeling would materially influence the obstinate body at Poughkeepsie, and bring matters to a crisis. This method of influencing public legislation seems to be peculiarly an American trait.

The morning was ushered in by a salute of thirteen guns from the Federal ship *Hamilton* moored off the Bowling Green. This vessel had been built for the occasion and presented by the ship carpenters. It was equipped as a frigate of thirty-two guns, twenty-seven feet keel and ten beam, with everything complete in proportion, both in hull and rigging, and was manned with upwards of thirty sailors, and a full complement of officers, under command of the veteran Commodore James Nicholson. It was drawn through the streets by ten beautiful horses.

The procession was formed upon a scale of vast magnitude. It was the first of the kind in New York—or in America, and nothing since has excelled it in magnificence of design or splendor of effect. A brief outline of its principal features will vividly illustrate the spirit of the age. It was marshaled in ten divisions, in honor of the ten States that had already acceded to the Constitution.

First came an escort of light-horse preceded by trumpeters and a body of artillery with a fieldpiece. Then foresters with axes, preceding and following Christopher Columbus, on horseback. Farmers came next, in farmers' costume, conducting a plow drawn by three yoke of oxen, followed by a number of gentlemen farmers carrying implements of husbandry, grinding and threshing grain. Next came the arms of the United States in sculpture, preceding the Society of the Cincinnati in full military uniform. Gardeners followed in green aprons, with the tools of their trade; then the tailors, the measurers of grain, then the bakers with ten apprentices, dressed in white with blue sashes, each carrying a large rose, decorated with ribbons. Then came ten journeymen in like costume followed by a large square platform mounted on wheels drawn by ten bay horses, bearing the "Federal Loaf," into which was baked a whole barrel of flour, and labeled with the names in full length of the ten States that had ratified the Constitution. Their banner represented the decline of trade under the old Confederation. The brewers paraded horses and drays with hogsheads ornamented with hopvines and barley. Upon the first, mounted on a tun of ale, was a beautiful boy of eight years, in close-fitting flesh-colored silk, representing Bacchus, with a silver goblet in his hand.

The second division was headed by the coopers; thirteen apprentices, each thirteen years of age, dressed in white shirts and trousers with green ribbons on their ankles, carrying keys under their left arms. They were followed by forty-two more in white leathern aprons, with green oak branches in their hats, and white oak branches in their right hands; upon a car drawn by four bay horses decorated with green ribbons and oak branches were coopers at work, upon an old cask, the staves of which all their skill could not keep together. In apparent despair at their repeated failures, they suddenly betook themselves to the construction of a new, fine, tight, iron-bound keg which bore the name "New Constitution." Butchers followed with a car drawn by four horses, each mounted by a boy dressed in white, and in the car was a stall neatly furnished, and butchers and boys busily at work; it also bore a fine bullock of a thousand pounds' weight, which was presented to the committee by the butchers and roasted on the ground during the afternoon. This car was followed by one hundred of the trade in clean white aprons. The tanners and curriers carried a picturesque emblem with the motto, "By union we rise to splendor." The skinners, leather-breeches-makers, and glovers were dressed in buckskin waistcoats, breeches, gloves and garters—with bucks' tails in their hats. The third division was happily and ingeniously conceived, and most effective in the novelty of its display; the cordwainers led, followed by twelve masters; then came the car of the Sons of St. Crispin, drawn by four milk-white horses with postillions in livery, upon which was a shop with ten men diligently at work.

The fourth division commenced with the carpenters, who numbered, altogether, upwards of two hundred; each carried a rule in his hand, and a scale of dividers hung

from his neck with a blue ribbon. The furriers attracted
great attention, their leader bearing a white bearskin; he
was followed by an Indian in native costume loaded with
furs; a procession of workmen, clad in fur-trimmed garments, a horse led by an Indian in a beaver blanket with
two bears sitting upon packs of furs upon his back, and an
Indian Chief dressed in a superb scarlet blanket, wearing
an elegant cap and plumes and smoking a tomahawk pipe.

The hatters wore blue cockades and blue sashes; the
peruke-makers and hairdressers displayed the arms of the
trade—a wig in quarters, with three razors for a crest. The
artificial florists carried a white flag ornamented with
flowers; the whitesmiths, an elegant pedestal of open scroll-
work supporting the arms of the trade—Vulcan's arm and
hand with hammer; the cutlers wore steel breastplates and
green silk aprons; the confectioners bore Bacchus's cup in
sugar, four and one-half feet in circumference, and an
enormous "Federal Cake." The stone masons displayed
the Temple of Fame supported by thirteen pillars, ten
finished and three unfinished.

The decorations of the societies were of the greatest
variety and significance, and the image of Hamilton was
carried aloft on banners in every part of the procession,
the Constitution in his right hand and the Confederation
in his left.

The upholsterers displayed upon a superbly carpeted
car, drawn by six horses, the Federal chair of State, above
which was a rich canopy nineteen feet high, overlaid with
deep blue satin, hung with festoons and fringes, gold and
glitter; and on the left was a figure in the character of
Justice, blindfolded and bearing the sword and balance.

The bricklayers with their motto, "In God is our trust";
the painters and glaziers, with various specimens of their
handicraft; the cabinetmakers, with a car drawn by four
beautiful horses, upon which a table and a cradle were

completed during the march; the chair makers, sixty or
more, with this motto upon their standard:

> The Federal States in union bound
> O'er all the world our chairs are found.

The ivory-turners and musical instrument makers, representing Apollo playing on a lyre, the lace and fringe
weavers, bearing orange colors elevated on a gilt standard,
paper-stainers, the civil engineers, carrying a design of a
dock for building and repairing men-of-war; the ship-
wrights, with Noah's Ark upon their banner; the black-
smiths and nailers, numbering one hundred and twenty,
who began and completed an anchor upon their stage
during the march; the ship-joiners; the boat-builders; the
block and pump makers, with a stage upon which they
made a complete pump on the route; the sail-makers, who,
in picturesque attire, with pine branches in their hats,
constructed a ship's foretopsail upon a car drawn by four
horses; and the riggers to the number of forty-one, bearing
a standard representing a ship in process of being rigged,
with the motto:

> Fit me well, and rig me neat,
> And join me to the Federal Fleet.

But by far the most imposing part of the gorgeous
pageant was the Federal ship with Hamilton's name em-
blazoned upon each side of it, heading the seventh division, its crew going through every nautical preparation
and movement for storms, calms, and squalls, as it moved
slowly through the streets. When abreast of Beaver Street,
the proper signal for a pilot brought a pilot-boat, eighteen
feet long, upon a wagon drawn by a pair of horses; when
opposite Bowling Green the President and members of
Congress were discovered standing upon the fort, and the

Arrival of Washington at New York, Murrays Wharf, foot of Wall Street, for Inauguration as our first President, 1789.

ship instantly brought to and fired a salute of thirteen guns, followed by three cheers. While abreast of Old Slip, the Spanish Government vessel saluted the *Hamilton* with thirteen guns, which was returned with as much promptness as though actually a ship of war upon the high seas. The Marine Society followed in the wake of the pilot-boat. The printers, bookbinders, and stationers came next. Upon a stage drawn by four horses was a printing press, with compositors and pressmen at work.

The eighth division consisted of three hundred cartmen in gay equipments; a horse doctor bearing a standard with a curious device; a band of mathematical instrument makers, with banner encircled by ten stars, exhibiting a Hadley's quadrant telescope, compass, and hourglass, with the motto, "Trade and Navigation"; a few carvers and engravers; coach and harness makers, preceded by a stage drawn by ten black horses, with men at work; coppersmiths, with a significant standard; tin-plate workers, exhibiting "The Federal Tin Warehouse," raised on ten pillars, with the motto:

When three more pillars rise,
Our Union will the world surprise;

pewterers; gold and silver smiths; potters; chocolate makers, with the device upon one side of their banner of a man with thirteen heads looking different ways, and upon the other ten men supporting "one presidential head"; tobacconists, numbering forty-five, with their arms encompassed by thirteen tobacco plants, and each carrying a hand of tobacco with ten leaves bound closely together; dyers dressed in various colors, their motto being "Give glory to God"; brush-makers with a beautiful banner, and carrying a large brush called a Turk's head, upon staves twelve feet long; tallow-chandlers, bearing a flag with thirteen stripes, beneath which was a picture of Washington on one side, and of Hamilton on the other—anticipating the administration of the first President of the new nation—and over the arms of the trade were thirteen candles, ten burning and three not lighted; and the saddlers, harness, and whip makers, followed by a richly caparisoned horse led by a groom with an elegant whip in his hand, and ten stable-boys dressed in character.

Every class of the population participated in this remarkable procession. In the ninth division marched the judges and lawyers in their robes, preceded by the sheriff, and coroner; John Lawrence, John Cozine, and Robert Troup bore the new Constitution elegantly engrossed on vellum, and ten students of law followed, bearing in order the ratifications of the ten States. The Philological Society, headed by its president, Josiah Ogden Hoffman, came next, the standard with its arms, borne by William Dunlap; Noah Webster, the great American lexicographer, was in the procession. The Regents of the University, and the president, professors, and students of Columbia College, all in their academic dresses, next appeared, their banner emblematical of science. Then the Chamber of Commerce, merchants and traders, John Broome, president of the Chamber, and William Maxwell, vice president of the Bank of New York, in a chariot, and William Laight on horseback, bearing a standard with thirteen stars about an oval field, and Mercury surrounded by emblems of commerce supporting the arms of the city. The tenth division embraced clergymen, physicians, scholars, gentlemen, and strangers, preceded by a blue flag with the motto, "United we stand, divided we fall." In the rear of the whole was a detachment of artillery.

Considering the small population of New York at the time, one must marvel at this truly magnificent pageant. Certainly no parade in modern times has ever approached it for color and interest. This parade, we are happy to say, had the desired effect. A day or two later the Legislature passed a resolution accepting the Constitution, thus making New York the eleventh State to sign. Connecticut followed the next year, leaving only one little lamb out of the fold: Rhode Island refused to sign until later. Prohibiting tariffs, vexatious restraints of trade and other annoyances were put into effect.

The adoption of the Constitution was largely a personal triumph for Alexander Hamilton, who labored day in and day out for its acceptance, and in the parade the Ship of State, named after him, was only a slight recognition of his patience and skill in the ultimate result.

Every year on the 17th of September a meeting, under the auspices of the Sons of the American Revolution, is held in front of Washington's statue on the steps of the Sub-Treasury, the site of old Federal Hall, to celebrate the adoption of the Constitution. It is rather a spiritless affair. Usually a fife and drum corps heads a few stragglers from Fraunces' Tavern to the Treasury. Some bigwig makes a speech which nobody can hear. Mystified bystanders wonder what it's all about.

"Constitution Day—they're celebrating the adoption of the Constitution of the U. S.," some one volunteers.

"Oh," says the anxious inquirer, and moves on.

The Constitution now finally adopted by all the States, steps were then taken with commendable promptness to select the executive officers to run it. A Senate and House of Representatives were chosen and these gentlemen now proceeded to elect a President and Vice President, the name receiving the largest number of votes to be President, the second highest to be Vice President. The balloting showed a unanimous vote for Washington; the next highest, John Adams. These gentlemen were immediately notified of their election and invited to repair at once to the

National Capital for their formal inauguration. There being no telegraph in these days, it was decided to dispatch the Secretary of the House, Mr. Thompson, on horseback to Mount Vernon. Another member performed a similar service for Mr. Adams.

Mr. Thompson reached the hospitable doors of Mount Vernon seven days after Washington's departure from New York. The announcement that his countrymen had again summoned him to lead their affairs at first filled him with dismay. He wrote to Knox that his "feelings were not unlike those of a culprit going to the place of execution"; and his diary records that his "mind is oppressed with more anxious and painful sensations than he had words to express."

Washington was then enjoying the languorous luxury of a Southern plantation. The previous eight years had been spent in such charming winter resorts as Valley Forge, White Plains, and crossing the Delaware on huge but unstable cakes of ice bearing aloft the stars and stripes which had not yet been invented. And the newspapers no longer teemed with such love taps as "Nero fiddled while Rome burned but Washington would have danced a jig." Even the benign and patriarchal Franklin could not resist the temptation of throwing a few bricks at him for accepting the presidency of the Cincinnati Society, whose uppishness riled the soul of the bourgeois philosopher. So the great commander hesitated. But only for a short time. The next day his mind was made up, and with Mr. Thompson was soon on his way to New York.

Whatever misgivings Washington may have felt were immediately dispelled when he commenced his journey. From far and near the people of the countryside gathered to see him and to cheer him on his way. His progress became a triumphal procession. At Gray's Ferry, over the Schuylkill, he was escorted through long avenues of laurels transplanted from the forests, and as he passed under the last of them, a youth concealed in the foliage dropped upon his head a beautiful civic crown of laurel, at which tumultuous shouts arose from the immense multitude. At Trenton a magnificent triumphal arch, supported by thirteen pillars, had been erected by the ladies; and as the hero passed under it on his white charger, thirteen lovely maidens, carrying baskets, scattered flowers plentifully before him, singing at the same time an ode composed for the occasion. At Elizabethtown Point he was received by a committee from Congress, of which Elias Boudinot was chairman, and by Chancellor Livingston, Secretary Jay, Secretary Knox, the Commissioners of the Treasury, the Mayor and Recorder of New York, and other dignitaries.

An elegant barge constructed for the purpose of conveying him to the city was in waiting, manned by thirteen masters of vessels in white uniforms, commanded by Commodore Nicholson, in which he embarked; and as it moved from the shore other barges fancifully decorated, fell into line. The glittering procession glided through the narrow strait between New Jersey and Staten Island, when, as if by magic, dozens of boats gay with flags and streamers dropped into its wake. All the vessels and sloops in the bay were clad in holiday attire, and each saluted Washington as he passed. The Spanish man-of-war, *Galveston,* displayed every flag and signal known among nations, as the presidential barge came abreast of her. Upon a sloop under full sail were some twenty-five gentlemen and ladies, singing an ode of welcome written for the occasion to the tune of "God Save the King." Another small vessel came up, distributing sheets of a second ode, which a dozen fine voices were engaged in singing. Bands of music on boats upon all sides, perpetual huzzas, and the roar of artillery filled the air, while over the whole exhilarating scene the sunshine fell from cloudless heavens.

The ferry stairs at Murrays Wharf at the foot of Wall Street where he landed were carpeted, and the rails hung with crimson. Governor Clinton received the President as he stepped upon the shore at which moment popular enthusiasm was at its climax. The streets were lined with inhabitants as thick as they could stand, and the wildest and most prolonged cheers rent the air. Military companies were in waiting to conduct Washington to the mansion prepared for his reception, but it was with difficulty that a passage could be pressed through the joyous throng. Colonel Morgan Lewis, aided by Majors Morton and Van Horne, led the way, and the various regiments were followed by the officers of the militia, two and two, the Committee of Congress, the President elect with Governor Clinton, the President's suite, the Mayor and Aldermen of the City of New York, the Clergy, the foreign ministers, and an immense concourse of citizens.

Every house on the route was decorated with flags and silken banners, garlands of flowers and evergreens. Every window, to the highest story, was filled with fair women and brave men. Every inanimate object seemed alive with the waving of handkerchiefs and hats. From the skies, apparently, fell flowers like snowflakes in a storm. And in every possible form of unique device and ingenious ornamentation the name of WASHINGTON was suspended from roof to roof, and upon fanciful arches constructed for the occasion. The multitude shouted until hoarse, and the bells and the guns caught up the echoes and with ceaseless clamor and deafening din proclaimed the universal gladness.

Upon reaching his destination, Washington was immediately waited upon and congratulated by the foreign ministers, statesmen, military celebrities, public bodies and private citizens of distinction. He then dined with Governor Clinton at the gubernatorial residence in Pearl Street.

In the evening the entire city was brilliantly illuminated.

No such beautiful marine pageant was ever before seen in the waters of our splendid harbor and none since has ever equaled it in splendor. Washington was greatly touched by the imposing spectacle and profoundly moved by the genuine affection with which the people greeted him. It was an occasion long to be remembered, and New York had reason to be proud of its efforts on this occasion, and justly so.

No sooner was the capital in smooth running order than the other States began to wish they had it. New York made valiant efforts to retain its possession. An offer was made to greatly improve its location. It was proposed to draw a line from river to river at the foot of Broadway and build on the lower end of the island, on the territory thus segregated, a series of buildings for governmental purposes that would put to shame all the palaces, châteaux and castles that existed in Europe. The possibilities of such a site were alluring. Nowhere else in the world would Parliamentary buildings enjoy such a magnificent marine setting as this would provide, and the spacious grounds which would surround it would insure delightful walks surrounded by beautiful trees and gardens. Additional land could be filled in as desired. Governors Island was to be included as the special residence of the President and his household. The proposal certainly had merits of no mean order. Had the plan been carried out, we would have had by this time a truly marvelous creation to greet the voyager on his approach to New York for the first time.

A specimen building was started on the site of the old Fort which had now outlived its usefulness and was condemned and removed. The new building was planned to house the President, Senate and Representatives in separate wings and also provide quarters for the State Legislature as well. Space was also provided for the accommoda-

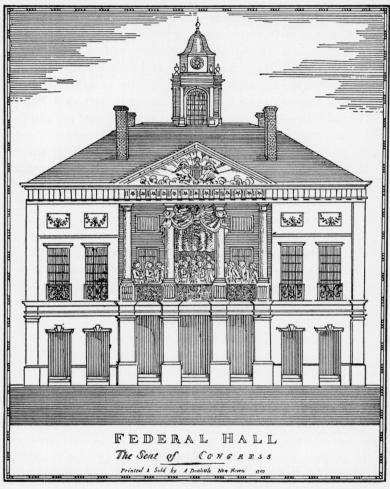

FEDERAL HALL
The Seat of CONGRESS
Printed & Sold by A. Doolittle New Heven 1790

*Washington being sworn in as President 1789. Present site of
Sub-Treasury Building.*

tion of visiting statesmen and distinguished guests. It was called Government House.

But it was not to be. That peculiarly American trait which blossoms forth when a new countyseat is to be selected, broke forth on this capital question in all its pristine glory. Hamilton, who had no local pride in his make-up, cared nothing about where the capital was located so long as he could muster votes enough to carry his great financial measure, which was to establish the credit of the country. What was it the old schoolbooks used to say? "He struck the rocks of National credit and a stream of gold rushed forth," or something like that. Anyway, he lacked two votes necessary to its passage. He agreed to let the capital go anywhere in return for these two votes. So the capital went first to Philadelphia. It was then to go to Boston or Baltimore and the other States in rotation. That plan, however, proved impractical. So Washington came to the relief of the perplexed statesmen by selling the swampy part of his farm on the Potomac for a new city in which none of the States would have any interest—a sort of no man's land. Virginia and Maryland agreed to give enough additional land to make a whole city—a hundred square miles. And in this way the District of Columbia came into being. It belongs to all the States, though it is not a State itself. It is ruled by the commission appointed by the President and Senate, who act only upon such powers as are conferred upon them by Congress; and its Chief Executive is the President of the United States. Its name is the feminine of Columbus in whose honor it was named. The district and the city have no voice in national elections. Its name was originally the Federal City. The river which laves its shore was at that time called the Tiber, and a little hamlet on its banks was called Rome. The name of the chief landowner on its banks was Pope.

Under this arrangement no one State had any advantage

over the other. Major L'Enfant, who had remodeled the old City Hall in Wall Street into a Capitol building, was employed to design a plan for the new city which was to be called "Washington," and to be made the capital of the United States for all time. Later engineers were Stephen L. Hallett and Dr. Wm. Thornton. Of course, it has been much enlarged and greatly improved, but the original building with its dome and cupola still remains.

The development of this National spirit was a plant of slow growth. The Colonies, during all their existence, had looked to England as the source of all government, and apart from her there was not for the moment, in a spiritual sense, a satisfactory substitute. The mutual coöperation, which had existed among the group during the war, appeared to have no further cause for existing and each Province now realized the necessity of looking after itself. The turmoil and confusion, which at once arose from this mistaken idea, was soon seen to be harmful and threatened serious consequences. Each State began to enforce trade restrictions on the other. New York placed a tariff on farm produce from Connecticut and the frugal nutmeggers promptly retaliated with similar measures of their own. The other Colonies followed similar policies and all with deplorable results.

An influence that could hardly have been foreseen and which did much to wipe out imaginary border lines, was the work of the itinerant preachers of the Methodist and Baptist Churches whose crusaders tramped the country from one end to the other. To them there was no East, no West, no North, no South. It was one country; they could see no difference between one section or another. They were in contact with the common people everywhere. They comforted their sick and buried their dead. They rejoiced with them in their happiness and mourned with them in their sorrows. The ties that bound them to their flock were unfettered. And the planter of Virginia was as much their friend as the merchant of New York or the manufacturer of New England.

No great change in social progress is accomplished in the twinkling of an eye. A great people suddenly bereft of their parental throne are bewildered and groping. The blessing of a new great political Union had not yet made itself manifest. A thousand little incidents must point the way. The National spirit enjoyed by these Knights Errant of the Church was insensibly diffused among all the people. It was a valuable contribution to the idea, slowly but unconsciously forming in men's minds, that salvation lay in Union; that a nation divided against itself cannot stand.

The brotherhood of man was nowhere more abundantly in evidence than among the people of the little congregations to which they preached. And in the establishment of the Sunday School another leveling force was unconsciously added to the feeble flame that was kindling a fire soon to blaze with the divine spirit of a new National life. And another change was helpful. The austere dogma of the Puritans had relaxed.Oftentimes in the past their sullen gloom, their irritating intolerance and their holier-than-thou attitude had been unbearable. Yet their ability to recognize a new order of things, to grow in grace and liberality as the progress of the times demanded, was a revelation as welcome as it was unexpected. Their prompt recognition of the changed order of things, their adoption and spread of the Sunday School and the Circuit Rider, rendered, in these perilous times, a service of incalculable value to the State.

So we must record that in the development of this new National spirit, religion played no insignificant part. It is a spiritual possession without which no state can survive. We were fortunate that it made itself manifest at this critical juncture in our country's affairs.

Perhaps one of the most emotional experiences one can have in London is to visit the little cemetery of Bunhill's Fields on the road to Finchley. In this little graveyard one gets a curious thrill to encounter just a few yards from the street, the vault containing all that is mortal of Robinson Crusoe. A few steps further on is the sarcophagus of John Bunyan, and adjoining, that of John B. Owens, his life-long friend who finally succeeded in securing the release of Bunyan from his prison. A daughter and son-in-law of Oliver Cromwell are also here; but the stone with the most moving appeal is thus inscribed: "In loving memory of Sarah Wesley, mother of Charles, John, Joseph and sixteen other children."

Opposite the old cemetery is the Wesley Memorial Chapel and all around it are further evidences of this great branch of the Christian religion which was so largely instrumental in breaking the thralldom and intolerance of the Puritans.

In our own city in John Street there still stands the re-built first Methodist Church in America and in which (Praise God) are many relics still preserved belonging to Charles Wesley (Glory Hallelujah). Charles Wesley first came to this country as a secretary to General Oglethorpe at the time of the founding of Georgia.

Diplomatic relations with foreign nations occupied the attention of Washington's Cabinet. John Adams was sent to England. He noted with pleasure that his hotel, the Adelphi, was bounded by John Street, Adam Street, and Robert Street. This section was named in honor of the famous architects and decorators, the Adam Brothers, who built the Terrace now facing the Embankment. A former envoy, Josiah Quincy, had been sent to London on a confidential mission in 1774 just when relations between the two countries were greatly strained. He returned, charged with a message considered too important to be committed to writing. He died on the return voyage lamenting that he could not have talked for an hour with Samuel Adams. It is interesting but useless to speculate how far the counsels that died with him might have affected the course of events.

John Jay, accompanied by Rufus King, came a few years later to negotiate a treaty with England. Both these gentlemen were greeted with a shower of stones upon their return as a reward for their labors. The treaty did not meet with popular approval.

Rufus King succeeded Adams. Appointed by Washington, he served through eight miserable years—years during which the complicated relations between Great Britain and the United States required great tact and watchfulness on the part of the American representative.

Rufus King lived at No. 71 Broadway, now the site of the offices of the U. S. Steel Corporation. One son, James Gore King, was President of Columbia College. He was for many years a leading figure in New York's social, political and financial life. Another son was a member of the great private banking house of Prince, Ward & King, the House of Morgan in that day. The redoubtable Sam Ward, epicure and *bon vivant,* was a member of this firm and father of Julia Ward Howe. His country home was in Jamaica.

Jefferson was sent to France, where his services were interrupted by his election to the Presidency.

These names mark our entry into world politics. They are all of men who resided in our city at the time of their selection to their foreign posts.

CHAPTER XV

Famous Institutions of Early New York

NEW YORK can boast of having had the first playhouse—the first theater in John Street. During the occupancy of the city by the British during the Revolution, this was the favorite resort of Society and officialdom. Officers of the crack regiments and distinguished visitors were constant patrons of this little theater.

The noble art of the drama was suffering at this time from the prejudice engendered by the devoted followers of Puritanism against all such heathenish practices as play-acting, so the plays were always announced as for this and that worthy charity.

The John Street Theater was probably good of its kind. It was, undoubtedly, as fine a playhouse as the one in Williamsburg which Washington attended so frequently; but there is no record of any outstanding performances such as has come down to us in *Audrey*. The tragedies of Shakespeare were frequently given, but more often his comedies; also Sheridan's work, then popular in London, with some revivals of the work of Beaumont and Fletcher, Ben Jonson, Nash, Peele, Kyd, Greene or Christopher Marlowe (still looked upon in Canterbury, his birthplace, as vastly superior to Shakespeare).

Whether it was the custom of the day or affectation, we cannot determine. But certainly the majority of the plays presented at the old John Street Theater were of the heavy pedantic Sixteenth Century school. We could not endure them today.

An incident which specially endears the old John Street Theater to the New Yorker is the fact that when Washington first visited the playhouse, his appearance was commemorated by a special march composed by the leader of the orchestra, Mr. Fyles. Singularly enough, it has endured to this day and grows more popular as time recedes. It is "Columbia the Gem of the Ocean." The entire audience arose as the President and First Lady entered, and remained standing till the music ceased and he was comfortably seated. One of Washington's outstanding traits was that he was passionately fond of the theater.

But the rapid growth of the city soon left the little theater in its particularly narrow street only a fragrant memory. Harvard College has a splendid collection of old programs which cover practically its whole career. They were presented by Everet Jansen Wendell, an old New Yorker, and should have been given to the New York Public Library.

The John Street Theater was succeeded by the Park Theater on Park Row, now the site of the huge Park Row building. The little street running alongside this great structure, named Theater Alley, is a survival of the time when this was New York's chief and only theater. For its time, it was a remarkable structure. It was a mammoth affair in comparison with the John Street building and, in fact, with any public building then standing in the country. And for such a one to be devoted to no utilitarian purpose, but simply to amuse, was, of course, the subject of much comment and many dubious shakings of the head. Yet the theater prospered and some really great actors appeared there. It was also the birthplace of Italian Opera in this country, and the name of Malabran is still one to conjure with in this connection. New York went wild

Fraunces' Tavern, corner Broad and Pearl Streets. Where Jefferson opened our first State Department and where Washington bade farewell to his officers. Built by Ettienne De Lancey, 1720. Now headquarters Sons of the Revolution.

about this famous singer, and her popularity for many years was unbounded. It was her success that made the Astor Place Opera House possible, and her influence can be traced all through the opera days of early New York. She was solely responsible for the great popularity of this school of opera for more than a half a century and for its high standing today, and brought to New York her first opportunity for contact with the great works of modern composers.

It produced also the first American play by an American

author, Miss Cora Mowatt's extraordinary comedy drama, *Fashion,* a huge success in its day. It was recently reproduced by the Provincetown Players, largely to give an illustration of the early New York stage. It possessed so many excellent theatrical qualities that it was still able to delight many audiences. It was promoted from Greenwich Village to Broadway for a brief appearance and was much enjoyed by the few. It was, of course, hopelessly outmoded; but in many details it showed a thorough understanding of the principles of dramatic composition and was not at all a reflection on the taste and culture of the New York theater of a century ago.

Edwin Forrest, William Macready, Thomas Cooke, Charlotte Cushman, Charles Dickens, and many other world-famous men and women appeared at the Park during its lifetime. It burned down one night in 1840 and was never rebuilt. The spread of the town northward had already made its location too far downtown. But the memory of this first American theater not only in New York but in the country, was kept green for many decades.

It was Sidney Smith who asked caustically in that most famous of all British literary publications, the *Edinburgh Review,* "Who reads an American Book, goes to see an American Play or listens to American Music?" Well, there was a play written by Royall Tyler of Vermont, *The Contrast,* in 1790, given successfully and attended by one of the most celebrated first-nighters of his day—George Washington. It was subsequently printed in Philadelphia, and Washington's autographed copy of it turned up at an auction sale in New York quite recently. We had a Public Library in New York in 1754, which exists to this day in the New York Society Library, and Carlyle's *Sartor Resartus* first appeared in Boston, no English publisher having the nerve to publish this masterpiece by a then unknown author.

In the eyes of our English cousin, we were but slightly removed from barbarism in matters intellectual and scholarly; yet even as he penned these lines, all England was praising the *Sketch Book* of Washington Irving; furthermore, the Indian tales of Fenimore Cooper delighted British youth of those days and their popularity endures to the present. Only two years ago in London (1932), the publishers eagerly displayed fresh editions of *The Last of the Mohicans, The Spy,* and other old-time favorites issued to commemorate the hundredth birthday of their initial appearance. Rodman Drake's *Culprit Fay,* though sadly neglected by the present moving picture generation, ornaments American literature. William Cullen Bryant's "Thanatopsis" still lives, and Fitz-Greene Halleck's "Marco Bozzaris" is still a famous favorite with the amateur elocutionist. His lament for his friend Drake,

> Green grows the grass above thee
> Friend of other days.

is a fragrant memory of John Jacob Astor's old clerk whose aid to Cosgrove in the suggestion of a great public library to Mr. Astor helped in the founding of that noble institution on Lafayette Place. It is now one of the foundations of our great library on Fifth Avenue and Forty-second Street.

Irving was born at 135 William Street. Fenimore Cooper at Burlington, New Jersey, and Bryant lived on Twenty-third Street. Rodman Drake's grave in the Bronx is visited yearly by school children who decorate it each Fourth of July with American flags in honor of his "Hurrah for the Red, White and Blue."

We may not claim New York as the birthplace of Edgar Allan Poe, but it was here that he wrote his poems, "The Raven," "Annabelle Lee," the story, "The Mystery of the

Rue Morgue," and other weird and awful tales. He lived
in a little cottage which was in the path of Broadway at
Eighty-sixth Street and was almost demolished. It was
miraculously preserved and can now be seen in Poe Park.

Charles F. Brown was the first American author to gain
any celebrity in this country as a novelist. But it was Washington Irving who first gained attention for American letters in Europe. In spite of the ill feeling engendered by the
war of 1812 which raged during his first visit to England,
he was warmly received by Sir Walter Scott, who became
greatly attached to the young American whom he was glad
to have at Abbotsford and to introduce to his friends.
The result of this visit, *Our Old Home,* was warmly received by the British public, and his residence in London
as Chargé d'Affaires under Louis McLane of Delaware,
who was our minister in London at the time (1828),
brought him a wide acquaintance among the literati of
England's capital.

In the year following, Irving became secretary to Martin
Van Buren who succeeded as Minister.

Van Buren was of Dutch extraction. He and Irving
had many happy memories of England as the result of a
tour in an open carriage when they visited Oxford, War-
wick, Kenilworth, Marlborough Hall, Newstead Abbey,
Hardwick Hall, and the Red Horse Inn at Stratford-on-
Avon where Irving wrote the *Sketch Book.* There they
found the same obliging little landlady that kept it at the
time of the visit recorded in the *Sketch Book.* She produced a poker on which she had caused to be engraved
"Geoffrey Crayon's Sceptre," and which is the principal
ornament in the little twelve-foot parlor which he occupied.

His whimsical *History of the City of New York* to this
day is anathema to the old Dutch families of New York
and to the later pseudo-Dutch—particularly the latter, but

still remains among the steady, if not the best sellers. In its facts it is singularly accurate and its gentle satire is nothing any one should take seriously. The fact remains, however, that it created quite an uproar at the time of its appearance, and Mr. Irving lost his popularity in some directions but gained it in another. It is from this work that the name Gotham is derived, and also Father Knickerbocker, as applied to New York.

After his travels abroad and his services to the Government as Minister to Spain, Irving returned to New York to be regarded for many years as her leading citizen. At the dinners given to many distinguished visitors, Irving was frequently master of ceremonies. He was one of the original Trustees of the Astor Library and later on, one of the Commissioners for the development of Central Park. He had a charming country home, "Sunnyside," on the banks of the Hudson in a little village named after him, and he was a vestryman in the local church of that village. He is buried in Sleepy Hollow Cemetery in Tarrytown between the graves of Andrew Carnegie and Samuel Gompers. A relative, Mr. Dupont Irving, now occupies "Sunnyside."

The memory of Washington Irving was recently honored by Spain when Granada renamed in his honor the chief road leading to the Alhambra, that gorgeous castle of the ancient Moorish kings. The largest Spanish-American fiesta ever held in Granada concluded with a play by Sanchez Reina, written from one of Irving's tales. *The Alhambra,* written more than a century ago, is still used as a guide to the famous palace.

Among the men he met in Europe and with whom he formed a lasting friendship, was another New Yorker, unknown for the moment, but soon to wake and find himself famous. This young man was madly infatuated with the widow of Shelley to whom he had been introduced by Irving. But Mary wanted the whimsical Irving and not his

talented friend. And the shattering of this romance gave
rise to the stories that he was a disappointed man, bereft
of fortune and doomed to a life of cruel penury. Disappointed he certainly was, but not a victim of poverty. In
the ancient city of Milan they produced his opera *La Scala*.
It lagged for the first two acts; but an aria in the third
brought the audience to its feet in a frenzy of enthusiasm
and applause. It had to be repeated again and again. In
fact, the desire to hear it has never ceased. It is sung somewhere, at some time, every hour of the day.

> 'Mid pleasures and palaces though we may roam
> Be it ever so humble there's no place like home.

John Howard Payne, Irving's friend, knew from personal experience "the birds singing gaily that came at his
call." Although born in New York, he was raised as a boy
in his grandfather's house in Easthampton, now a public
museum, where the "lowly thatched cottage" is reverently
visited by thousands of his admiring countrymen every
year. His grave in Tunis, where he died, giving his birthplace as Boston, is an error.

The Government owed Payne when he died a small balance on salary account. It sent his estate a check for the
amount a little over a hundred years later!

Not so many years ago—there are still many old New
Yorkers who can recall it—there stood on Broadway between Thomas and Worth Streets, a venerable gray building half hidden by tall elms and sycamores, which formed
a graceful approach to the stately pile. This was the first of
New York's great public philanthropies and came into being before the Revolution—the Society of New York Hospital. When Nobel discovered dynamite, he saw in it only
a great boon to humanity. Roads were to be built, the
earth leveled at will, and even the courses of rivers could

be changed. The world would be immensely benefited by
his humane invention. But sinister minds subverted Nobel's great idea and made of it also an engine of destruction. And an unfortunate occurrence known as the Doctors' Riot, while not quite so devastating in its results, yet
hampered the great work of this Hospital for many years
and deprived the sick poor of our city from enjoying its
beneficent services in the generous measure it was able
and willing to provide. Fear, unreasoning, terrifying fear,
was the unseen foe with which they had to combat, and
how that came about is the reason for this story.

In those days, it was quite legitimate to obtain a supply
of dissecting subjects from Potter's Field and other public
burying grounds. But the purveyors of cadavers were, perhaps, not always particular whence came their supply, and
doubtless operated occasionally in forbidden fields.

Be that as it may, the young students at work in the dissecting room were constantly annoyed by small boys climb-
ing up a ladder to see what was going on. One afternoon
when this nuisance had been particularly aggravating, one
of the students brandished an object in the face of a particularly annoying Peeping Tom, saying at the same time,
"This is your mother's arm; get off that ladder or I'll hit
you." The boy fled in terror and never stopped till he
reached home where he related the incident to his father,
a laborer.

Now, by a curious coincidence, it so happened that this
boy's mother *had* actually died only a few weeks before
and the lad's story caused the father to get some friends to
go with him to the cemetery. To the horror of everybody,
the grave was empty! Parts of the broken coffin told the
story only too plainly.

News of the outrage spread rapidly among the poorer
classes and a mob quickly formed. In a short time, the
hospital was surrounded, the doors broken down and a

howling, frenzied mob entered. The doctors, sensing the danger, sped across the fields and took refuge in the jail, then in City Hall Park, where they were with difficulty protected by the hastily summoned militia.

The mob swore vengeance on all the doctors in the city. They wrecked the interior of the hospital, destroying a valuable collection of anatomical specimens, instruments, etc. They then started for such homes of doctors as they could find. The house of Dr. Cochrane, a well-known physician, was ransacked from cellar to garret and completely demolished. Fortunately, they did not think to open the scuttle and look out upon the roof, or they would have discovered Dr. Hicks, of whom they were in special pursuit. He was hiding behind a chimney. In the height of their fury, they destroyed the home of Sir John Temple, mistaking "Sir John" for "surgeon." They almost leveled the building to the ground.

As night wore on, the mob grew smaller in numbers and the trouble seemed over. But in the morning the crowd was greater than ever, having been joined by sailors on shore leave from vessels in the harbor and the usual hard characters that infest the waterfront.

They attacked the jail, breaking the windows, tearing down the fences and seeking to drag out the luckless doctors to hang them. Innocent citizens suffered. John Jay was hit by a stone thrown through his carriage window. Governor Clinton called out the militia. Mayor Duane was loth to order the soldiers to fire. Hamilton, who had joined the officials, strove with soothing tongue to disperse the mob. Baron Steuben, in the goodness of his heart, was remonstrating with the Governor against attempting to quell the riot with firearms. He had just finished an impassioned plea to the rioters when a brickbat struck him in the head and he fell bleeding to the street, but not before he called loudly to the Governor, "Fire, Governor, Fire!"

Society of the New York Hospital. Their first building facing Broadway from Thomas to Worth Street and extending to the River.

The order was given and, at the first volley, five of the rioters fell dead and seven or eight were badly wounded. The mob fled in terror and the worst of the trouble was over. It took weeks, however, to bring things back to normal. Baron Steuben was carried to the home of Lady Kitty Duer where he received attention. Doctors were obliged to take every precaution not to show themselves too publicly or to enter suspected or forbidden precincts.

The saddest result of the affair was the deep-seated prejudice against hospitals engendered in the minds of the poor. It was most unfortunate and was doubtless responsible for much needless suffering. There are traces of this feeling on the East Side to this day, but happily it is only in isolated instances. From a practical standpoint, it has virtually died out and no longer exercises any influence. In its splendid service to the public for more than a hundred and fifty years, the Society of the New York Hospital has had a useful and distinguished career. Even its remote connection with the "Doctors' Riot" is known to but few, and has long ago been forgotten even by them, in the face of the magnificent services which this splendid institution has ever rendered to the poor people of our city and still continues to do.

The origin of this historic hospital goes back to the days when George III was our sovereign lord and King.

During the commencement exercises of Kings College, in old Trinity Church on the morning of May 16, 1769, Dr. Samuel Bard, Professor of Medicine in the College, had the pleasure of awarding the first diplomas ever bestowed upon students in this department of learning. The number was small—only two contestants being thus honored—yet it was the beginning of the good doctor's great ambition to see this science become one of the leading features of his beloved college.

Taking advantage of the opportunity, Dr. Bard, "with

great Pathos and Strength of Argument," the old record tells us, "dwelt upon the great necessity of establishing in this city, a regular hospital for the reception of the poor sick." In a city containing upwards of twenty thousand persons, there was not a single place where this much needed service was provided. The appeal met with immediate response, Sir Henry More, Governor of the Province, then and there heading a subscription list for the proposed project. Other subscribers promptly added their names, and Drs. Peter Middletown, John Jones and Samuel Bard were appointed a committee to draw up a suitable charter for the new philanthropy.

A few months later, the Earl of Dunmore, who had succeeded Sir Henry More as Governor, received from His Most Gracious Majesty King George III, a royal document incorporating certain persons, including John Watts, John Leake (who afterwards founded the Leake-Watts Hospital), Owen De Lancey, Isaac Roosevelt, Robert R. Livingston, Leonard Lispenard, William Bayard, James Duane, Archibald Kennedy, Charles Ward Apthorp, Roger Morris, and all the other social-registerites of the day, under the title of "The Society of the Hospital in the City of New York in America," and the new organization was an accomplished fact. A silver seal with the legend of the Good Samaritan accompanied the charter, and the original die is still used by the Society.

The old and somewhat cumbersome name was retained by the corporation for many years after the Revolution, but in 1810 it was shortened to the "Society of the New York Hospital" which is the name by which it has since been known. The celebrated Dr. David Hosack, who afterwards became Professor of Botany in Columbia (late Kings) College, was the first visiting physician of the Medical Directors. It was he who afterwards founded the Elgin Botanical Gardens further to extend the studies of his department in the College. This garden, soon exceeding the good doctor's modest income, was subsequently procured for the College by a joint purchase by the City of New York and Columbia. It covered about twenty acres on Fifth Avenue to Sixth. Part of this land on Madison Avenue was selected by the College as its first uptown location when it moved from its first home on land given it by Trinity Church on Murray Street. This property, now known as Columbia Leaseholds, provides a considerable part of the University's royal income (variously estimated at between thirty and fifty millions), and enabled it to purchase from the Society of the New York Hospital, the eighty-seven acres in Bloomingdale on which stood the department of the Hospital devoted to the exclusive treatment of mental cases. It is this ground that is now covered by the buildings of Columbia University, Cathedral of St. John the Divine, the National Academy of Fine Arts, the Woman's Hospital, and Barnard College.

It would be nice to add a little sketch of Dorothy Dix who first instituted humane treatment of insane persons in old Bloomingdale. Before that, sufferers from mental upsets had a sorry time. Confinement in the few places then available for maladies of this sort, whether public or private, were worse than the disease itself. Cruelty and neglect was the fate of the unfortunate victims of this illness.

From York Lodge, in England, managed by some Quakers, Miss Dix got the idea of substituting kindness and patience in place of savagery. The methods introduced by her commended themselves to both doctor and layman, and the great work then begun at Bloomingdale has since spread all over the country.

The beautiful trees and foliage which adorned old Bloomingdale while in New York are a reminder of the tie between the Hospital and the College, as the plants, trees and flowers came from the Botanical Gardens. In White

Plains, to which the Hospital moved in the early '70's, this horticultural beauty has been maintained and expanded. There is no church or hospital that can match the gorgeous displays of flowers that are a feature of the Easter Sunday and Christmas celebrations in White Plains. And the rare trees and decorative plants that are everywhere in the grounds of the hospital cannot fail to have a beneficial effect on the patients. All New York is proud of its pre-Revolutionary Hospital.

CHAPTER XVI

George Washington Dies

SHORTLY after 11 P.M. on Saturday, December 14, 1799, the last year of the century, the last month of the year, the last day of the week and the last hour of the day, New York was greatly shocked by the news that Washington was no more. Signs of mourning instantly draped the city and flags were at half-mast. A feeling of personal loss was everywhere apparent.

Washington was tenderly attached to our old town—a feeling which was warmly reciprocated. Here the greatest moments of his life occurred. It was through her streets that he led his ragged but exulting army to witness the final departure of British troops from American soil, and it was here that he was made ruler over a new nation.

No doubt, sitting on his porch at Mount Vernon, that supreme moment in his life would often rise before him. He would recall mounting the little stairway to the balcony. He would not know that we have piously preserved the little iron rail on which his hand casually rested on the way up and that it now helps the sick and distressed as they seek shelter in Bellevue Hospital, and that the very stone on which he stood, now hangs on the wall of the Sub-Treasury, a loving memory and a sacred treasure. He would recall the Chancellor's solemn words, "Do you, George Washington, swear to be faithful to the Constitution, to protect and defend this Union against all evil?"

and his own voice saying, "I do," adding impulsively, "so help me God!"

And the tearful farewell at Fraunces' Tavern with his comrades in arms for eight long weary years, and his final departure from Whitehall Ferry when like Cincinnatus he returned to his plow. Yes; there were many memories that bound the heart of Washington to Old New York, and all glorious.

It was here that he had a providential escape from capture at the beginning of the war. Not realizing his proximity to danger, he, with some aides, had landed just below Fort Washington during the severe fighting on Harlem Heights. Fifteen minutes after his departure, the spot on which he stood was surrounded by a special detachment from the enemy. The story spread through the British Army that he had been caught, and an American soldier as tall as Washington was mistakenly paraded before the camp as leader of the enemy forces. As such, he was the victim of indignities and insults all the way on the march to the city with other prisoners. But Washington, having seen his pursuers approaching, leaped into a waiting rowboat and was safe from pursuit.

And it was here, when he came to be inaugurated, that he received the most enthusiastic and loving greeting from his countrymen ever vouchsafed any citizen before or since. The roadside all the way from Mt. Vernon to New York was lined with cheering crowds who bade him Godspeed as he passed by.

No nobler figure ever stood in the forefront of a nation's life. Washington was grave and courteous in address. His manners were simple and unpretending; his silence and the serene calmness of his temper spoke of perfect self-mastery; but there was little in his outer bearing to reveal the grandeur of soul which lifts his figure, with all the simple majesty of an ancient statue, out of the smaller passions, the meaner impulses of the world around him.

What recommended him for supreme command was the renown won in Braddock's campaign; his experience in border warfare with the French and Indians; and Franklin's letter to Samuel Adams:—"I have met a young Virginian colonel down here who would make an excellent Commander-in-chief. His name is George Washington."

It was only as the weary fight went on, that the Colonists learned, little by little, the greatness of their leader: his clear judgment, his heroic endurance, his silence under difficulties, his calmness in the hour of danger or defeat. The patience with which he waited, the quickness and hardness with which he struck; the lofty and serene sense of duty that never swerved from its task through resentment or jealousy; that never, through war or peace, felt the touch of a lower ambition; that knew no aim save that of guarding the freedom of his fellow-men and no personal longing save that of returning to his own fireside when their freedom was secured. It was almost unconsciously that men learned to cling to Washington with a trust and faith such as few other men have won. The country at large hardly realized his real greatness till death set its seal on him, and Richard Henry Lee, with tears streaming down his face, bade him a last tender farewell and passionately acclaimed him as "First in war, First in peace, First in the hearts of his countrymen!" And in that lofty sentiment his memory is forever immured.

During the obsequies, business was suspended everywhere. Church bells tolled mournfully. It had been arranged to bury him in a crypt in the new National Capitol building in the city named after him, part of which had been designed as an American Westminster and in which a vault had been reserved for him. At the last moment, however, it was discovered that Washington expressed in

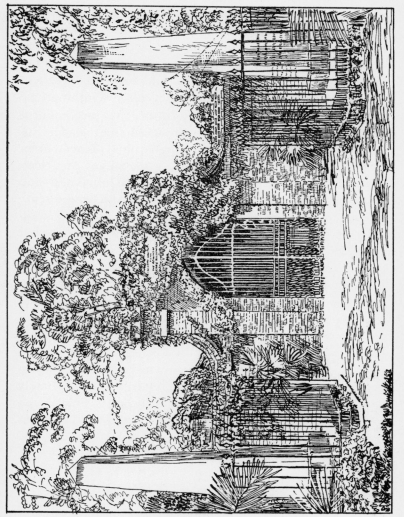

Gateway to Tomb of Washington, Mount Vernon.

his will a wish that he be buried in the garden of his old home at Mount Vernon in "what is commonly called the Vineyard Enclosure, on the ground which is marked out," so this final tribute of affection was reluctantly abandoned. The space thus reserved for him, however, can still be seen in the Capitol. It has never been used for any other purpose.

A stone is over the entrance to his vault, on which is carved—

> I AM THE RESURRECTION AND THE LIFE: HE THAT BELIEVETH IN ME, THOUGH HE WERE DEAD, YET SHALL HE LIVE.

On the gateway is this inscription:

> WITHIN THIS ENCLOSURE REST THE REMAINS OF GENERAL GEORGE WASHINGTON.

Providence left him childless, that his country might call him Father. But he gave us the Declaration of Independence, the Star-Spangled Banner, and the Constitution of the United States.

The news reached Sallie Fairfax at her home in England. She received it in silence.

But that night she retired to her own room early. She went to her desk and withdrew from a secret drawer three letters—two yellow with age. She sat by the fire and read them over. Two were from the camp in the Wilderness half a century before; the other, the one he sent her a few months before his death imploring her to return to Old Virginia and end her days in her girlhood home. She read the last one. It is dated "Mount Vernon, 1798."

Five and twenty years have nearly passed away since I have considered myself the permanent resident of this place or have

been in a situation to indulge myself in a familiar intercourse
with my friends otherwise.

During this period, many important events have occurred,
and such changes in men and things have taken place as the
compass of a letter would have given no idea of: none of which
events however, nor all of them put together, have been able
to eradicate from my mind the recollections of these moments,
the happiest in my life, which I have enjoyed in your company.

The fire glowed brightly. If she had consigned these
letters to the flames, the world would never have known
that she was Washington's only love; that in his thoughts
he had ever been to her as a faithful chivalrous knight of
the Middle Ages whom he so closely resembled.

But—Sallie was only a woman after all. She rose, walked
slowly to her secretary, unlocked the secret drawer and
placed them within. She resumed her seat by the fire. And
through her tears Sallie Fairfax smiled.

The letters came to light a hundred and twenty-five
years later, and were first published in the *New York
Herald* in August, 1875.

The tall obelisk erected to his memory in the city named
after him was the first public monument to be erected by
our Government.

A stone in this Monument, contributed by the Government of Switzerland bears this inscription:

THIS BLOCK IS FROM THE ORIGINAL CHAPEL BUILT
TO WM TELL IN 1338 ON LAKE LUCERNE, SWITZER-
LAND, AT THE SPOT WHERE HE ESCAPED FROM GESSLER

The Historical Society of Switzerland has since written
that no such persons as Tell and Gessler ever existed.

A very pretty custom was inaugurated by an American
Naval officer passing Mount Vernon shortly after Washington's death. The sailors manned the rails, the ship's bell

tolled, the flag was dipped, while every man stood at attention. President Franklin D. Roosevelt has the original copy of the letter written by the American Naval officer who first saluted Mount Vernon in this fashion. Since then, every American vessel on the river has followed the ceremony thus originated.

The origin of Washington's Birthday as a holiday was New York's idea. It came about as the result of a casual meeting of a few of his friends in New York. On February 22, 1783, a number of them met in Fraunces' Tavern to celebrate their great General's birthday. They agreed to assemble in future on that day, and to celebrate it with odes and toasts. Washington's ascendance shortly after to the Presidency gave a new significance to this friendly gathering, so that in time the idea became general, and finally grew into a "legal holiday," the people demanding it as a tribute to their departed leader. It is now thus gladly observed throughout the Union he created.

Washington declined a third term and his example has had an enduring effect. No man has ever yet been elected to the Presidency for a third term and probably never will be. And no man was ever unanimously elected to that high office except Washington.

With Washington's death we end the eighteenth century and with it, a distinct cycle in the history of New York. Henceforth, the city was to develop along lines almost wholly removed from the atmosphere in which the Nation was born.

CHAPTER XVII

A Tragedy in New York

JUST a few years after the death of the illustrious Washington, New York was called upon to mourn the death of a son whose every waking moment had shed luster on the city of his adoption. In the very zenith of his powers, at the most productive period in life, Alexander Hamilton was laid low by a bullet. The duel between Burr and Hamilton is now known to have been nothing but a brutal murder. Hamilton all along had decided to refrain from firing his pistol. Burr for weeks had practiced at a target in the garden of his home at Richmond Hill in Varick Street. At ten paces Hamilton had absolutely no chance for his life, and Burr knew it.

The most astonishing thing about the duel is the coldbloodedness shown by Burr after the encounter. Knowing Hamilton to be mortally wounded, Burr returned calmly to his residence. Reaching the shore at the bottom of his garden at Richmond Hill, he slowly entered the house and repaired to the dining-room. A nephew from Canada, who had unexpectedly arrived that morning, received an affectionate greeting from his uncle and was cordially bidden to breakfast.

Throughout the entire conversation during that morning repast, many subjects were briefly discussed, but not one word did Burr utter about the duel. Not until the young man had proceeded well into the city was there any suspicion in his mind concerning such a tragedy. As he neared the more densely populated business section, he noticed signs of increasing public excitement. Alighting from the Greenwich stagecoach which had brought him to the city, he crossed the street, joining a crowd that had gathered before a hastily contrived placard pasted on the window of a tavern. To his horror, he read that Alexander Hamilton had been fatally shot that morning in a duel with Aaron Burr. The young man could not believe his senses. "Impossible," he exclaimed, addressing no one in particular, so great was his excitement. "Why, I left him less than an hour ago. We breakfasted together and he said nothing about it." Resuming his journey still further

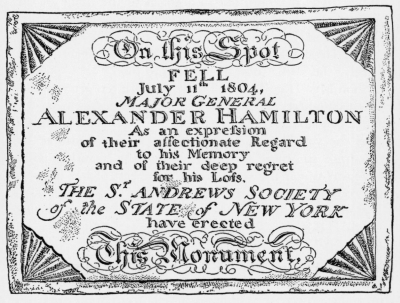

Tablet marking site Hamilton-Burr Duel in Weehawken.

The exact "spot" where the duel was fought was on a stretch of level ground on the shore about half a mile from Hoboken in the town of Weehawken. There was no way of scaling the Palisades where the marker now stands, and "the stone on which his head rested" pointed out to the visitor is, only another sentimental harmless myth. It was on this same stretch of ground that Hamilton's eldest son also met death in a duel a few years before.

downtown, he noticed the crowds growing larger and the public anger greatly intensified. At the Merchants Coffee House on Wall Street was posted the latest bulletin from the most celebrated physician in town, Dr. David Hosack. He read with sinking heart that Hamilton was rapidly failing; that he was surrounded by his family and that the last tearful farewells were being spoken.

Pendleton, who had borne Hamilton off the field, soon saw that nothing could be done to save him. Hurrying into a boat, he made desperate efforts to reach the New York shore where medical help could be obtained. With all possible dispatch he and his friend took the almost lifeless body of Hamilton in a coach to the home of the nearest refuge, which happened to be the house of James Bayard at 8 Jane Street. Dr. Hosack was the first to respond. He shook his head despairingly. "Better notify the family," he said, "there is no time to lose."

Soon Mrs. Hamilton and their six children arrived. His eldest daughter, Alicia, who had never recovered from the shock occasioned by the death of her brother in a similar duel the year before, was now completely prostrated by this fresh and more terrible disaster. The beautiful child gave way under the strain and for the rest of her life was the constant care of her mother.

Hamilton realized the nearness of death, embraced each of his children, and lapsed into a coma. The end soon followed.

Public indignation knew no bounds when the final news reached them. Although a man of strong convictions and ever the object of venomous attack from some quarter, foes for the time being became friends, and only his great public services, his patriotism, his services on the field of battle and his high character were remembered. Since the death of Washington, he had been the first citizen of the

Republic and the idol of New York. His death was a disaster of the first magnitude.

On the day of his funeral, business was everywhere suspended. Flags were at half-staff on every public building and mourning was displayed throughout the city. An immense concourse filled the interior of Old Trinity and every important organization, not only in the city but in the country, was represented. His remains were interred in the old graveyard. A simple monument now marks the spot close to the Cedar Street side. Mrs. Hamilton survived her husband for more than half a century. It seemed that with Hamilton's death a great gap had been left, which could not be filled. He was only forty-seven years of age, and had only begun to make provision for his growing family. His life hitherto had not been engaged in gainful

Richmond Hill. Residence of Aaron Burr at time of the duel with Hamilton. (On what is now Charlton St., between Varick and Macdougal Sts.)

pursuits, but his great reputation and his preëminent legal abilities bade fair to repair speedily his neglected fortunes. His sudden ending caused great suffering and deprivation to those whom he so greatly loved and this knowledge added unspeakable misery to his last moments.

Public abhorrence of the crime caused Burr to flee for his life. Although dueling had not yet become outlawed, the circumstances of this particular encounter were such as to secure the indictment of Burr for murder. Late that afternoon in a rowboat he made his way down the river and in the morning reached the home of a friend in Elizabeth. He was a ruined man and spent the remainder of a long life for the most part in dire poverty. His closing years, after many other vicissitudes, were spent with his friend Jacob Swartout in a modest dwelling on Staten Island.

As a lawyer Burr was reputed never to have lost a case. The choicest pickings of the New York Bar were divided between him and Hamilton. Both could have rounded out wonderfully useful careers but for Burr's tricky nature and abominable temper.

Thus ended one of the great dramas in the early history of Old New York.

CHAPTER XVIII

Streets and Schools

THE first comprehensive plan of streets and avenues in our city was the result of a Commission appointed in 1807, which finished the work five years later.

When the map was submitted, it was accompanied by a few observations dealing with the problems presented and solved in the course of their important undertaking. It reads in part:

> To some it may be a matter of surprise that the whole island has not been laid out as a city; to others it may be a subject of merriment that the Commissioners have provided space for a greater population than is collected at any spot on this side of China. They have in this respect been governed by the shape of the ground. It is not improbable that considerable numbers may be collected at Haerlem before the high hills to the Southward of it shall be built upon as a city; and it is improbable that (for centuries to come) the grounds north of Haerlem flat will be covered with houses . . .

In justifying their adoption of the checkerboard plan, instead of embellishing it with circles, ovals, stars, etc., the Commissioners said:

> They could not but bear in mind that a city is to be composed principally of the habitations of men and that straight sided and right angled houses are the most cheap to build and the most convenient to live in. The effect of these plain and simple reflections was decisive.

312

No better idea of the rapid and enormous growth of our city can be had than by reference to this plan and its quaint remarks about the huge population thus provided for "centuries in advance" of the probable requirement.

At the time this plan was filed, there was still good shooting in the lowlands between Sixteenth and Twenty-third Streets on the West Side—woodcocks, snipe and rabbits. Huge farms extended clear across the island from about the Bowery Village at Ninth Street. No streets had yet been formally laid out and one crossed cornfields, potato patches and other indications of bucolic ruralness. A beautiful stream—Minetta Water—made its way down Fifth Avenue from Twenty-third Street and turned off at Washington Square toward the river. It was renowned for its purity and clearness and many a pleasant stroll was had upon its leafy banks. The path along Twenty-second Street where the stream joined the Avenue was known as Lovers' Lane.

The city has been laid out very nearly in accordance with this original plan. The huge space reserved for Training Bands has however been greatly curtailed. Starting at Union Square, a huge block extending to the north side of Thirty-fourth Street was set aside as a Parade Ground for our citizen soldiers. That has now totally disappeared leaving only Madison and Union Squares to remind us of the noble space that was originally set aside for public use. It went to Sixth Avenue on the West and Third Avenue on the East.

There was in effect, at this time, a law requiring every citizen between the ages of sixteen to forty-five to report once a year for the "Train band." It was a popular holiday for many years and practically all of our citizens were soldiers for a day. They went through the Manual of Arms, marched and counter-marched.

It was an interesting sight. The citizen soldier dressed

as he liked. He might wear a Revolutionary uniform, War of 1812 uniform, etc. Gradually these genuine military clothes disappeared and all sorts of substitutes took their place. These rapidly became absurd and the mockery of the town. Excessive drinking marked the end of the demonstration and "Training Day" soon became a pest, and was, in consequence, discontinued.

With the exception of this huge space for training grounds, the building of the city has followed closely the plan of the Commissioners of 1809.

We have elsewhere in these pages made casual reference to Adam Roelantsen, the first schoolmaster in the City of New York, and we now take up the organization of our present magnificent public school system of which we may be justly proud.

If one should go in that section of the city made famous by the splendid work of Miss Lillian Wald, we would come upon Public School No. 1, at the corner of Henry Street and Oliver. On the site of this imposing plot, stood the first little schoolhouse in which the children of the city, who were without money, could enjoy the privileges of a good education. The free school system, which was organized to carry out this idea, derived its chief impetus from President William A. Macy, whose early days were spent as a cabin boy on board a Nantucket whaler. There is still in existence the log book kept by this little boy when he was less than sixteen years of age and a member of the crew that sailed around the world. The family today is well known in New York and perhaps its most recent distinguished member was V. Everitt Macy, whose great public service for Westchester County is much in evidence in its marvelous system of State roads and public parks. The William A. Macy, who had so much to do with this free school system, was a neighbor of Rowland H.

Wall Street, showing Trinity Church and Federal Hall, site of present Sub-Treasury Building, 1789.

Macy who gave to New York the now famous dry goods company of R. H. Macy & Co.

The discovery of oil in Pennsylvania brought a change in the business of the Nantucket Macys, who then came to New York to continue the whale oil business to which they added this new mineral oil found on dry land. It is perhaps unnecessary to add that in the due course of events the Macy business was absorbed by the Standard Oil Company with which the family has ever been closely identified.

W. Kingsland Macy, who is known as the leader of the Republican Party in the State, is a descendant of the Macy who helped organize the first Free School. In the New York Historical Society there is still preserved the original roll containing the names of the subscribers to this school fund which marked the beginning of free public education in the great city of New York.

It would be interesting to print this list in full if space permitted. It is, perhaps, not too much to say that few citizens have been able to realize such magnificent results from their public spirited work as have the signers of this first list.

Our splendid Public School System of today is the ultimate flowering of the work of this modest group who founded the first free school in our city.

CHAPTER XIX

America Right or Wrong

"OUR country, may she always be in the right; but our country, right or wrong." This very charming sentiment made its first appearance at a dinner held in the City Hotel given in honor of Stephen Decatur upon his return from his most successful attack on the pirates of the Barbary Coast. Our genial friend, Washington Irving, was toastmaster on this occasion, and in the assemblage was practically every man of distinction then present in New York.

Decatur was fresh from his brilliant exploit off Tripoli. Commodore Bainbridge, too eagerly pursuing an enemy ship, ran the *Philadelphia* on an uncharted reef and was obliged to strike his colors and surrender with 300 men. To the great disgust of the Americans, the Tripolitans managed later, to float the *Philadelphia* and tow her safely to anchor under the protection of their batteries, where she was a constant irritation to the Americans in the offing.

Decatur sailed to the stranded *Philadelphia* in a small ketch, boarded her and bound the crew. He then filled her with combustibles, set her on fire and made his escape through a shower of badly aimed shots from land batteries and ships in the harbor. It was a magnificent deed of daring and the whole country rang with his praise.

When he had called for volunteers, every man-jack aboard the ship stepped forward. The dinner was New York's tribute to his reckless courage.

It is, perhaps, not quite possible to realize adequately the importance of Commodore Decatur's work in freeing from American commerce the murderous and ruinous attacks made on American ships by these organized pirates of the Mediterranean. For years they had terrorized the governments of Europe, most of whom were in the habit of buying immunity by heavy tribute. Even under Washington the same policy was followed by the United States, and we were annually mulcted to the sum of a million or two to purchase freedom from molestation on the part of these voracious pirates.

Upon the accession of Jefferson, however, to the Presidency, with James Monroe as Secretary of State, a wholly different attitude was adopted. In the language of Charles C. Pinckney, Ambassador to France, word was sent to the pirates of the Barbary Coast that we now had "millions for defense but not one cent for tribute." Under Preble and later Decatur, a section of our young Navy was sent to patrol this part of the world's highway on the seas and many spirited conflicts ensued.

The Napoleonic Wars in Europe at this time were raging and England, which up to this time had been the great carrier of the world's commerce, was hard put to find men and ships to handle this important branch of her trade. The new Republic along the Atlantic seaboard of the Western World became the natural successor of this lucrative business.

The East River in New York became a hive of shipbuilding. All along the shore from Coenties Slip clear up to the Dry Dock Ward, the air was heavy with the scent of freshly cut pine, and the heavier odor of tar and pitch. Anvils rang out and the blows of many hammers made South Street one of the busiest and most picturesque sections of our city. The variegated garb of the seamen of all nations suggested the departed days of piracy, and the

number of privateers that left New York every week gave
one the impression that this ancient industry was having
a new lease of life. Almost every nation was at war with
either France or England and the peaceful merchant ships
of these two nations were fair game for almost any ad-
venturer. In addition to that, the preoccupation of their
fighting fleets deprived them of the customary protection
of these warships. The shipbuilders of New York were
quick to seize their opportunity.

Embargo Acts, Navigation laws and countless other
measures designed to interfere with the free movement of
trading vessels were constantly being enacted by Napoleon
who finally decreed that all commerce with England
should cease. But maritime laws in time of war amount to
nothing without the power to enforce them. England,
proud mistress of the seas, promptly retaliated by similar
inhibitions on French shipping. The situation lacked nothing to entice all and sundry who were willing to risk their
necks for the certainty of a huge monetary reward. And
New York never lacked for a large supply of just such
adventurers to whom blockade-running was second nature.

So seriously did the various orders in council, letters
of reprisal, etc., interfere with American commerce, that
Jefferson threatened to place an embargo on American
shipping and thus cut off an important source of food supply and other necessaries. This measure was not at all
popular with the country at large, especially in New England, which was reaping a rich harvest from the present
situation. Nevertheless, Jefferson could see no other way
out of the dilemma and an embargo was accordingly ordered.

It is said that this embargo laid the foundations for the
Astor fortune. According to the story, John Jacob the
first, picked up a Chinaman somewhere and dressed him
in all the gorgeous regalia of a mandarin of highest rank.

Thus equipped, Astor made representations to the Government that this mandarin was a guest of Astor's and that he was morally bound to return him to his own country in the grand manner. As China was a far-off country and in no wise affected by the war in Europe, Jefferson consented that the *Beaver* should be allowed to depart. Since no ship had left an American port in several months, it was morally certain that any cargo it would obtain would surely find a rich and immediate market.

So the *Beaver* sailed under this special order with no examination concerning its manifest. Its prompt return with an enormously valuable shipment of teas, spices, silks, etc., to a country that had received nothing of this kind for months, naturally produced a huge profit. It was generally conceded that Astor cleared over $400,000 on this venture alone, a perfectly amazing sum for those days and worth probably ten times that amount according to present-day values.

England, in the meantime, driven to desperation by her lack of seamen, suddenly decided to seize and search every American ship found on the high seas. If any of the crew were found to be British subjects, they were at once impressed into British service. Such an utter disregard of the rights of a neutral nation, to say nothing of its sheer illegality, naturally strained the relations of the two countries. No relief being offered, Jefferson finally declared a state of war between Great Britain and the United States.

This contest was marked by several unlooked-for surprises and the perpetration of some unusually exasperating military movements.

General Ross with a force of four thousand men captured Washington and burnt its public buildings to the ground. "Few more shameful acts," wrote the great English historian Green, "are recorded in our history and it

Broadway looking down from present Post Office, in City Hall Park, to the Battery, one hundred years ago. 1835.

was the more shameful in that it was done under strict
orders from the Government at home."

Dolly Madison fortunately had time to cut an oil painting of Washington by Stuart from its frame before the
pillage began. That portrait hangs in the Blue Room today. The fire was quenched and the British troops compelled to return to their ships before the building was
completely demolished.

While these curtain raisers were being enacted, New
York was feverishly engaged in preparing something in
the way of defense. All night long here, citizens worked on
entrenchments, barricades and fortifications against an attack from Canada in the rear. Facing the harbor, the
newly erected fort on Governors Island was strengthened
and additional ordnance installed. An entirely new fort
was erected on an island that then stood about two hundred yards from the mainland at the foot of Broadway.
It was named Fort Clinton in honor of New York's first
Governor. It subsequently achieved world-wide renown
as Castle Garden, through whose portals as poor emigrant
boys passed such great figures as Andrew Carnegie, Alexander T. Stewart, Jacob Schiff, Michael Pupin, and scores
of others equally famous. Jenny Lind gave her first con-
cert here under the management of the celebrated P. T.
Barnum. For years it was one of New York's most popular
amusement resorts. After almost a century of unexampled
usefulness, it is now the Aquarium and draws a larger
attendance of delighted spectators every year than ever
before in its history.

One other notable memory of this war remains prominent in New York—the grave of gallant Capt. Lawrence
of the *Chesapeake* in old Trinity Churchyard with its
famous legend, "Don't give up the ship."

Lawrence somewhat recklessly accepted a challenge from
the British ship *Shannon,* much superior in size and

weight of armament. Notwithstanding the courage and dauntlessness of Lawrence, this superiority of guns proved fatal to the *Chesapeake* and it was captured by the *Shannon*. The body of Lawrence was courteously surrendered by the commander of the *Shannon* and was buried with every honor which the young captain could have desired.

Not far from Southampton, where most of our liners dock in England, there is a little inn, the beams and rafters of which are said to have been taken from the *Chesapeake*.

For some reason not now understood, the war was tremendously unpopular in New England. Upon receipt of the news that hostilities had been declared, shipping in Boston lowered its flags to half-mast. Massachusetts and Connecticut both declined to furnish money or men, and cries of secession began to be heard. The old Bay State, in the terrible distress brought about by the blockade and the complete ruin of her commerce, even went so far as to appoint delegates to confer with delegates from other New England States "on the subject of their grievances and common concerns." Yet New York suffered in exactly the same way, but stood behind Jefferson.

At one time it looked as if Our Lady of the Snows would be annexed to the States. The American forces cleared Lake Ontario, captured Toronto, destroyed the British flotilla on Lake Erie and the force of nine thousand Peninsular veterans who accompanied it. A second force, under Gen. Packenham, attacked New Orleans but was defeated by Old Hickory, who killed half the invading army while losing only a handful of men himself. General Jackson's success was largely due to the Battle of Fayal fought by a New York man, General Reid. This was a remarkable conflict and has few parallels in the annals of the sea. Reid inflicted such damage on the British ships convoying troops to New Orleans that the fleet was detained several precious weeks, giving Jackson time to collect an army, hide it behind an improvised fortress of cotton bales, and conduct a fight without exposing a man. The British were mowed down like sheep. They lost 700 killed, 1400 wounded, and 500 prisoners, while the Americans had only 8 killed and 13 wounded—a most extraordinary result.

The Lafitte brothers, notorious pirates in the Gulf at that time, were offered prodigious sums to pilot the British ships up the devious and tortuous channel of the delta of the Mississippi, but resolutely declined. It was the same Lafitte brothers with whom our amiable friend, Capt. Randall, of Sailors' Snug Harbor, associated. In recognition of their invaluable services on this occasion, the Government issued to them a pardon for all past offenses.

The war had a curious and sudden ending. All through its course England had been handicapped by her struggle with Napoleon. That was now over. Waterloo had been fought and Napoleon was a prisoner. England was now free to turn her entire strength against an enemy whom she no longer despised, and a long and bloody struggle loomed ahead. Strange to relate, the men who were of the greatest and most unexpected assistance in helping our Peace Commissioners to effect a satisfactory basis on which to negotiate a treaty were none other than Lord Cornwallis the Iron Duke himself, Wellington, aided by Czar Alexander of Russia.

Neither side yielded anything and the impressment of seamen which caused the outbreak, is not even mentioned in the Treaty. England, however, was decent enough never to offend in that direction again. There has been no armed conflict between the two nations since; common sense and mutual forbearance have enabled us to settle all disputes amicably. Though there have been some that have strained relations almost to the breaking point, yet they have been smoothed out.

In New York, the announcement of peace was received everywhere with shouts of joy and the utmost thankfulness. The city had been a terrible sufferer. The war had come just at a time when the town was preparing for the immense foreign commerce that was hers to take, a goodly share of which had already gone to Boston. So with the end of this war, shipyards began to hum, industry and trade sprang into vigorous action and the population of the city increased by leaps and bounds.

CHAPTER XX

Sailing, Packet, and Clipper Ships

WHEN the chimes of old Trinity greeted the advent of the New Year in 1800, it also joyously recorded the fact that New York had passed all other cities in point of growth and population. Boston had long ago been distanced, leaving the City of Brotherly Love as the sole rival to New York; and Mr. Penn was now obliged to doff his hat in token of surrender. New York was, as she has ever since remained, the most populous city in the country.

The growth of her ocean-carrying trade had vastly increased. The supremacy of New England in the matter of shipbuilding was now to be challenged; and Donald McKay, the most renowned of her builders, creator of the *"Flying Cloud"* and the *Sovereign of the Seas,* was soon to open here.

All along South Street, shipyards sprang up; the odor of piny wood, fresh shavings, Carolina pitch and fragrant spices made the old street one of the most unique in town. These yards stretched all the way to the Twelfth Ward, known then as the Dry Dock. Some of the world's greatest shipbuilders were located here—William Webb, Jacob Westervelt, Christian Bergh, father of Henry Bergh, the horse's friend; Smith & Dimon; Bell & Brown who built the North River steamboats—*Rochester, James Kent,* and *Oregon;* George Steers, destined to become famous as the designer of the yacht *America*, built for John R. Stevens of Castle Point, Hoboken; also Henry Eckford & Co., who had the credit of building what was the first ocean steamer, although that honor is usually bestowed on the *Savannah* which came from that port and made the run to Liverpool from New York. But the *Robert Fulton,* of which we speak, depended upon her machinery all the time, while the *Savannah* used sails most of her trip. She was owned by David Dunham & Co., her machinery also being of New York manufacture—by Allaire & Co. She ran regularly as a packet from New York to Charleston, Havana, and New Orleans. Her time was eleven days, including stops.

All along the waterfront from South Ferry to the Dry Dock at the foot of Twelfth Street were to be seen splendid deep-sea-going ships in every stage of construction. Vast crowds used to view them every day. Besides the ship-building yards, there were rigging lofts, sail lofts, the shops of boat builders, block and pump makers, ship chandlery stores, gilders, iron, brass and copper workers. Skillful wood carvers who made those famous mythological and historic figures which adorned the prows of these swift sailing beauties; mast and spar makers; little shops where everything required on shipboard from a palm to a mar-linspike, a ball of yarn, anchor or chain could be obtained besides slickers, sou'westers, boots and other needful articles. And the stores selling hardtack, jerked beef and other comestibles were legion. South Street in those days was one of the great sights of the city. No foreign quarters in Shanghai or Stamboul could rival it in picturesqueness or romance. The Tower of Babel was a kindergarten in comparison with the jargon of strange tongues and stranger peoples who thronged its streets. Malay and Lascar, Portuguese and Scandinavian, East Indian and Japanese, walked cheek by jowl with Yankees and Britons. At night the street glowed with blazing torches, whale-oil flares and charcoal fires. The air resounded with the strident cries of itinerant hawkers, with their wares on modest two-

"Flying Cloud"; Queen of the Clippers. Record run, New York to San Francisco 84 days.

wheeled hand carts or spread out on the ground. The din was terrific, and through it all the mirage of gold—yellow gold—in the background, for there was big money in ships.

Even as late as the '70's this district and its adjoining neighbors, Cherry and Water Streets, south from Roosevelt, was the popular rendezvous of Jack ashore and was a picturesque section of the city. Water Street was a street of all Nations, and each house of call floated a flag designed to attract the class of trade it sought to secure. One house would hoist the Spanish ensign, another the British, and another the tricolor of France, and so on down the line. The denizens of these resorts sat on improvised "settles" built within the stoop line. They were a sorry, bloated-looking coterie of frumps, whose main object in life was to rob the poor fish who swam into the net. The average sailors' boarding house was no better. It was simply a hell-hole in which drugs were freely used and shanghaiing was a daily practice. Many a poor devil woke up in the morning to find himself aboard a strange craft bound for the ends of the earth with no idea of how he ever got there. It was to correct such abuses that the Seaman's Institute was established, and it has done a world of good. The old brothels of Water Street have long ago disappeared and the region is now a business section. The glory of Cherry Street in its days of prosperity is almost wholly forgotten in its later career of crime and debauchery. But at one time it was a choice residential neighborhood.

When a packet finished loading, she dropped down the East River and anchored off the Battery, there to ship her crew and wait for a favorable turn of the tide. There were no towboats to take her to sea, and with a favorable breeze any of these powerful ships would sail to Sandy Hook much faster than they could be towed. One of these deep-sea beauties getting under way was a beautiful sight and was always watched by an enthusiastic crowd.

A "sailing day" was an event in which a large number of persons were interested. Many had friends on board. Others had valuable consignments of suitable merchandise for some foreign port, and all were engaged in a hazard of new fortunes.

One of the chief attractions for the people who gathered at the Battery, then a very fashionable section of the city, was undoubtedly the chanty singing of the sailors. They could be heard far up Broadway. These sea songs were an important element in sea life, giving zest and cheerfulness to those on board. It used to be said that a good chantyman was worth four men in a watch, and this was true; for when a crew knocked off chantying, there was something wrong—the ship suddenly became lifeless.

These songs originated early in the last century among the black stevedores of the levees in Mobile and New Orleans, who sang them while screwing cotton bales into the holds of northern packet ships. That's where the clipper sailors learned them. The words had about the same intelligence as the average radio croon song, but there was a wild inspiring ring in the melodies that made a man pull, whether he would or no. In course of time, they became unconsciously influenced by the pungent briny odor and surging roar of the gale at sea. No landsman can imitate them. They belong to square-rigged sweethearts of the deep and no man can take them from their natural surroundings.

As the flood tide begins to slacken and the packet swings to the wind, the order is passed along to man the windlass and heave short. The ship is getting under way. The mate sings out in a cheery voice, "Now then boys, heave away on the windlass breaks; strike a light, it's duller than an old graveyard." And the chantyman, in an advanced state of hilarious intoxication, gay as a skylark, breaks into a chanty that can be heard on land all over the Battery and well up into Broadway; it is, however, utterly impossible in cold type to reproduce the stirring effect of these weird, enchanting melodies. The soul of brevity was conspicuous by its absence. To the landsman they lacked both rhyme and reason; but on shipboard they were as a flaming sword to the laggard.

One of the great stand-bys was a saga of poor Paddy who worked on a railway. There were so many verses that they could easily take up the rest of this book. Here is the first —the million that follow it have about the same high literary and artistic quality:

> In eighteen hundred and forty-six
> I found myself in a hell of a fix
> A-working on the railway, the railway, the railway
> Oh! poor Paddy works on the railway.

The thread of the narrative has a wide latitude. At one time the hero shifts his location but not his vocation.

> In eighteen hundred and forty-seven
> When Dan O'Connell went to heaven
> He worked upon the railway, the railway, the railway
> Poor Paddy works upon the railway.

In the next verse, he is bound for the Golden Gate, but he is still "working on the railway." Next, he is on the Black Ball line, etc. It seems passing strange that though a dyed-in-the-wool deep-sea sailor, his idol is a man who works on land.

However, these chanty songs were indispensable on shipboard. To hear them on land as the sails filled up and she slowly turned on her heel, was one of the most engaging sights ever witnessed from the old Battery and was something long to be remembered.

There were a great many Whitehall boats kept at the lower end of the Battery, and to be a Battery oarsman was to be among the blue ribboners of the waterfront. The time when these men shone at their best was when a California clipper put to sea.

A busy scene it was, as they put the crew and dunnage aboard, one or two lots at a time accompanied by a boarding-house runner, the sailors being in the various stages of hilarious spiffiness as was the immemorial custom. Those who had completely passed out were hauled over the side in bowlines and stowed away in their berths to regain their senses when the ship was well out to sea and escape hopeless. These men had been drugged and robbed of

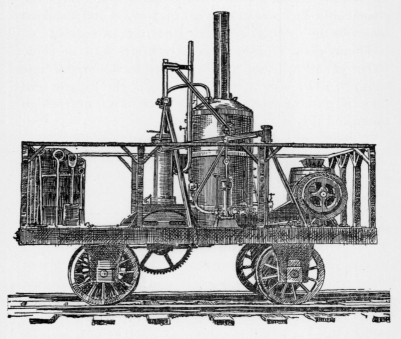

"Tom Thumb." First railroad engine 1830, built by Peter Cooper, New York for the B. & O. R. R.

their clothing. In a few hours they would come to and find themselves at sea on board a ship they never heard of and bound they knew not where.

The mate considered himself fortunate if he could muster two-thirds of his crew able to stand up and heave on a capstan bar or pull in a rope. This condition had been anticipated and a gang of longshoremen was on board to lend a hand in getting the ship under way. The provident among the seamen brought well-stocked sea chests; the less thoughtful found moderate-sized canvas bags quite large enough to hold their possessions. Occasionally, one optimistic mariner would carry his outfit for the Cape Horn voyage tied up in a nice bandanna handkerchief, the parting gift of a Cherry Street damsel—who kept the change. But Jack was in a jovial, tipsy mood and appeared happy in the recollection of his Don Juan experiences.

There was a crisp northeasterly breeze and the blue waters of the bay danced and sparkled in the bright June sunshine. The crew were all on board, the captain and pilot in consultation on the quarterdeck; it was nearly high water and the tide would soon run ebb.

As the crew mustered on the forecastle, they appeared to be a motley gang, mostly British and Scandinavian with a sprinkling of Spaniards, Portuguese, Italians and one or two "down-easters." Some wore thick coarse red, blue or gray flannel shirts; others blue dungaree jumpers or cotton shirts of various colors; their trousers were in a variety of drabs, blues, grays, browns, supported by leather belts or braces. They wore stiff or soft felt hats or woolen caps of many colors. But no clothes ever invented could disguise these men, their bronzed, weather-beaten faces and sunbaked tattooed arms, with every swing of their bodies betraying them as sailormen and good ones, too, above even the average. They would no more submit to putting on a

uniform of the man-of-war than they would think of eating food with a knife and fork.

And what wonderful chaps these captains were! They
knew nothing of fear. Once aboard their ships, they were
czars. Their word was law and gospel, and they held the
power of life and death over any of the crew. It was well
for the sailors that they were men as a rule, vastly superior
to the ordinary run of seamen.

One of the important vessels built in New York at this
time was the *President,* a forty-four-gun frigate, sister ship
to the *Constitution.* She was launched from the yard of
Forman Cheesman at Corlear's Hook—by far the largest
ship built up to this time in New York.

Among the famous New York packet captains, and there
were many of them, were William Skiddy, an older brother
of Francis Skiddy; Joseph Delano, Benjamin Trask,
Charles H. Marshall, F. A. De Peyster, John Johnston and
Robert C. Cutting. It required an unusual combination of
qualities to command these western packet ships successfully. Above all things, it was necessary that the captains
should be thorough seamen and navigators; also, that they
should be men of robust health and great physical endurance, as their duties often kept them on deck for days and
nights together in storm, cold and fog. Then there were
frequently desperate characters among the crews and steer-
age passengers who required to be handled with moral
courage and physical force, while the cabin passengers
were usually persons of good breeding, accustomed to
courtesy and politeness, which they expected to find in
the captains with whom they sailed. So the calling developed a superior type of man to what is generally
understood in a sailing captain.

The profits of the shipping business in those days were
enormous. It was not an unusual thing for A. A. Low &
Bro., Wm. T. Coleman, Howard & Aspinwall, Grinnell,

Fort Clinton, afterwards old Castle Garden and now the Aquarium, as it appeared when erected during the War of 1812. Jenny Lind sang here. Land was filled in 1851.

Minturn Co., N. L. & G. Griswold, and other New York men to earn in one trip the entire cost of the ship itself. The *Samuel Russell,* to quote only one instance, received $72,-ooo for her first trip to California, which was considerably more than the entire cost of ship, wages and all other expenses. The return trip with tea from China was all "velvet." Most of the great fortunes before the Civil War came from shipping.

The opening of the Erie Canal in 1825 gave a great impetus to the ocean-borne commerce of New York. As a result, lines of packet ships for Liverpool were established with regular fortnightly sailings, to which were added packets to Havre, and to New Orleans.

Fast on the heels of the Liverpool packets came the California Gold Rush and the Australian rush. This trade called for an entirely new type of ship and thus began the most enchanting chapter of American Merchant Marine— the never-to-be-forgotten Clipper Ship era, of which we shall speak later.

At about the same time the whale-fishing industry began to attract the attention of Hudson River men. The town of Hudson, settled largely by men from Nantucket Island, took the lead, followed closely by Newburgh and Poughkeepsie. Richard Henry Dana, in *Two Years Before the Mast,* mentions the fact that the *Pilgrim* met up with a Poughkeepsie whaler, but does not think much of the crew, whom he says "appear to be farmers and ought to be at home cutting hay." There is a reminder of these far-off days in Poughkeepsie to this day in a dock still called the Pacific Dock. The city was also considered as a U.S. Navy Yard. There are plans still in existence, showing what was proposed. Difficulty in keeping the channel deep enough for the new style boats finally killed the scheme.

The most remarkable thing about these ships prior to 1800 was the smallness of their size. None of them was what we could today call large; on the contrary, they were ridiculously small—the average being not much over a hundred feet long and many not even that. To look at them today one would not credit them with being able to navigate the perils of the Chinese monsoon or the terrific winds that sweep the Caribbean Sea. Yet they not only survived these tempests but made excellent time. The crews were small, making up in skill and stamina what they lacked in numbers.

But they rapidly increased in size as the shipbuilder increased his knowledge of marine architecture and the demands of commerce warranted the construction. And these little ships sailed the world over and were a familiar sight in all the ports of the Orient. They were as well known in Singapore as in Calcutta, and in Liverpool as in New York.

New York trading ships were now everywhere. They had been swift to seize the opportunity providentially opened to them by the European wars, and were now strongly entrenched among the contenders for the riches of the tea trade. Whampoa, Shanghai and Hongkong were familiar headlines in news dispatches.

Howland & Aspinwall, Grinnell, Minturn & Co., Archibald Gracie, Robert Lenox, John Jacob Astor, Cornelius Vanderbilt, Tileston & Co., Sutton & Co., A. A. Low & Bros., Chas. H. Mallory, Robt. Sedgewick, Warren Delano, Chas. H. Marshall, Daniel Fearing & Co., Ward, Oliphant & Co., are only a few that come to mind.

Almost all of these firms were engaged in the Far East trade which embraced all the Oriental ports except the Hermit Kingdom, Japan, which was closed to European commerce till it first was opened by Capt. Matthew Perry, brother of Commodore Oliver Hazard Perry of Lake Erie fame, in 1853.

In addition to this foreign trade there was also, of course, the vast and continually expanding passenger traffic between New York and Liverpool with weekly sailings. There were the famous Black Ball Line, The Swallow Tail Line, the Red Ball Line, the Collins Line, the Dramatic Line, etc.

In the port of Marseilles, at the beginning of the last century, there dwelt two brothers—Anton and Pierre Roux. These enterprising young artists would watch the arrival of American ships from the Orient preparing for the long run across the Atlantic. They usually spent a week or so in Marseilles repairing sails, rigging, and sprucing up generally. While the ships rode at anchor, these young chaps would go out in a small boat and make a "portrait" of the ship and sell it to the captain. But for that, many of our best-known early ships would have left no record of their existence and we should never have known what they looked like. These portraits were naturally few in number and of these few, not many have survived. Consequently, their value has now reached such a high level as to make them beyond the reach of the average pocketbook.

Chapter XXI

The Romantic Hudson River

It is rather hard to convey to the New York of today an adequate idea of the importance of the Hudson River in the early development of New York. It was one of our main "streets" in the fullest sense of the word, and more traffic passed over it going and coming, than through any of our other thoroughfares. From the day that Hudson sailed its waters to the head of navigation, down to the present, it has contributed in many ways to the comfort and well-being of the city.

It has rejoiced in many names: Norumbega, Rivere Grand, Mauritious, North, and Hudson. By a singular oversight the name of its discoverer was never attached to it till almost two hundred years after its discovery. In 1809, on the two hundredth anniversary of the founding of New York, as we have already related, it was by common consent finally accepted. All maps, and other drawings of the river, thereafter, used this name on their publications and all others gradually disappeared except one—North. That is still applied to the river as it sweeps past Manhattan Island. Beyond that, no one thinks of calling it anything but the Hudson.

The origin of this use of the word North is Indian. The early Red Men used it to indicate that the river came from the north. The Dutch used the same term to denote the territory claimed by them which was bounded on the south by the Delaware and on the north by the Hudson.

339

So these two words were merely used in a descriptive way, as in a real estate deed. It has no relation at all to its geographical position to the city, as it lies directly west. The use of the word Hudson to cover the river as it flows past Manhattan Island, is gradually extending and in time will doubtless be universal. The advertisements of the railroad and steamship lines that invariably use the number of the pier, adding North River to distinguish it from the East, will, however, continue to prolong the use of this centuries-old error.

Travel by land on the Island from its most northerly point was in its early days almost impossible. A canoe trip by water was infinitely easier and much less laborious. So to reach the Fort at the foot of Broadway, most of the red men preferred the river and the white man soon followed suit. Like all islands lying on the water, little clusters of tents or small farm houses would form and ultimately become villages. So we find, on the shores of the Hudson, many interesting names on old maps that recall these villages. On the west side were Chelsea, Greenwich, Carmansville, Manhattanville, Bloomingdale, Washington Heights, Tubby Hook, Inwood, Spuyten Duyvil and Harlem. On the east side were Manhattan Island (a small island just off Grand Street, now filled in), Turtle Bay, Jones Woods, Yorkville, Hell Gate, City Island. A good many Indian villages bordered the river in aboriginal days, but with the exception of Sapponican, now Greenwich Village, no record has come down to us. Beyond the Island and as far up as Albany, there were, of course, numerous tribes, but they were a nomadic lot and the names of but few of any permanent abiding places have been preserved.

Trading with the white settlers on the Jersey Shore and with the Walloon and Dutch settlements in and around Albany, was conducted wholly by river, and of course all of the fur and peltries brought to New York by Indians from the Mohawk Valley likewise used the Hudson. So, long before roads, horses, stagecoaches or sloops, the main traveled highway to New York was the river. The growth of its career as a street, so to speak, is one of the most interesting chapters connected with our city. No other single possession did so much for the growth of New York as its beautiful and practical river.

In these early days, it was also a wonderful provider for the hungry people of New Amsterdam. No elaborate preparation for fishing was necessary. A few nets secured to stakes in the river would yield every spring morning a plentiful supply of shad, which for culinary delight could not be surpassed. Eels, crabs and a variety of salt-water fish were caught all along the shores of the city; while perch, bass, whitefish and other dainty fresh-water fish were had in abundance a little further up. Between the fish in its waters and the fruit and grain on its banks there was food and enough for everybody. No more beautiful stream was ever vouchsafed man. Shad are still fairly plentiful above Poughkeepsie, but nothing in comparison with former days. As a meal ticket for early New York, its record is unparalleled. Before the advent of steam, it was nothing unusual to count from thirty to forty sloops within a mile, all leisurely making their way up or down the river.

It enjoyed the honor of being chosen for the trial trip of the first vessel ever propelled by steam as already related. It also gave to our country that invaluable and humanitarian organization now in use along all our seaboards and inland waters wherever men are exposed to danger on the sea—the U. S. Volunteer Coast Guard Service.

The story of how this originated is a romance in itself. A young lad in the city coming casually into contact with this phase of metropolitan life, devoted the hours left after a hard day's work to prowling around the waterfront to be of help in case of mishap. His services were unfortunately frequently in demand. A few of his intimates joined him in this singular work, which brought no pecuniary reward. Finally some interested persons, realizing what was going on, contributed a small sum, but sufficient to provide warm shelter for the boys at each end of their route. They covered the lower end of town on both rivers from about Peck Slip on the East to Twenty-third Street on the West.

Some more spectacular rescues than others finally brought this work before the public and moved some citizens to give a dinner to the boys and enlist some financial support for their work. A Capt. Boynton, who was well known in those days by reason of his efforts to popularize a non-sinkable bathing suit, presided at the dinner. He was genuinely interested in saving lives from drowning and made an eloquent speech in behalf of the work undertaken by these lads. The boys were not able to speak for themselves; but the story of their unselfishness and their heroism told by others made a deep impression. The result was the subscription of enough money to open two more stations, this time adequately equipped with life preservers and a couple of rowboats. Influential citizens brought the matter to the attention of the Federal Government, and shortly afterwards the system was made part of our Lighthouse Service. Its use was later largely extended and is now not only part of our lighthouse routine but has become an adjunct to every popular bathing beach in the country.

So the old Hudson River can add to its steamboat laurels, its indescribably beautiful scenery, and its matchless record as a servitor of New York, that of having introduced one of the most humane and valuable institutions ever devised for the benefit of the public on land as well as at sea.

With the opening of the Erie Canal, the Hudson en-

Broadway looking South from about Liberty Street, 1835, showing small retail shops.

tered into a new and larger service to New York. It is not at all too much to say that the Canal and the River have had practically everything to do with placing New York at the head of all the commercial cities of our country. A year or two after the opening of "Clinton's Ditch," as it was derisively called, New York passed Philadelphia in population and grew so fast that it has ever since led all other cities in wealth and numbers and has placed it in a class by itself.

As population grew and the river played an ever-increasing rôle in the city's growth, it developed a type of boat peculiar to its need—the Hudson River Sloop.

The winds on the river are treacherous. They sweep down from openings in the high hills with a suddenness that is appalling. In addition to that it is a breeding place for violent storms with their accompanying and destructive squalls. It is nothing unusual to see the sky turn from blue to black before your very eyes and a crash of thunder herald the approach of what they would call in the West, a small cyclone. They disappear as suddenly as they come, but in half an hour cause great destruction among its floating population. From bitter experience the Indian knew what to expect with a sudden shift of the wind to the west or northwest, and speedily sought shelter in some convenient cove.

Although the white man always used sails, the Indian with his little canoe could easily outstrip him in speed; and when he traveled in his warship with a dozen or more men at the oars he made wonderful time in his trips from Albany to the wigwams of his pale-faced brothers. For many years, trade with the Indians on the upper Hudson was the main business of the settlers. Furs were brought from the interior to the rendezvous at Albany and from thence transported by canoes to New Amsterdam. As pop-

ulation increased, the river became a busy highway. Before
the advent of steam, it was no unusual sight to see from
thirty to forty sail within the space of a mile or two, besides several strings of barges with a population of their
own who knew no other home.

The Hudson River Sloop was a boat peculiarly adapted
for this river. It was rather wide, had a rail running
around the deck and a single mast stepped well forward
with an enormous boom. It was roomy and was designed to
carry both passengers and freight. It carried an immense
spread of canvas. It resembled the familiar catboat of the
harbor and bay, but differed slightly in the more forward
step of the mast and, unlike the cat, it carried a foresail.
Perhaps its great advantage was in the fact that it could be
easily handled by two men. In a sudden squall, the sail was
lowered from the peak or sheeted in altogether. Sometimes
the force of the wind, if from the rear, was sufficient to
send her along scudding under bare pole at a great rate.
Her one great fault, and a serious one, was her promptness
to "jibe" in a sudden gust of wind. In that event, the
huge boom would start to swing from one side to the other
of the schooner and in that event, if you were in the way of
the boom, it just swept you overboard. Sometimes, the victim would also be stunned by the boom striking his head;
in which case, he generally sank. Despite all precautions
and the warning always given by captains to their passengers, accidents of this kind occurred with painful regular-
ity. The temptation to become entranced with the gorgeous scenery on a lovely summer day, had much to do
with the failure of the luckless passengers to heed the captain's warning cry. Aside from this, the Hudson River
sloop was a delightful mode of transportation, and very
popular. In head winds, however, the trip to Albany was
likely to stretch into many more days than the schedule

called for. Nevertheless, this type of boat retained its popularity till the marine engine drove it off the river. Its disappearance was sincerely mourned.

These sloops connected at Albany with a line of canal boats going north to Buffalo and the Great Lakes. Business soon increased to the extent that regular daily sailings from New York had already superseded the occasional departures heretofore. A boat would advertise to leave New York on completion of a certain number of passengers and the requisite amount of freight to make the trip pay. Considerable amazement was aroused when cards were one day distributed stating that henceforth a certain sloop would leave every day at 3 P.M., rain or shine, freight or no freight. Business justified this step and presently the daily sailing became a regular thing. And an attempt to land passengers at a certain hour in Albany was a further inducement to forsake the stages. That also helped and presently both means of transit were at your disposal; and despite the competition, business increased on both lines. It was certainly a delightful and leisurely way of traveling, especially on the canal boats. They had spacious decks covered with awnings and fairly comfortable chairs. They passed through a beautiful country. The mules traveled leisurely but surely. When you came to a lock, there was always a small crowd gathered to look and listen. They sold fruit and flowers. You had time to go ashore and spend an hour looking over the little town with its half-white, half-Indian population. The latter were getting so scarce as to be now included as one of the attractions of the trip.

Long strings of freight barges loaded with lumber, grain or produce would pass you on the way. These barges would be made up into long strings at Albany after steam was invented and proceed to New York towed by two or three powerful tugs. On the way to the city, these barges were frequented by "bum boat" women who carried the contents of a general store in their little craft. There was a small resident population in these barges whose homes were in the rear of the boat. Several rooms were given over to the wives and children of the captains. So these itinerant merchants in small rowboats could depend on quite a staple market. Small fancy articles, candy for the children, tobacco, fruit and all sorts of knickknacks found a ready sale. The proprietor would be hauled aboard the barge, her own boat tied behind. Her visits would last long into the day if the barge was a long one as each family had its own separate home. It was a curious and picturesque feature of Hudson River life and lasted well up to the close of the nineteenth century. In winter, these barges anchored in that wide slip at the foot of Coenties Street. There the children went to school. When the ice was out of the river, they went back to the only life they ever knew.

A very pretty feature of Hudson River boats at one time was what you might call Honeymoon boats. It was not at all an unusual thing for young people of sufficient means to charter one of these boats for their own use exclusively for the honeymoon trip. The rear of these boats had spacious rooms tastefully decorated and completely furnished. Bedrooms, dining-rooms, parlors and cheerful sitting-rooms were part of every passenger steamer of that type on the river for the use of the usual passengers. Thus, for a comparatively small sum, one had a private yacht fully commissioned and staffed with a highly trained crew.

As most of these young people were connected with the old manor families along the Hudson, it was a pleasant way of spending a fortnight or more. When they came in sight of the home they were next to visit, a few sharp blasts of the whistle was all that was necessary to give advance notice of their arrival. By the time the boat had tied up at the private wharf of the big house, the grinning faces of the black servants with resplendent carriages, would be ready and waiting. On the spacious veranda would be waiting aunts, uncles or cousins and the bridal couple would receive a royal welcome. The stay might be only for the afternoon or it might be extended to three or four days. The big boat would be waiting meanwhile. When the visit was ended, the young people sailed away to the next stop. Practically all the old New York families had countryseats on the River between here and Albany. A large number are still standing just as they were in Colonial days, particularly in the neighborhood from Hyde Park to Clermont, home of the Livingstons. For many years before the Civil War and Newport, it was the favorite country-seats of our best-known society, from Riverdale to Albany. President Roosevelt lives in one of these old homes at Hyde Park. The pictures which illustrate this article are from his private collection.

It would be hard to imagine a more comfortable and delightful way of spending one's honeymoon. It was much better than traveling by private coach or stage. There was at each stop practically your own home always at hand ready for any contingency.

No royal progress could ever be more enjoyable. Life was more leisurely and, in some ways, more elegant. And under such conditions, it was well-nigh perfect. It would be hard to imagine a more delightful experience. We are always painting pictures to hang on memory's walls. A trip like this would undoubtedly produce a large and valuable collection.

In its present-day capacity the river provides what is easily the most spacious and most beautiful recreation ground for the people of a great city that exists anywhere in the world—Palisades Park and Bear Mountain Park, extending for miles along the west bank of the river from a point opposite Grant's Tomb, provide camping grounds,

Traveling by Canal to the interior from Albany.

picnic grounds and bathing beaches of priceless value for the purpose.

Private individuals, especially Mr. John D. Rockefeller Sr., were responsible for initiating this great public improvement at the beginning; but now the State, in a modest way, shares in the expenditure. Aside from this great outdoor playground for all the people, the Palisade Interstate Park Commission has rescued for all time those natural wonders, the basaltic cliffs known as the Palisades, which were in imminent danger of destruction at the hands of quarry men. Posterity will ever be grateful to the present generation for this thoughtfulness, and the whole country is the gainer.

It is not possible to enumerate the manifold beauties of this beautiful river; it is no exaggeration to say that its equal does not exist in this section of our land. However that may be, the Hudson needs fear no rival.

One of the greater glories of the Hudson, is the fact that it was the scene of the *first* launching of the *first* practical steamboat built in the New World. Many other inventors were at work on the same idea, but the credit of being the first to demonstrate its feasibility belongs to Fulton. His *Katherine of Clermont,* afterwards shortened to *Clermont,* made the voyage from New York to Albany in 1807 and returned a few days afterward. It demonstrated successfully that man need no longer be at the mercy of wind and tide. His mastery over the sea was now an accomplished fact.

He was a country lad born in Lancaster, Pa. His original intention was to be an artist and he studied for a time under Benjamin West, who afterwards became President of the Royal Academy in England and one of the leading British painters.

Fulton had discontinued his art studies. We next hear of him in England. He was conducting an experiment for the

British Admiralty. It was an under-sea boat capable of blowing up the finest and heaviest ship in the British Navy without detection. The Admiralty provided him with an old hulk for an experiment. Fulton's torpedo boat blew it out of the water before their astonished eyes. It was too dreadful an engine of destruction, the Admiralty concluded, and Fulton left for France.

The amazing Napoleon failed to grasp the weapon offered him by Fulton, and the chance to invade England and bring the proud Mistress of the Seas in humble supplication at his feet, was lost. This important matter had been referred to a stupid under-secretary. He reported to his great master that the scheme was ridiculous and impractical.

Fulton's first idea was evidently in the direction of an under-sea boat. James Gallatin, whose father, Albert Gallatin, was then our Minister to France, tells a most interesting story about Fulton at this time. This was before he had done anything beyond sketching his plan on paper. He was without funds to build a model. Mr. Gallatin says:

I was told such an interesting story about Robert Fulton today. It seems during the Terror he was in Paris; wishing to go to England on business he obtained a permit and passport. By accident it was made out to Mr. and Mrs. Fulton. Arriving at Calais he was detained as there was no packet crossing. In the evening at the *auberge* where he was lodged, he noticed a young woman who seemed in an agony of mind—this was rather a common thing in those days. At last she summoned up courage to speak to him, saying, "I throw myself on your mercy. I see you are a foreigner. I escaped from Paris where I had foolishly gone to try and save some important documents. My husband would have gone, but he is very ill in England, and I persuaded him to allow me to do so. I am without a passport, and hardly dare to embark as there is a price on my head, and I am certain to be arrested and sent back to Paris. Can you help me?" Fulton said: "I will do my best. I have my American passport; oddly enough by error it was made out for myself and wife, but she is in America. If you are willing to pass as Mrs. Fulton, you are welcome to the little protection I can afford you."

As the lady in question was disguised and very simply dressed, the plan succeeded and with many expressions of gratitude, she parted with him at Dover without revealing her name.

Some years later, when Fulton was in Paris trying to raise money to put his submarine into practice, he strolled one night into the Theatre Français. Looking around the auditorium, he spied, much to his astonishment, in one of the boxes, the lady of his adventure splendidly dressed and covered with jewels; at the same time, she recognized him, and waved her fan, sending her husband at once to escort him to her box. It was through her that the money was found to carry along his experiments with his submersible. One rarely hears of such gratitude. It was the Duchesse de L——.

Meanwhile, Mr. Robert R. Livingston, had been appointed Minister to France. His friend Mr. Joel Barlow was visiting him and the conversation drifted to the new idea of propelling boats by steam. A Frenchman had just made a demonstration of one on the Seine. Livingston was all attention:

"There's a countryman of yours over here with the same idea. I met him only yesterday. He is trying to interest Napoleon in his boat. Says it would be no trouble at all to invade England with a fleet sailed by steam."

"Who is this chap?"

"Fulton, I think is his name—an artist, I believe, studied under one of your men now prominent in London—Benjamin West."

"Could I meet this Mr. Fulton?"

"Certainly. I'll arrange it for you."

So Livingston met Fulton. He was captivated by Fulton's idea of a commercial steamboat. They purchased an engine in England and returned with it to New York. To-

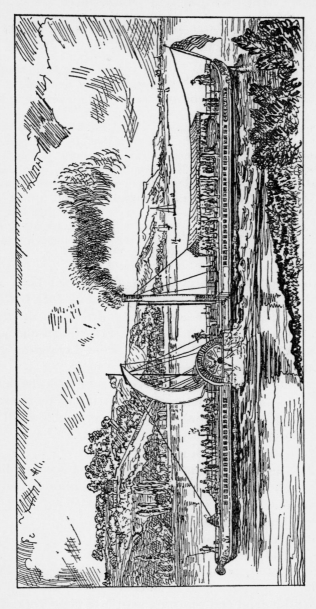

The "Clermont" plying the Hudson, after improvements and enlargements over first model.

gether they quietly proceeded to construct a vessel for peaceful pursuits: for the transportation of goods and passengers in more sheltered waters than the open sea. A shop was opened in a small building in the rear of No. 1 Broadway. Along the river-front and in the market places, men discussed with much merriment the design of the mad artist. It was everywhere spoken of as "Fulton's Folly."

"Excuse me for laughing, gentlemen, but I must bring up that bill of the Chancellor's for a boat to sail by steam," remarked Dr. Mitchell to the members of the Assembly in New York in the Winter of 1797.

"Oh! I say," answered one of the group, "you are really not serious in asking us to grant a patent for a steamboat to ply the Hudson and all other inland waters of the country, are you? What is a steamboat, anyway? Is it good to eat?"

"I don't know. It's some crazy scheme to propel a boat without the use of sails, I believe. The vessel is to go regardless of wind or tide."

"Fiddlesticks! Do you want us to be the laughingstock of the whole country? A *steam* boat! Ridiculous!"

"I know it, but the Chancellor wants it. He's a good fellow and we all want to oblige him. It won't do him any good nor us any harm. And I'd like to oblige."

"We all would, for that matter. Let's see. We've had that bill before us for almost a year. None of us want to father such a crazy scheme. Can't we get rid of it in some way? Well, suppose we pass it and say what everybody will know to be the truth—that we did it only out of consideration for a dear friend and it cost the State nothing."

"Not a bad idea."

So the bill granting Robert R. Livingston a perpetual right to navigate the inland waters of America by means of a steamboat was passed amidst shouts of laughter and much good-natured raillery by most of the members.

At length the great day arrived. *Katherine of Clermont,* named after the Chancellor's favorite daughter and Fulton's fiancée, cast off from her dock at the foot of Cortlandt Street and made her way to midstream. She was holding her own against the swift outrushing tide of the Hudson. Her admirers on the dock cheered. Her opponents were silent.

Suddenly the *Clermont,* caught in the gap of the tide, was slowly forced downstream. Her walking beam was motionless. It was "Fulton's Folly" after all!

Livingston, with a sinking heart, saw the boat slowly drifting toward the open sea. Fulton, on board the craft, had doffed his tall beaver hat and his blue-skirted coat and was working feverishly at the stalled engine. Minutes passed, minutes fraught with agony to the watching Livingston, and half an hour was gone. Fulton emerged from his task, surveyed the scene in one final look, gave the order to start. Slowly but surely she stemmed the tide. Then gradually she gathered headway and at last moved *up* the river against wind and tide to her triumphant first voyage *up* the Hudson. When she had covered a mile, all doubts were dispelled. The pent-up emotion on the dock and on the ship found relief in a paroxysm of cheers and shouting. Fulton was seized by the hand by those nearest him and ecstatically congratulated. The sea-going world was on the eve of a mighty revolution and a band played "The World Turned Upside Down."

Fulton and Livingston enjoyed their monopoly for nearly thirty years. It was finally declared invalid in the famous case of Fulton vs. Gibbon, in which the real defendant was not Gibbon, but old Commodore Vanderbilt, who had graduated from his first venture in transportation the Staten Island ferry and was now reaching out for wider fields to conquer. He employed Daniel Webster.

With this obstacle removed, Vanderbilt started in to develop business along the river. As the Hudson was then practically one of New York City's principal streets, it is quite proper that we include a little history of it in our story of the city.

In this connection, it is of great interest to read of the work done along this same line by the Stevenses. It is to this family we owe the famous schooner yacht *America*. What Col. Basil M. Stevens has to say on early steamboats is worth reading:

At the same time at Castle Point, Hoboken, his countryseat, Colonel John Stevens of Number 7 Broadway, a brother-in-law and neighbor of Livingston, was at work endeavoring to improve some of his earlier experiments with steam boats.

In 1799, Stevens designed and supervised the making of the first condensing double acting engine that was built in America. To quote Mr. John Hewitt, father of the first Mayor of Greater New York, the Honorable Abram S. Hewitt: "that engine was put in a boat in which I traversed the route from Belleville to New York and Back again, John Stevens being the owner, the builder and the Captain. . . . And we came to New York in that boat nine years before Fulton put the *Clermont* on the Hudson." This boat had a stern wheel, as distinguished from a propeller.

Not satisfied with its performance, Colonel Stevens, during the next five years, and while Livingston was in Paris, devoted much energy to developing numerous improvements connected with steam navigation. In 1802, he began experimenting with a single screw propeller, and on April 11th. of the next year, patented his invention of the multitubular boiler. One day in May, 1804, John Renwick, then a student but later Professor of Natural and Experimental Philosophy at Columbia University, and an authority on many subjects, joined a "crowd" running through the gate of Battery Park. As he, later, described it, "on reaching the bulkhead by which the Battery was then bounded, we saw lying against it a vessel about the

size of a Whitehall rowboat," (approximately thirty-two feet
in length and six feet beam), "in which there was a small engine *but no visible means of propulsion.* The vessel was
speedily underway." Thus, the little *Juliana,* equipped as she
was with a multitubular boiler, and with twin-screw propellers
of a shape resembling those now in use, embodied the first
known successful application of steam to this "invisible means
of propulsion." On this memorable occasion the crew consisted
of but two men, both sons of Colonel Stevens; the helmsman
was John Cox Stevens, later the first Commodore of the New
York Yacht Club; and Robert Livingston Stevens, a younger
brother, fulfilled the duties of engineer and fireman.

Stevens, then nearing his sixtieth year, immediately began
planning a larger craft, but, deciding that the boilers of his
day were incapable of carrying sufficient steam pressure for
propellers, he concluded to revert to paddle-wheels, such as
those advocated by Nicholas Roosevelt, with whom he and
Livingston had collaborated ten years before. This larger boat
was to be one hundred feet long and twenty-six feet wide.

During the weeks that Fulton was at work on the strange-
looking craft which caused wonder to the inhabitants of the
Hudson Valley, and in which he placed a Bolton & Watts
engine imported from England, John Stevens and his son,
Robert, were engaged in building the *Phoenix,* and equipped
her with an engine designed by Colonel Stevens, and built
under his supervision. Launched on April 6, 1807, she was not
completed until about six weeks after the *Clermont's* first trip
on July 18, 1807.

Prior to his departure for France, and after he had signed a
partnership agreement with his brother-in-law, John Stevens,
and Nicholas Roosevelt, Livingston had obtained an exclusive
grant to run steamboats on the waters of New York State from
the Legislature of the State. Despite his previous agreement,
Livingston had, while in Paris, entered into partnership with
Fulton. When the *Clermont* met the requirements of the grant
upon her first trip, the Chancellor's monopoly became effective.

Prevented by the monopoly from running the *Phoenix* on
the Hudson River, Colonel Stevens used her to transport
passengers from Hoboken to New Brunswick, until the mo-
nopolists placed another boat upon the same route, with a
passenger-rate one third as high. This cutthroat competition
compelled Stevens to seek other fields.

CHAPTER XXII

Why the Erie Canal Was Built

AMONG the vast public improvements urged upon the city of New York early in the last century, the astounding proposal to build a canal connecting the Great Lakes with the Hudson is the one that for sheer boldness and originality stands out most vividly. We are frequently called upon to criticize the Federal Government for building million-dollar Post Offices in five- and ten-cent towns, but in comparison with the howl of derision with which the building of the Erie Canal was greeted at the time it was projected, these criticisms become pæans of praise. There was nothing too scandalous to heap on the defenseless head of De Witt Clinton; and "Clinton's Ditch" was the highest encomium it received during the tedious process of its construction.

No doubt, the monopoly of steam transportation owned by Fulton and Livingston on all our inland and coastal waters had much to do with this undertaking. Some public utility of this nature must be owned by the State. Possibly Clinton envisaged the future growth of the West with its teeming granaries and foresaw the time when cheap transportation would place New York in the van of all other cities in the competition for this business. Yet that is not likely. He probably saw only the rapid growth of his own State. He could see endless Conestoga wagons wending their way from Philadelphia through the Cumberland gap, and countless droves of cattle on foot making their way

slowly to the great cities of the seaboard from the fertile
valleys of the Mohawk and the plains of western New
York. To divert all this unregulated commerce into one
definite and dependable route no doubt made its appeal to
him. Then again, stage coaches were not practical save
where sufficient local traffic could support them, and long
journeys were therefore virtually impossible for the occasional traveler. A canal, once made, would be inexpensive
to maintain, would form a connecting link with the frontier villages and in every way would minister to the wants
and necessities of a growing State. It was an alluring picture, and Clinton managed to communicate his enthusiasm to the people at large, who consented to the allotment
of the gigantic sums necessary for its completion. The City
of New York was, of course, the backbone of the enterprise. Her merchants were enterprising and apparently
farsighted. And so the Erie Canal was built and has demonstrated the wisdom of its projectors and justified the
enormous capital outlay in countless directions. Great
cities have grown up along its route. Sleepy little villages,
to whom the coming of a canaller was like the arrival of
the week-end train at a summer resort today, have now
grown to be huge and prosperous manufacturing centers.
The vast foreign immigration which now set in was quickly
absorbed, providing every year largely increased business
for this "ditch." Farmers in remote regions were brought
into contact with ready markets, and prosperity everywhere followed the plodding mules along the towpath.
They furnished romantic backgrounds for the start of
many of our public men and it was no mean recommenda-
tion to point with pride to their humble beginnings as
riders of the prancing steeds along the raging Erie Canal.

A very delightful adjunct was the passenger traffic that
soon made its appearance. The boats added an attractive
superstructure and made an upper deck that was at once

popular and comfortable. In variety of scenery of novel experience, there was no end. Indians by this time were considerable of a curiosity. The noble red man had fallen like the famed leaves of Vallombrosa before the advancing power of the whites. Yet in many parts of the State he still lingered in fairly generous numbers and he never failed to meet a canal boat when it stopped at a lock. It often happened that an hour or two was at the disposal of the passengers at these changing points, and they spent the time most agreeably strolling around the little village or chatting with the natives at the landing stage.

The women passengers in fair weather carried neat little sunshades, wore poke bonnets and daintily colored cotton frocks distended like a balloon with hoop skirts. White stockings were invariably worn, and low-cut satin slippers. They were usually young, and, with their saucy little ringlets peeking out from the bonnet, were not at all obtrusive objects on the landscape.

Passenger service on the canal boats began at Albany. As the system developed, many transfer points were established. It was quite possible to go far in many directions because of the rapid growth of canals, and they were run at stated hours very much the same as our present railroads. It must have been a delightful way of traveling.

The completion of the Erie Canal was celebrated by an imposing demonstration at New York. Mr. Clinton, the hero of the occasion, attended by many dignitaries and high City and State officials, occupied the center of the stage. The boat on which he appeared carried a barrel of water from Lake Erie. The marriage of the Lakes to the Sea was symbolized by pouring this lake water in the salt water of the harbor. A very pretty conceit and splendidly carried out. In the evening there was the usual banquet where innumerable toasts were drunk.

The canal proved a wonderful asset to the city and is

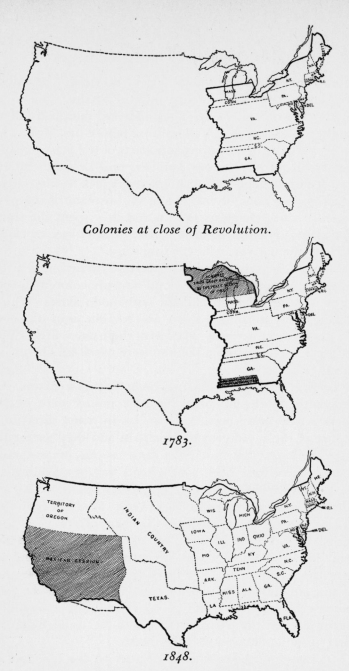

Colonies at close of Revolution.

1783.

1848.

**How the rest of the Country expanded to keep pace
with the growth of New York.**

probably entitled as much as any other single force, to the preëminent position which New York occupies today among the great cities of the world.

The success of the Erie started a mania for canal building, which well-nigh ruined the country, culminating in the fearful panic of 1837. Canal shares, like our own stocks, soared in price like rockets and came down like sticks. Human nature does not seem to learn much from experience.

In the summer of 1825, had you been a passenger on one of the many sailing ships that came to New York, you might have noticed a man of rather more than usual height leaning against the rail and gazing somewhat earnestly across the water in the direction of the approaching land. He was no longer young, but of distinguished bearing and his features were strongly marked. A shawl was loosely wrapped around his shoulders.

With one of the passengers he has been more than passing friendly, inquiring much about the cost of travel in the States, a subject which seems to possess a deep interest for him.

"Have you ever been in America before?"

"Oh, yes. But that was many years ago. All the friends of those days have since passed away. That is more than half a century ago. I shall be a stranger in a strange land."

Next morning the vessel passed Sandy Hook Light and was soon running through the Narrows. The two friends gazed delightedly at the fascinating scene before them. To their great surprise all the shipping was gayly dressed in flags and the great guns of the Forts boomed forth a rousing welcome and the harbor was alive with barges and small boats rowing merrily out to greet the oncoming vessel. There was no mistaking the reason for the scene. The welcome was meant for the incoming vessel. Signals fluttered from deck to deck and thus it was that the lonely traveler coming to a land where he thought himself unknown and forgotten, extended its welcome. The great nation, which he had done so much to help in her hour of need, was eagerly awaiting his arrival.

Lafayette was coming to visit the scenes of his youth—to live over again the moments spent with Washington, Hamilton and the other great figures now part of History.

Lafayette landed at what has now become the official landing stage for all distinguished guests arriving from the sea. It is next to Pier One on the North River. Its record of famous arrivals almost equals the record of Old Castle Garden. It would be interesting to have the complete list. The most famous in recent years was that of Lindbergh, though during the World War we welcomed most of the great leaders in that conflict and many of the statesmen.

Lafayette's visit was in response to an invitation from this Government. The vicissitudes of his life since the Revolution, his incarceration in prison for many long years, had left him in his old age much reduced in fortune and sadly impaired in health. His visit to the United States greatly improved both. Congress voted him an honorarium of a quarter of a million. Our cities vied with each other in doing him honor. No foreign visitor ever before or since enjoyed a triumphal progress such as was accorded this old friend of Washington's. Memories of these dark days with their stirring stories were revived and the few men still, like Lafayette, alive to tell of them, found eager audiences.

Lafayette was barely twenty when he offered his services to America. There were thousands of adventurers anxious for high and lucrative commissions from all the great countries abroad, but Lafayette was the only one who asked neither high position nor remuneration. His youth, his high spirits and his attractive personality were something that the serious-minded Commanding Officer could

Fifth Avenue and Broadway a hundred years ago. The small house became Thompson's Cottage and site of the old Fifth Avenue Hotel when the avenue was cut through.

not resist. A charming affection sprang up between this young chivalrous soldier of fortune and the leader of the Revolutionists. Washington loved him almost as a son, and that affection was warmly and unaffectedly returned. No wonder that Lafayette had moments of sadness amidst all the festivities, when the thought intruded itself upon him that all his old companions-in-arms had passed on.

He was then in his seventy-eighth year. His present visit would in all probability mark the closing scenes in his own career. He greedily enjoyed every moment of his experiences. No man could have had a more delightful time. Cities, towns and villages turned out to do him honor. Every possible homage was paid him and he was almost worshiped. Every house he visited, every school and every public building complimented by his presence, now cherishes the memory of that visit and has caused some memento to be erected of the event. Boulevards, streets, parks and cities have been named after him, and it is safe to say that of all the foreign officers who were engaged in the Revolution, none so completely won the hearts of the American people as this brilliant, dashing, romantic young officer on Washington's personal staff.

Chapter XXIII

When New York Burned

AT THE foot of Pudding Lane in London is a tall monument erected to commemorate the start of the great blaze which almost destroyed the city in 1665. The inscription at the base of the column is in Latin, and is to the effect that the fire was undoubtedly started by the Catholics. Charles I stood on London Bridge watching the rescue work of the fishmongers of Billingsgate Market who were harboring as many refugees as they could on their fishing boats moored in the river and beyond the reach of danger. Moved by the kindliness and neighborliness of these humble fisher folk, he decreed that ever afterward boats could anchor outside the market in the Thames free of wharfage or charges of any kind. Today the Londoner dates many interesting events from "Before the fire" or "Just after the fire," as if it was of quite recent occurrence.

No commemorative tablet marks the beginning of a similar catastrophe which overwhelmed New York one zero night in December, 1835. It raged for two days, and when finally stopped by blowing up the buildings in its path with gunpowder, it had laid the wealthiest and most valuable business section of the city in ruins. Practically every building south of Wall Street and east of Broadway was destroyed. It was as if a similar conflagration today should wipe out our whole financial district.

Merchants and other business men had gone to their homes that evening leaving everything in their offices the

same as usual. Most of them lived not further away than
Canal Street, and many still nearer. The evening meal had
been dispatched, slippers took the place of shoes and the
head of the house composed himself before the glowing
grate fire for a quiet perusal of the evening paper or a discussion of family affairs. It was a bitter cold night and the
wind blew a gale. The streets were deserted.

Along about eight o'clock, an alarm of fire rang out and
the signal indicated a location in the business section.
Those who were members of the fire company in their
neighborhood heaved a sigh of relief that the alarm was
not in their district—it was no night in which to be out.

Within what seemed but a few minutes a second alarm
sounded, and this time the bell indicated a nervous ten-
sion, so sharply was it rung. A third and fourth alarm followed. By this time a feeling of anxiety seemed suddenly
to pervade the city and in every block the slam of closing
doors indicated that the householder had ventured forth to
ascertain what all the alarms meant. The sight that met his
gaze confirmed his worst fears. The sky in the lower part of
the city glowed with a vivid red. Above the housetops
could be seen tongues of flame darting above the buildings.
Dense clouds of smoke hung like a pall over the downtown
streets and bells in all parts of the city were clanging as if
help was needed from every one.

The streets were soon filled with excited citizens hasten-
ing to the scene of disaster. Fire engines from the upper
part of the city were encountered rushing madly along far
from the district to which they belonged. The ferries from
Brooklyn and Jersey City also discharged engines and
crews. It was evidently a fire of unusual dimensions. Constables were met crying for help and urging all who could
to repair to the scene of disaster. From Wall Street down,
the city was a seething furnace.

The Merchants Exchange was a burning caldron. Most

Collection New York Historical Society.

*The Great Fire of 1835. Burning of the Merchants Exchange on
Wall Street site of present National City Bank.*

of the great banks were on fire. The flames spread to the
warehouses on Broad Street, filled to their doors with the
costliest merchandise. Building after building toppled into
the streets, and the flames, fanned by the fierce wind and
by their own draft, reached out greedily for the next victim. Burning embers carried by the breeze fell on buildings
across the street and sometimes blocks away. There was no
means of quenching these incipient blazes and soon the
fire was raging in a dozen places at once. Men in silk hats
and evening dress, as well as men in corduroy and overalls,
worked manfully at the pumps or passed buckets along.
One might as well try to dam Niagara with a mop as to
quench this roaring furnace with a bucket or a hundred.

The city appeared to be doomed. The intense cold added to the misery. Water froze as it fell, when water could be had. Most of the pumps were useless. The situation was desperate. Nothing would save the city unless the fire could be checked and that could be done only by blowing up the buildings in its path. And there was no gunpowder to be had.

Volunteers were called for, to man a boat and secure the needed explosive from the Navy Yard in Brooklyn. A dangerous and perilous trip in the teeth of the bitter gale in the turbulent waters and its swift tide. A boat was finally launched; but the night went on and it did not return.

As the morning dawned, the lower part of the city was hidden by a huge cloud of black smoke shot through with flaming tinders which, falling at a distance, kindled new fires and spread the devastation. A high northwest wind, bitter cold, added to the misery of the situation. At nine o'clock the *Courier* issued an Extra: "There is no telling when the fire will be stopped; the hydrants are exhausted, the hose of many of the engines are frozen and useless; the flames are extending; Wall street from William to the East River, totally destroyed; from 700 to 1000 buildings are said to be gone."

Presently the newspaper office itself was reached. A final edition said that the fire was almost upon them and they were moving out.

Some odd happenings were reported. A fine old sycamore tree, near the corner of Beaver and William Streets on the premises formerly occupied by Cadwallader Colden, stood uninjured among the ruins.

A gallant effort was made to save the statue of Hamilton in the Merchants Exchange. A young officer from the Navy, with four sailors, had actually succeeded in moving it from its pedestal, when the danger from the approaching fall of the roof compelled them to seek safety in flight.

Just then the boat was seen, bringing supplies of gun-powder from the Brooklyn Navy Yard. The *Courier* said: "We have seen nothing more characteristic than the *sang froid* with which the sailors of Capt. Mix's party carried about, wrapped up in a blanket or pea jacket as it might happen, kegs and barrels of gunpowder amid a constant shower of fire as they followed their officers to the various buildings indicated for destruction."

There were no papers published that day, and the news as it reached other cities and the country generally produced a sensation beyond description. It was not until Saturday—four days later—that the news reached Albany. The meager reports available served only to increase the dismay—the imagination furnishing from the scanty material even more dreadful accounts of the calamity than the reality. It was reported in New Haven, that the entire city had been destroyed—not a building left.

Philadelphia and Baltimore sent all the fire-fighting machines they could muster and almost a thousand firemen. But traveling facilities were inadequate in those days and the gallant volunteers from these cities were mostly stranded at Perth Amboy where the congestion was inextricable.

The blowing up of houses finally stopped the onrushing flames, and on the third day the worst was over. But only a heaping pile of blackened ruins marked what had been the busiest and most important section of our city; the streets were everywhere strewn with valuable merchandise and looting began on a large scale. This was promptly checked by orders to shoot to kill.

When some accurate measure of the disaster, which had overtaken the city, could be taken, it was stated in the papers: "It is not probable that the destruction of any given section of any other city in the world of equal extent would have involved a greater destruction of capital or

Broadway, junction Park Row and Vesey Street, 1833. St. Paul's Chapel occupied during Revolution by Society Library. Residence of John Jacob Astor at corner Vesey Street on which he subsequently built the Astor House.

ruined the fortunes of a greater number of men." Daniel Webster brought in a Bill in Congress for the relief of the sufferers.

About the only thing the fire did not destroy was the courage and the credit of the merchants of Old New York. Their stocks were gone, their buildings were gone, their money was gone and not a company was left who could even think of paying insurance. For a time it looked as if life wasn't worth living after all. Yet in less than two years a finer city had risen on the ruins of the old—more beautiful buildings, better-paved streets—and the calamity proved a blessing in disguise. Perhaps its greatest achievement was the introduction of running water into the city. Looking backward, it seems incredible that a city of over 160,000 inhabitants should have been content with the improvements of a third-rate village.

Work was immediately started on the Croton Aqueduct. So the fire created a modern up-to-date city in place of the shambles it was before.

The money loss was prodigious for that period—over twenty millions of dollars. What that meant in suffering and anxiety cannot be computed. But there was no repining, no post-mortems. It was still the great receiving and distributing city of the Western World and it had no thought of letting envious rivals usurp its proud position.

The old merchants of New York were a sturdy, self-reliant lot!

The young city that now lay prostrate in the ruins, was by no means dead. A new, a broader and a nobler life was to rise from its charred and blackened débris. The mighty force of steam had entered the world.

The Indian trail, which gave way to the planked road, became but a legend; and the man on horseback, symbol of advancing civilization, followed the trail into history. Huge iron bands were soon to stretch across the illimitable, untamed prairies and the mysterious Pacific was to be linked to the Atlantic. The lumbering stagecoach that made its trip from New York to Boston in the incredibly fast time of four days and seven hours, stood on the brink of oblivion.

The sea, where man for centuries had been helpless alike in calm and storm, had at last yielded to his mastery. He now rode the wave regardless of wind or tide and there was no shore upon which the prows of his ships might not dash. The crushing burden of heartbreaking labor was to be lifted from the backs of men. Women everywhere were to emerge from worse than slavery.

Jefferson, riding up to the gates of the Capitol, took his place as the last heroic figure to wave farewell to a vanishing world; to hail the splendor of a new era—a greater, more dazzling, more glorious Renaissance than rose from the ruins of the Roman Empire.

The little hamlet on the rim of an unknown continent —the far-flung outpost of an ancient civilization—was no more. The New York we had known for two centuries was gone. In its place arose a new city of such surpassing grandeur, such imposing greatness, that men were awed by its majesty, by its sheer magnificence.

That story, however, must wait for another book.

THE END